THERE'S A
DEVIL IN THE DRUM

THERE'S A
DEVIL
IN THE DRUM

by

JOHN F. LUCY

THE NAVAL & MILITARY PRESS
MCMXCIII

"I sought them far and found them,
 The sure, the straight, the brave,
 The hearts I lost my own to,
 The souls I could not save.
 They braced their belts about them,
 They crossed in ships the sea,
 They sought and found six feet of ground
 And there they died for me."

A. E. HOUSMAN

Introduction to 1992 Edition

'Before mounting the steps on the opposite side of the wide barrack-square I looked back, and Jim was still standing there, motionless against the lighted windows—the personification of comradeship between men, and the symbol of all his kind for me—the case-hardened war-time members of the sergeants' mess, the senior non-coms who were the backbone of the army, who soldiered well automatically, and fought and led in war without supervision when their officers were killed. I was proud now to be an officer, but prouder far to have been a Regular sergeant with those chaps.'

This eloquent and moving tribute to the senior N.C.O.s of the old army expressed the feelings of the author when, in June 1917, he moved from that close comradeship of the sergeants' mess to the officers' mess, translated from Sergeant J. F. Lucy, 2nd Battalion Royal Irish Rifles to Second Lieutenant J. F. Lucy of the same regiment and battalion. This is essentially the story of a battalion of the pre-war army and the opening months of the Great War—Mons, Le Cateau, the Marne, the Aisne, La Bassée and First Ypres. It is the story of a man who took an immense pride in being a regular soldier and in his Irish regiment. It is an exceptionally good book on the Great War, a rare example of an account of the fighting in 1914 as seen by a young N.C.O.

It is, however, something to be regretted that all the names in the narrative are pseudonyms and the true identities are not easy to establish with any certainty. As a battalion record, it suffers in that respect in comparison with another great book, *'Old Soldiers Never Die.'* For some reason, too, the author was reluctant to identify the pre-1914 stations in which he served; thus his depot is in 'an Ulster town,' he joins his battalion in 'one of the old southern English Cinque ports, and the battalion moves from there to a 'purely garrison town near Salisbury.' It seems strange that he could not have written Belfast, Dover and Tidworth respectively.

The book neatly divides itself into three phases: 1912 to 1914, an interesting account of soldiering in the ranks and the moulding of young recruits into the dedicated professionals that were soon to win imperishable fame; August 1914 to the end of 1915, by which time that superb army had passed into history—and this phase takes up most of the book; and finally the epilogue, covering four months in 1917 as a Second Lieutenant in his old battalion—Third Ypres to Cambrai where the war ended for him, wounded in sixteen places.

John Lucy was born in Cork, the son of a cattle dealer and one of a family of three boys (he was the middle one) and a girl. According to family records his birthday was on 1st January 1895, but according to army records, and therefore the date he must have given the recruiting authorities, it was 3rd January 1894, a date more consistent with the very few clues about his age that appear in the book. His mother died while he was a teenager, and after an altercation with their father, John and his younger brother Denis, presumably about a year younger, left home in the winter of 1911. After an unsuccessful period of employment in a newspaper office, John was persuaded by his brother to enlist, and they did so on 3rd January 1912 for seven years with the colours and five in the reserve. This was his eighteenth birthday, the minimum age for enlistment at the time. It is not clear what line the younger Lucy took, but evidently there were no problems at the local barracks where they joined up. In *'Old Soldier Sahib'* Frank Richards says that he added eighteen months to his 17½ years when he enlisted in 1901—no questions asked and no birth certificate demanded; he looked big enough. Denis Lucy was bigger than his older brother.

He comments that they took the oath of loyalty with 'some national qualms of conscience,' a reflection of their origins in the South, and to alleviate the pangs they evidently felt they chose an Irish regiment. The local regiment for Cork was the Royal Munster Fusiliers with Tralee as the location of the depot, but for reasons not explained they opted for one at the other end of Ireland, the Royal Irish Rifles with its depot in Belfast. And yet, despite the South and North dilemma the author served on in the regiment after it had become the Royal Ulster Rifles in January 1921, eventually rising to command a battalion of the regiment in World War II.

At Belfast they underwent their basic recruit training, graphically described, which was then something of a make or break routine, and many indeed broke under it or resorted to any length to get their discharge. The brothers survived and at the end of six months became trained recruits, and in due course they were posted with their squad to the 2nd Battalion, then stationed in Dover where it had relocated from Aldershot in September 1909. When the Lucy brothers joined, the battalion was occupying the Citadel. The battalion commander at Dover was Lieut. Colonel Frederick John Hamilton Bell whom Lucy describes as a 'taciturn Englishman, suffering from old war wounds;' and yet Bell had been commissioned into the Royal Irish Rifles in 1883 and served with them throughout his military career (wounded in the Boer War) which suggests someone of Irish rather than English stock. His successor, however, was from an English regiment as described later in this introduction.

There is a problem, at this stage, in reconciling the dates, or implied dates, in the narrative with those of the regimental history and the Army List. Lucy states they completed six months training at the depot in Belfast, which takes them to July 1912, and then, 'in due course' they were drafted to the 2nd Battalion in Dover where they were still classified as recruits for 'some further months.' According to Lucy they were dismissed the square, *i.e.* were considered to be proper soldiers, in the summer of 1913 when they took part in battalion training and, in the autumn, in army manœuvres, after which they moved to another garrison, near Salisbury (Tidworth).

But the regimental history shows the battalion left Dover in 1912, stating: 'At the close of the Army manœuvres of 1912 the battalion proceeded straight from Cambridge (they had found themselves near that town when the 'Stand Fast' sounded) to their new station at Tidworth, which place they reached about 3.30 a.m. on the 20th September 1912 ...' This was one year before the date given by Lucy, and the Army List confirms the move of the battalion to Tidworth in September 1912. It is hard to explain this discrepancy, unless the twenty four years that had elapsed before he began writing the book played tricks with Lucy's memory. He does relate that in November 1914, in a fit of depression, he burned his diary, but it is not clear whether he began the diary when he enlisted or when he arrived in France. He does plead this as an excuse for any inaccuracies in dates or other lapses subsequent to its destruction.

In Tidworth the battalion formed part of 7th Brigade, 3rd Division. The brigade commander was F. Q. N. McCracken, late R. Berkshire, who would take the brigade to France in August 1914 and would subsequently rise to the command of a corps. The divisional commander at the time was Henry Rawlinson who would rise to even greater heights. He was not, however, commanding the division when war broke out; he had been replaced in June 1914 by Hubert Hamilton who, in October 1914, would be the first divisional commander to be killed in action.

The battalion C.O. was now Lieut. Colonel Wilkinson Dent Bird, D.S.O., who had assumed command on 23rd September 1913 (his predecessor retired after handing over). He had been commissioned in The Queen's (Royal West Surrey), only transferring to the Royal Irish on assuming command. He had received his D.S.O. in South Africa where, like Lt. Col. Bell, he had been severely wounded. He took the battalion to France and was again badly wounded on the Aisne in September 1914, losing a leg. Despite this he continued in the army till retiring in 1923 as Major General Sir W. D. Bird, K.B.E., C.B., C.M.G., D.S.O. He was Colonel of The Queen's from 1929 to 1939.

During the first half of 1914 both brothers were promoted to lance-corporal, and by the time war broke out John Lucy had received another promotion, to full corporal. They sailed for France with the battalion on 13th August 1914, both section commanders in 'A' Company, each with eight men under command. Lucy remarks that he was twenty years old and his brother only nineteen.

Although the 2nd Battalion Royal Irish Rifles suffered few casualties at Mons, rather less than a dozen all told, they inflicted heavy losses on the Germans as they advanced in solid phalanxes. This first clash between the B.E.F. and units of the German First Army is vividly described. Lucy's opponents were the 75th Infantry Regiment (1st Hanseatic) and in their attack on the brigade position they lost 5 officers and 376 men (Official History)—swept away by the rapid rifle fire of the British regular soldier.

The Retreat from Mons ('Sleep-marching') and the battle of Le Cateau are related with a similar eye for detail and with impressively descriptive writing. II Corps losses at Le Cateau were close to 8,000 and Lucy, who must have had recourse to the regimental history for casualty figures, puts his battalion's loss at a hundred officers and men. The history breaks this down to 5 officers and twenty nine other ranks wounded, and sixty killed or missing, and the majority of these were missing. But it was during the Aisne crossing that tragedy struck when, on 15th September, John's young brother was killed. The two had been very close all through their service, and his account of his brother's death is simple but extremely moving. The occasion was an abortive attack by 'A' and 'D' Companies on enemy trenches near Rouge Maison, about a mile north of Vailly on the north bank of the river. While waiting for his turn to advance John watched his brother's platoon go forward with Denis well in front of his section: 'Forward he went, and out of my sight for ever.' The body was never found, and his name is on the memorial to the Missing at La Ferté-sous-Jouarre.

October 1914 was, for the B.E.F., the worst of those first four months of the war; in fact in terms of dead, missing and P.o.W. October's figure was only exceeded twice during the eighteen months January 1915 to June 1916—in May 1915 (Aubers Ridge and Festubert) and September (Loos). Lucy's account of the fighting and of the virtual destruction of his battalion in the Battle of La Bassée (10th October–2nd November), with the dead alone numbering some 200, makes grim reading. For him the battalion was never the same again; of the thirty-two corporals who had sailed for France just over two months earlier, he observes, only four had survived. After receiving a draft of two hundred the battalion moved north to the Salient, in time for the last desperate effort by the Germans to break through on 11th November, the occasion of the attack by the Guard and 4th Divisions. Lucy's account of this action and of those on the Aisne and at Mons feature as three separate articles in the first volume of Sir John Hammerton's *'I Was There.'*

By the end of the year the battalion had been brought up to strength with drafts numbering some 800 officers and men and Lucy had again been promoted—to Orderly Room Sergeant. When, in response to the adjutant's question about his age Lucy replied he would be twenty-one next January [1915], the adjutant commented that he had never seen a twenty year old sergeant before. Even in war this was a very young age for a member of the sergeants' mess, especially one with such a responsible position in the battalion; that he should have been thus singled out is an indication of his ability, personality and character. This is further borne out by the fact that three months later he was asked to consider taking a commission, but he decided against it. He felt that after seven months of war he was more fit for a sanatorium than commissioned rank.

The passing of 1914, notes Lucy, saw the passing of the old regular army and the end of the type of warfare for which it had been so well trained. Now it was trench warfare, a totally new concept where new tricks had to be learned. In just two pages (299 and 300) he gives what amounts to a superbly practical guide to the art of staying alive in the line; he calls it the technique of life and death. It would have done as a *vade-mecum* to be issued to all soldiers going into the trenches for the first time.

At the end of 1915 John Lucy was sent home, a sick man. He remained at home throughout 1916, and in the second half of the year he decided to apply for a commission which he received on 15th June 1917. He had been asked for by the C.O. of a Royal Munster Fusilier battalion, but he had learned that he could stay with his own regiment which he regarded as an honour at any time and in war a distinction. At the end of July 1917 he rejoined his old battalion, now in 74 Brigade, 25 Division, to which it had been transferred in November 1915, just before he went home. Third Ypres began on 31st July, and on 10th August the division assaulted Westhoek Ridge; Lucy's battalion captured the village with two intact strongpoints in it, and his account of this action paints a vivid and terrible picture.

Towards the end of October, Lucy went home on what turned out to be his last leave from the

Western Front. When he returned, the battalion
had been transferred again, this time to 108 Brigade in 36th Ulster Division, and he found it in
reserve for the forthcoming battle of Cambrai.
This was his last fight; during the German counter-attack in the first week of December 1917 he
was badly wounded in the trenches by a German
heavy grenade, the fragments of which put sixteen holes in him. At the end of the month he
was evacuated to England in a hospital ship; his
case sheet read: 'Shell wounds; very severe—
knee, buttock, thigh, abdomen, back and
forearm.'

John Lucy stayed on in the army after the war
and while recovering from his wounds he was
employed under the Ministry of Labour. His regiment became The Royal Ulster Rifles (R.U.R.)
on 1st January 1921, though it was some years
before he rejoined it. From 1921 to 1926 he was
seconded to the King's African Rifles as a company commander, and in 1928 he was posted to
Bombay as a staff officer where he remained till
1932. Here he married Mary Carver, whom he
had first met in Nyasaland and they had two
sons. After home leave he rejoined his old 2nd
Battalion in 1933 in Milton Barracks, Gravesend,
and not long after, on 4th April 1935, he retired.

After an unsuccessful venture into the world of
business in Dun Laoghaire, he took up journal-
ism and became a well known commentator and

interviewer for Radio Éireann. He began to write his book in 1936 and it was published by Faber & Faber in 1938. It was widely acclaimed by the critics and received excellent reviews; *The Times Literary Supplement* called it 'an exceptionally good war book' and *The Irish Times* regarded it as 'easily the best written by an Irishman about the war.' For *The Tablet* it was the book of the week, and extracts from it were read to a party of officers visiting the Aisne battlefield, so accurate and detailed were the descriptions held to be. There is no doubt that all this praise was well deserved.

He joined the Reserve of Officers in August 1939 and served with the B.E.F. in France as a staff officer in 1940, managing to escape from St Nazaire in a destroyer. Back home he became a training officer and achieved much success in that role, eventually being given command (in January 1942), with the acting rank of Lieutenant Colonel, of the 70th Young Soldiers' Battalion, R.U.R.; surely a most satisfactory conclusion to service that had begun thirty years earlier as a private in that same regiment. He was appointed an Officer in the Order of the British Empire in 1945; he died on 1st March 1962, in Cork, where he had been born sixty eight Years before.

Terry Cave
Worthing, July 1992

Introduction

ACKNOWLEDGEMENT

I would like to acknowledge the assistance given by Gerald Gliddon who not only provided the book but also, through his contact with John Lucy's next-of-kin, biographical details of the author.

Contents

Contents

Part One

MY BROTHER AND I

Chapter One

'THERE'S A DEVIL IN THE DRUM'

The pre-war soldier, when asked why he enlisted, explained that one afternoon, while his mother was entertaining some casual friends in the peerage, he had the misfortune to spill his tea on the grand piano, and of course one could not expect his mother to put up with that kind of conduct.

If at the time of the question he was not in the inventive mood which produced this or similar fantasies he replied: 'I 'listed for me pound.' The soldier's pound was his daily ration of army bread, and unemployment and the need of food had really driven him to the colours.

So it was with most of us who marched to Mons. We had indeed one or two strange characters in the ranks, but these were the exception. There was a taciturn sergeant from Waterford who was conversant with the intricacies of higher mathematics, and who was very smart and dignified and shunned company. There was an ex-divinity student with literary tastes, who drank much beer and affected an obvious

13

pretence to gentle birth; a national school teacher; a man who had absconded from a colonial bank; a few decent sons of farmers. The remainder of us in our Irish regiment were either scallawags or very minor adventurers.

My brother persuaded me to join the army. We had hardly left school. Our mother had just died, and we had gone a bit wild. We were locked out for coming home late one night. It was 9.30 p.m. when we knocked at the door, and we were told by an outraged father to stay out. It was winter, and having no place to go, and no money, we climbed an orchard wall and slept that night in a summer-house.

The next day we found work in a newspaper office and set ourselves up in lodgings. We did not stick that for long. My brother took French leave for two days after Christmas, and on being reprimanded by the newspaper manager told him to go to blazes. He was sacked, and I walked out in sympathy.

We were tired of small wages, of lodgings, and of having to cook our own food, and the landlady viewed us with a hostile eye.

She had been very difficult about the matter of a fire. One of us had left a lighted cigarette in our only room before we set out to a theatre one night, and on returning we found our lodgings ablaze. The fire brigade was in occupation and had made a mess of everything. The water they had spilt was enough to put out a burning hotel.

Our meagre belongings were ruined, and every-

thing smelt of burnt brown paper. The furious landlady is still associated with that smell in my mind. I
forget our excuses.

We were tired of landladies and mocked the meaning of the word. We were tired of fathers, of advice
from relations, of bottled coffee essence, of school,
and of newspaper offices. The soft accents and slow
movements of the small farmers who swarmed in the
streets of our dull southern Irish town, the cattle,
fowl, eggs, butter, bacon, and the talk of politics
filled us with loathing. Blow the lot.

As a matter of fact we were full of life and the spirit
of adventure, and wanted to spread our wings.

We got adventure. We enlisted.

Avoiding the recruiting sergeant, because I objected to presenting myself to any of that bluff, florid
beribboned type, we walked into the local barracks
and took oath to serve and protect the King and his
relations, and to obey the superiors set over us by
him for a period of seven years with the colours and
five in the reserve.

We swore with some national qualms of conscience.
As a sop to our feelings we chose an Irish regiment,
and one stationed far away at the other end of Ireland.

We were given two shillings and ninepence each,
the King's shilling, and one and ninepence for our
first day's rations, and told to report the following
day at the railway station in time to catch a train for
our depot in Ulster. Ulster, the province of the O'Neil

of the Red Hand, and of Cuchullain and the Red Branch Knights.

The date of our attestation was the 3rd of January 1912.

Chapter Two

BARRACKS IN ULSTER

We passed north through Dublin, feeling we were great travellers, and at the end of our journey we were met in the Ulster town where our depot was situated by a soldier wearing side arms, who conducted us to the barracks, and handed us on to an older soldier who was in charge of what they called the reception-room. This older soldier possessed himself of our civilian clothing when we later got into uniform, and he was particularly anxious that we should not give our shoes to anyone else.

It was cold and dark when we arrived, and the reception-room was dimly illumined by two naked gas-jets. The flickering light showed up a floor scrubbed white as the deck of a ship, and along the walls on either side of the length of the room rows of uninviting black-painted iron beds. Sets of iron pegs and shelves were fitted in the white-washed wall over each bed. A rough table on iron trestles and a couple of low wooden forms completed the furniture. We felt homesick and cold, and our gaze shifted on to the occupants of the room; four young men grouped round a low-burning fire.

They were sharp-featured and clothed in rags, and were all four fine specimens of corner boys. We approached them and exchanged information. Two of them hailed from Dublin and two from Belfast. The Belfast men called it 'Bilfaust'.

We found it difficult to understand any of the four, and our accent seemed strange to them. They joked at us. One of the Belfast men had opened up the questioning by asking our names, and then asked with a fair imitation of our way of speaking: 'Are you from Corrk?' We answered: 'We are, are you?' This evidently was the stock answer of all Cork men, and was greeted with gusts of laughter.

One of the Dublin men protected us from further banter by saying: 'Here, here, what do yez think yez are on? Let up, let up.' We felt small, and very provincial in the eyes of the Belfast guttersnipe.

The old soldier showed us our beds, and told us to go and report ourselves as present to the orderly sergeant in the main barrack block before we retired.

He pointed out the room in which we should find the non-commissioned-officer, and we walked over. The barrack-room door was closed and we knocked. A young soldier in shirt and trousers opened it, and stood abashed at our polite inquiry as to the whereabouts of the orderly sergeant. We stood outside waiting to be asked in, and became the butt of all in the room, thus learning that one did not knock at barrack-room doors, nor wait outside, nor did one say: 'Please would you tell me?'

A loud commanding voice caused immediate silence: 'Who are those two diseased idiots?' The man at the door shouted: 'Recruits, Corporal.' The loud voice ordered 'Show 'em in.'

We went in blushing, and approached a dark-faced stocky man who was busily engaged writing at a table in the middle of the room, and who continued at his task for some time, ignoring us.

At last he lifted his head, looked at us gravely, and spoke to us gently. He asked us how we were, did we enjoy the train journey, were the old people at home all right, if we were tired and other solicitous matters.

We were pleased. We liked this first real kindness shown to us since we left our town, and, quickly responding, told him we were all right and thanked him.

The soldiers in the room, quiet up to this point, laughed loud and uncontrolledly. The corporal was evidently a wit, and we had been taken in again. It later dawned on us that our manners, and our school caps, which we still wore and had mistakenly doffed on entering, had provided quite a comic turn for that barrack-room.

The corporal marked us present and dismissed us to the reception-room. There we examined our beds and found them to consist of three small, hard sections called biscuits, which laid together made a mattress, on which were spread two dirty-looking coarse brown blankets. At the head of the bed was a hard coir-stuffed pillow without a slip, and there were no sheets.

Following the lead of the protective Dublin man, we knelt down and said our prayers. After that night we resolved to say them in bed.

In the morning we found that the blankets were lousy.

Chapter Three

WE ARE EQUIPPED

A bugle-call startled us at dawn. For the first time we heard the 'Rouse':

> *Jump out of bed,*
> *Jump out of bed,*
> *You lazy donkey.*
> *Roll up your kit,*
> *And get on parade.*

It sounded romantic.

The old soldier shook us up, shouting: 'Show a leg.' We washed ourselves under running taps in a common wash-house, not caring to use the indifferently cleaned zinc basins set in a row on the wet slate slab under the water-taps. It was miserably cold. We were too young to shave, and, our simple toilet completed we went back to the room, pushed in our concertina beds and folded our bedding on the top under the direction of the old soldier.

After a light meal of washy coffee and one biscuit each we were invited to earn our pay. We were each allotted a section of the floor to clean. We scrubbed it with hard hand-brushes, soft soap, and caustic soda. The caustic was supposed to burn the dirt out.

It burnt our soft hands too, while we reflected that scrubbing floors in the dawn of a winter's morning with icy cold water and caustic soda was poor kind of soldiering for schoolboys familiar with the work of Lever.

We then had a good breakfast of strong fresh tea, porridge, and liver and bacon, which was served in tinware on the rough bare table, and afterwards we blackleaded the grate, the fire-irons, and the table trestles, and polished coal-boxes and ration tins with brickdust. There was no idling in this army business, and already romance was beginning to pale.

We were marched, too shy to keep step with our comrades (some of whom were ex-Militia men) to another medical inspection.

Then we met a gentle person in the commanding officer, who, after more questions, finally approved of us and made us real soldiers with army numbers.

I wobbled from the presence to commands of 'Left turn', 'Quick march', 'Right wheel', 'Mark time', 'Right turn', 'HALT!'—the last order being given in a devastating *fortissimo*. I was taken unawares, and only realized that it was my duty to pull myself together when given a twisting push in the direction of the door by our corporal friend of the previous night while I was still gazing admiringly at the rather kind-looking, white moustached, elderly gentleman who commanded the depot.

We are Equipped

We were next marched off to the quartermaster's stores, where we received a free issue of an enormous amount of kit, all smelling of camphor. I forget the number of uniforms we had thrown at us. My possessions rattled me. We got two sets of most things— green, khaki, and white suitings, large rough boots, canvas shoes, grey socks and shirts, suspenders, hats, badges, blankets, kitbags, a jack-knife and an ordinary knife, a fork, a spoon, a razor, a comb, holdalls; tooth, hair, clothes, shaving and blacking brushes, towels, buttons, soap, blanco, and other cleaning materials.

The sense of carelessness emanating from the storeman, who appeared to be rapidly throwing stuff away in all directions, created an atmosphere of abandon about me. I reflected, and was caught again asleep from the army point of view. The corporal addressed me rudely. I obeyed him, and lifting a bulging blanket full of articles of kit which I had no time to memorize, I staggered away in the wake of the other recruits to a soldier who stamped our kit with the army numbers we had received that day.

He expected a tip for this office. My brother and I gave him one, not knowing that it was for doing his duty, but none of the others rewarded him. In fact one of the Belfast men invited the number-stamper to kiss his Irish backside.

This incident did not mark our introduction to soldiers' language—our Dublin friends blasphemed softly and easily, and the slum adjective for fornication preceded every noun they uttered. The staccato talk of the northerners was interspersed with obscure or obscene words, which we soon discovered was simply the mode and entirely meaningless.

We, too, acquired the habit of colouring our speech a trifle, just for the sake of being understood.

Chapter Four

BREAD AND SORROW

Our clothing, casually issued by sizes in the quarter-master's stores, did not fit, so our next expedition was to the regimental tailor, who after many changes made us quite presentable. Incidentally he drew our attention to other articles of clothing for sale in his shop, and pestered us so much that we bought stuff we did not require. The shoemaker also had excellent civilian boots for sale. We had just given away our footgear, but we obliged him too. There was no need to pay ready cash, it was explained, as these things could 'go down to our account'. We were fools, being fleeced.

We were posted to the barrack-room of the corporal who had referred to us as 'diseased idiots', and were still very uneasy when we entered it again. Our strange, hard serge uniforms irritated and our many possessions bothered us. We dumped our belongings near two unoccupied beds and looked in dismay at the high piles of neatly folded and colour-graded kits on the iron racks above the beds of the older recruits.

Each man's number and name were beautifully painted in white on a black kitbag, reinforced inside with an oblong board to the length of which each article of kit above precisely conformed. Everything in the room was spotless, and similarly squared off, even the beds, which were dressed along one of the lines of the floorboarding.

We despaired, agreed not to compete just then, and started packing everything pell-mell into the big wooden boxes under our beds, but were interrupted by the corporal, who ordered a tall bugler, one of the depot permanent staff, to show us how to make our beds and fold our kits, which demonstration he carried out in an amazingly swift and thorough fashion, talking a lot the while.

This bugler gave us to understand that we were only 'red arses'—a term of contempt for recruits; that we would probably never learn to do anything for ourselves in our puff (life); that our undue delay in not presenting him with a cigarette was past forgiveness; that we had peculiar names, and faces, and figures; that the army was going to bloody hell anyway; and that he was possessed of a thirst which he would hesitate to exchange for a pension.

We cottoned on, and gave him beer money. He immediately gave us a mass of really useful hints, a second demonstration of kit-folding, and several stories of his own recruit days.

Eventually he left us experimenting by ourselves and wandered off in the direction of the canteen,

quite grave with the suspicion that we might turn
out well, after all, under his guidance. He nearly
poisoned us a week later by doping bread with some
white powder he bought in the town. He was a drunkard and did not eat bread. He left his daily ration in
the open barrack-room cupboard, instead of locking
it away in his box, as was the custom with the hungry
recruits. Our work was too hard for growing youths,
and we devoured everything edible we could lay
hands on. The bugler's bread supplemented our soup
issue every evening at eight o'clock, when he was usually out, boozing in the town.

He tried to discover the bread-stealers in order to
make money by selling it, but none of us would confess, so he resorted to sterner measures the effects of
which kept six recruits galloping for hours out into a
cold winter's night, spurred on by the pangs of a violent and recurring diarrhœa. My brother and I were
among the groaning runners.

A second coup by the same bugler forces his memory
on me for ever.

On the evening of a certain pay-day he received a
wire from Dublin telling him his mother had just died.
He was distracted, and mournfully stalked the floor of
the barrack-room, all the recruits commiserating with
him. It was pathetic to see the tall strong soldier in
sorrow. He slowly unfolded his best uniform and
dressed in it. We all helped to polish up his boots,
belt, and medals. We brushed his hat and clothes.

He told us he had got special leave, and was going

at once to Dublin to attend the funeral, but he was very short of cash.

He actually wept. My heart warmed, melted, and flowed out over my comrades, each of whom had just received six or seven shillings pay. I started a subscription, and raised about eighteen hard-earned shillings for the orphan. He left us silently, and we went to bed discussing his hidden virtues.

Sorrow arouses godly feelings, and is a great bond.

The next morning we were startled by the notes of the 'Rouse' alarmingly near. Looking to a corner bed we saw our bereaved bugler, too drunk to get up, but conscientiously blowing his instrument out through an open window; with his legs and the lower part of his body still in bed.

He would not give a single answer to any of our angry questions.

Chapter Five

YOUNG SWEATS

We had a stiff time in the depot. The bugle bullied us out of our beds at dawn. We dressed rapidly, putting snow-white canvas suits over our khaki uniforms.

The canvas suits were a curse, as we had to have a clean one every day. Elbow-grease and soap gradually bleached the yellow cloth white. The suits were stiff and difficult to wring out, and some men, to save labour, resorted to rubbing them with chalk, and got into trouble for their ingenuity. Our boots, equipment, rifles, and dummy cartridges had to be spotless, and our hair had to be cropped.

If the inspecting N.C.O. instructor found no fault with our clothes and accoutrements, our teeth, and even our finger-nails were looked at, and some martinets went so far as to examine our undervests, or to unbutton our tunics in a search for dirty necks. We received extra drill or fatigues for any delinquency.

The N.C.O.s of the old army had the power to punish on the spot. If the entire squad displeased in any way it was made to double round and round the

barrack-square until perspiration dripped on clothing and rifles slipped from wet hands. I fainted at the
double one morning. I had had no coffee before the
first parade, and was literally run off my feet. A stinging north wind added to the gaiety of life by seeming
to freeze the sweat on the skin of my empty stomach,
and my harnessed carcase was left spiritless on the
bleak parade ground.

My brother saw that in future I got my early morning coffee. I had refused to join in the scramble for
the washy stuff and so lost my share to my fellows,
who had little control in the matter of food.

We drilled, and drilled, and drilled; the bugle bul-
lying us on to parade after parade. Our weak muscles
were wrenched at physical exercises at which everything for a solid hour was executed on the tips of our
toes. This was our worst experience. We sprinted
from one kind of torture to another while our mouths
went dry, our bodies clammy and stale, and our limbs
trembled.

'If you broke your mothers' hearts, you won't break
mine.' A tall, lithe, elastic-muscled English sergeant
put us through it. He demonstrated every exercise
himself first in a completely effortless manner, and
bounced about as if on springs. He taught us good
manners too. 'Good morning, Class.' 'Good morning,
Staff.' He was always deathly pale. His hand-clap,
two rapid explosions, brought any defaulter to
' 'shun' and 'Round that post and back, Dubbul.'

Punishment immediately followed crime. Our

bodies ached. A whisper in the ranks, and the exercises ceased. The hand-clap paralysed us to attention. The most painful exercise was chosen as a corrective: 'On the hands down, arms bend, stretch, bend, stretch, bend, stretch, stick that backside down, you're not a bloody camel.' A strong rubber-soled shoe pushes the offending part into alinement and the strain continues, while a sharp pain, half physical, half mental, gnaws at the back of the head: 'Bend, stretch, bend, stretch . . .' for an interminable period. Then back like a shot to our interrupted exercise: 'In front of the beam, double!' The fellow was diabolical. We hated him, and aped his manners and way of speech in the security of our barrack-room. It was a rotten life, and we were very, very sorry for having enlisted.

To allay our own disgust we took a perverse pleasure in watching the other squads doing their training. The corporal who dubbed us 'diseased idiots' operated on a party of recruits in our vicinity. 'Diseased' was his pet word.

He was diseased himself from regarding the quaint postures adopted by his disciples. He actually had a torso like a bull's, and he swung his body about like a monkey.

Standing in a religious attitude he called on heaven to witness the iniquities of the sweepings of mankind in his hands: 'This is too much for any bloody man. I wish to God I was dead, dead and out of me misery taychin' swabs like yous. Have a look at yereselves,

go on, go on, have a look at yereselves, and you,'
he roared at a drooping pupil, 'you standing there
like a drowned duck in the family way, where were
you got? Merciful God, look at him. Where did you
say? Donegal! Never in Ireland. We don't projoos
things like you. You're not a man, you're a mystery,
a bloody awful mystery, a cross for me past sins.

'For the love of our sufferin' God have mercy, lads,'
he wheedled. 'I'm only a poor old corporal, only nine
years to go for pension. Let me live. I'm diseased, I'm
bloody well diseased. Straighten your chicken chests
a bit, can't yeh, and let on to be swaddies just to give
us a hand, or be the Lord God I'll chuck this, and
join a regiment for a change. I'll join the lousiest
English regiment I can find and soldier for a change
instead of wet nursin' diseased idiots. . . .' Then he
stage-whispered: 'I'll tell yeh what I'll do. I'll turn
my back and you can walk out the bloody gate, and
no questions asked. Bugger off. No one wants you,
and no one'll look for you, except the diseased blind-
eyed son of a bitch of a recruiting sergeant who enlisted you when he was in the rats, and he won't be
able to see you.'

He looked at the barrack clock and his attitude
changed again. 'Now I'm going to jerk you up. You're
not on a blasted picnic, you're in a muscle factory,
and with the help of an almighty God and my poor
diseased efforts I'll straighten your backs or I'll
bloody well break 'em.' His voice dropped gently to
the order that without warning closed his discourse;

a softly spoken order, almost a request, in sharp contrast with the staccato outbursts of our instructor, yet like his pregnant with all the power of the military machine, and one that exacted a similar swift obedience—'To the wall bars, DOUBLE.'

Hanging with grasping hands back-twisted on the bars, like poultry in a shop window, the recruits raise their shaking legs forward and up to the level of their hips, and lower them to the word of command, until their faces writhe with the effort. If they are in the slightest degree slack they are left hanging. That hanging developed in the thoughtful some kind of appreciation of the pains of crucifixion. Our language became perfectly foul.

One day my brother refused to obey an order.

As leader of our squad in the gymnasium he was the first man told off to climb a rope to where a narrow plank was swung high up under the roof. He was to clamber off his rope on to the end of the plank, and to walk it without the protection of a net underneath.[1] He coolly explained that he was ready to climb any rope, but, as he had no head for heights, he would not venture the high plank. I thought the world had ended, and we were all as astonished as the sergeant, who was speechless with anger. I became terrified of the results. My brother was always too bold and independent. Our set policy from the beginning was to avoid guardrooms, and charge-sheets in which minor offences of neglect or carelessness were described as 'crimes'. We

[1] Since abolished as a dangerous exercise.

had the Irishman's loathing of enforced confinement, and the pride that made us fear the stigma of punishment. After a short pause the sergeant simply said 'Right', and took us off to the easy obstacle course outside the building. I am still puzzled as to why no punishment was inflicted on the culprit. The incident was not referred to again by the N.C.O., and none of our squad ever walked the plank.

Another time my brother interrupted a drill-sergeant whose personal remarks galled him by saying: 'Don't be sarcastic, Sergeant,' but the N.C.O. merely replied: 'There is no sarcàsm in the army.'

The strain of training to be a soldier was so hard that many broke under it. Some men went bad deliberately to 'work their tickets'.[1] They committed open crime in the town, by beating the police, breaking windows, or stealing in daylight, and so got imprisonment and freedom. Some developed an insolent obstinacy, became dirty and disobedient, and experienced the whole gamut of military punishment from simple confinement to barracks to imprisonment with hard labour, passing, still incorrigible, through the hands of hard-hearted and bitter provost sergeants and prison warders. One admired them in an oblique way for their persistent efforts, and wished them luck with their hard-won discharge. Others failed physically, their underfed bodies and weak muscles being unsuitable to produce the swiftness of limb and coordination of action required in the British infantry,

[1] Procure their discharge.

and they were released labelled 'medically unfit', or 'not likely to become an efficient soldier'.

The minor criminals, punished for untidiness or slackness on parade, had a very thin time. These 'defaulters' seemed to spend every moment in the intervals between parades, from dawn until ten o'clock at night, sprinting from their rooms to prove their presence in barracks by attending roll-call outside the quarter-guard, in answer to bugle calls purposely blown at irregular intervals. As a further punishment they did scavenging and any odd job that appealed to the imagination of an inventive provost sergeant, such as picking grass or stones, and white-washing or polishing articles that were already spotless. They also did pack drill, parading in full marching order to drill, march, and double until such time as the provost sergeant thought fit to dismiss them. This pack drill was so ferocious, that nowadays there is a time limit fixed for the duration of each punishment parade, and doubling is not allowed.

I have seen a case-hardened defaulter—a reckless fellow of cheerful temperament—sob like a tormented child at the treatment meted out to him by the provost sergeant. He was reputed to have once duped the sergeant by coming successfully through a punishment with a light pack, that is one stuffed with straw and boards instead of heavy field kit. For this or some other reason known only to himself the provost sergeant had purposely prolonged his punishment parade, and the unfortunate defaulter had no time to make the complete change necessary in clothing and equipment so as to appear in good time for the next routine parade. The result, as we all knew beforehand, was that the man was crimed again and got another dose of pack drill for late turning out on ordinary parade.

The military authorities sought to educate us in addition to making us into soldiers. We were forced to go to school every day for an hour, except Saturdays, in order to win a third-class certificate of education; a qualification which, combined with skill in marksmanship, would earn us proficiency pay in the dim future when we ceased to be recruits.

This education business was a farce and a scourge as well. I told the teacher that we brothers would like to have a shot at the first-class certificate at once, but his hobby was certificate collecting, and he discouraged us.

We therefore wasted hours and hours practising simple addition, multiplication, and division, and wrote letters full of lies to imaginary friends on 'Why I Joined the Army'.

We always finished first, and drubbed idle pens while we watched curiously the tortured faces and clutching hands of our labouring neighbours. On fine days it was agony to sit there in the stuffy dusty room, listening to the larks and eyeing the blue spot of sky through the windows of the church that served us as a school.

As it was necessary to get the third- and second-class certificates first, it took me eighteen months to gain the highest certificate, which I could easily have taken on enlistment. This first-class educational certificate turned out quite harmful to me in my second year of service. I was the only soldier in my company who had it, and was regarded as an educated bloke and a freak by my comrades. One colour-sergeant went out of his way to be rude about it by blaming me for having it, and coupling it with any failure of mine to come up to scratch in my ordinary duties.

The military vocabulary, minor tactics, knowledge of parts of the rifle, route marches, fatigues, semaphore, judging distance, shooting, lectures on *'esprit de corps'*, and on the history of our regiment, spit and and polish, saluting, drill, physical training, and other, forgotten subjects were rubbed into us for the worst six months of my life. We became insensitive, bored, and revolted, and talked seriously of deserting after three months of the life. We spent our meagre pay on food. I was 'put down' for a new blanket in order to adjust the accounts of an unctuous, dishonest hypocrite of a colour-sergeant.

Officers had little to do with us, and we preferred them at a distance. They paid us, and watched our training, sometimes even inspecting us on parade. They disappeared in the afternoons.

Gradually the older recruits were drafted to the home battalion stationed in England, and our squad became the crack number one, and reached a high standard.

Young Sweats

In time we effaced ourselves. Our bodies developed and our backs straightened according to plan. We marched instead of walking, and we forced on ourselves that rigidity of limb and poker face that marks the professional soldier. Pride of arms possessed us, and we discovered that our regiment was a regiment, and then some.

Romance revived, despite our queer way of attaining manhood, and of the fact that we had become mere mechanical numbers of an infantry unit.

We were young, both still under nineteen years, but in the strangest circumstances we would not have batted an eyelid, except in quiet understanding as an encouragement to each other.

Chapter Six

A WEE DANDER

The grey prison-like barrack-gate, on a Saturday afternoon in the early summer of 1912: Two brothers in natty green uniforms rifle-step from the adjoining guard-room, having been inspected by the guard commander as to correctness of dress and written permission before proceeding beyond the confines of the barracks.

Precise, upright, every movement of one conforming to that of the other, they march out for an hour's relaxation. The general effect of swagger canes, highly polished black belts and fittings, neat square-pushing boots, creases in black trousers fit to cut one's throat, handkerchiefs peeping from sleeves, and hats at the slightest of angles, reflects much credit on their efficient and blasphemous mentors.

A friend, a defaulter in dirty canvas carrying coals to the guard-room, greets them in passing:

'What cheer, boys.'

'What cheer, Bill.'

'What are yez on?'

'Oh, goin' for a wee dander.'

'Mind Mingy Maggie don't get yez.'

'No bloody fear.'

'Ha-ha, look at mammy's darlings, on the Cross. Well, look out for the lousy Red-caps.'

The provost sergeant in charge of prisoners comes round the corner with the injunction: 'Shut that bloody row, and get on with yer job,' and Bill, an adventurous spirit, who is suffering for the sin of breaking out of barracks by climbing over the wall at night, purses his lips and silently lifts his coal-box.

Outside we ignore two pairs of very glad eyes.

An old soldier then staggers towards us, widely rounding the last corner that leads to the barrack-gate. He hiccups as he passes the sirens, and we hiss: 'Look out. Nobby's at the gate.' He knows Nobby, the provost sergeant, but in the contemptuous manner of the old sweat spurns our warning with a lordly wave of the hand. We halt to watch his progress.

He recovers, straightens up, rapidly inspects himself, hitches the buckle of his belt to the centre front, adjusts his cap, and marches upright in through the gate. Marvellous to us, and we wonder if he will hold out. He does, head up, and past the sergeant, whose eyes twinkle. He is a man of experience and good judgement who literally loves the well-behaved drunk. He addresses the back of the disappearing old stiff: 'Been piddling up, Ginger?' 'Aye, Sergeant. Been piddling up.'

We break into well-controlled laughter, under the

critical eyes of two coasting Red-caps, and turning about walk on into the town. We begin to have a queer affection for all those comrades of ours, and even talk admiringly of the N.C.O.s. We meet our physical training instructor. 'Good evening, Sergeant.' 'Evening, lads. Don't get into trouble.' 'No fear, Sergeant.'

We steep in the military atmosphere, and swap impressions as we walk. We now have a good word for all, but we cannot help thinking that the hungry, illiterate, hard-swearing youths who are our soldier comrades are hardly the cream of Ireland, and that if England really valued their services as she appeared to do Ireland's best would produce a rattling army.

This disgusting impression we held for about a year, until we came to know our fellows better still. Then we understood them, and when the war came we reversed our opinion entirely.

I had a shilling, and my brother had nothing. He was like that.

Now the best way a young soldier could spend a shilling in 1912 was on food, so we resolved to blue the bob on coffee, eggs, bacon, rice, and prunes at the local Soldiers' Home, and all that lot we could have for fivepence each. We would have a little music for the remaining two pence from the automatic music-box as we ate.

Chapter Seven

BIFFING UP, STACKING, SALVATION

In the depot we had very little spare time, and even the intervals between parades were devoted to spit and polish, which the soldiers called 'biffing up'. We scrubbed floors, polished the rough barrack utensils, cleaned windows, and prepared uniforms, arms, and equipment for the next parade.

'Biffing up' was essential; therefore wise authority glorified it. But we could take no pride in the drudgery. It was menial work, and dull, no matter how much one might admire an organization that made one fend for oneself in every way that did not ask for initiative. The soldiers met every domestic requirement. 'A place for everything, and everything in its place,' was the motto, and everything was in its place, and spotless as well.

The last parade of the day was the hated school attendance, and we suffered the limit of boredom listening to the Cockney schoolmaster, as he juggled with h's, k's, and g's, and dictated the rivers and towns of England, or expounded the magic of the decimal point. All the scholars were lumped together, complete illiterates and past pupils of the Christian Brothers. Some of us could have taught our schoolmaster, but had learned to be humble. The north of Ireland men were frightfully ignorant, and slow and stupid in the schoolroom. They compared badly with the men from other parts of Ireland, who invariably had had some scrap of education, and were not worried by the simple Army School tasks, but the northerners more than made up for their failing in these abstruser matters by being slick and smart on the barrack-square.

As a counterblast to the repressive system of training which robbed us of our independence, we enjoyed a certain amount of self-assertion in quarrelling amongst ourselves, and as a word was immediately followed by a blow there was a good deal of blood-letting. Our rough fellows had but a rough idea of the sporting spirit.

Party songs were rightly forbidden, but one day my neighbour, an uncouth hairy fellow from Derry, sang *The Boyne Water*, an Orange War ballad, sitting astride his barrack-room box, polishing his boots, and leering meaningly at me as he sang. His beady eyes and thick wet mouth got me on the raw, and I shouted: 'Put a sock in it.' He immediately socked me, and I retaliated by butting him hard in the stomach with my head, and he fell back over the box. He got up and came at me with dropped jaw and wrinkled forehead, like a great angry baboon. I bolted behind a table, from which he snatched a heavy pudding-basin and pitched it at my head. I ducked and it smashed to pieces on the wall behind me. He followed up, but luckily for me, the other men in the room surrounded him before he reached me.

Another day I was accused of snatching the biggest dinner by a hard-faced, ambitious little fellow from Belfast, and an excellent soldier, who was jealous of my school certificate. 'Bloody liar,' said I, and he invited me to repeat the insult in the open air, which I did, and we fought it out with bare fists behind the barrack-room.

I made a nasty mess of his lower lip, and closed one of his eyes, but he ended the fight by knocking me clean out. It was my first knock-out, and I felt weakly indignant at the surprising sensation. I felt no pain in my head as my knees turned to water and I sank slowly to the ground.

My brother, though younger, was bigger than I, and a tiger for fighting. We were both hot-blooded, and we backed each other up to such an extent that the soldiers found it uncomfortable to interfere with either of us. Any one quarrelling with one of us had to take on both, and the man who knocked me out got a bad beating afterwards from my brother. So we were soon respected and left alone, no one being so keen as to want to fight a family. We were quick to notice that, whether one lost or won, it was a good thing to fight, and agreed as a matter of policy never to refuse to 'stack', as they called it.

Biffing Up, Stacking, Salvation

Fights always took place in the evenings, and our usual excuse for our battered appearance next day was that we had fallen off bicycles—an explanation always accepted, but one which made officers and N.C.O.s smile. They appeared to know all about it, and as a matter of fact the N.C.O.s always openly advocated 'having things out in a soldierly fashion', and they occasionally attended a performance.

The presence of N.C.O.s at fights was disliked, because they insisted on having rounds and proper timing, and sometimes went so far as to suggest boxing gloves in the gymnasium; but we preferred the rough and tumble knock-down game with bare fists, which ended quickly, and one did not really feel very much after the first few cracks.

Still, one had to walk warily. I remember one Kerry man catching an opponent by the shirt collar and butting his nose and mouth into a bleeding mass. Then there were certain rules as to the nature of verbiage —one might call a fellow a bastard or use the most offensive personal terms without hurt, but one could not in any way refer to a mother or a sister, though the indirect 'son of a bitch' was an accepted form of reproach, and even of endearment.

Guard duties brought another relief from the monotonous routine. There is a thrill about one's first sentry duty, and I always found the work pleasant, especially at night. It was good being alone on a sentry beat under the stars, and the temporary power to challenge officers and N.C.O.s as well as men added piquancy to a drab existence—and then, too, there was also the important matter of the extra rations which are issued to men on guard duty.

The commercial northern garrison town was a strange place to us. Slogans: 'To hell with the Pope', and 'No Rome rule', were white-washed on the gable ends of the houses in the poorer districts. Bigotry reigned here, surviving ironically in Ireland's quarter of progress. Most of the inhabitants were mill-workers. They were undersized and underfed, but dressed extravagantly, and boasted of the amount of money made in their town. We saw with regret that some Catholics living here seemed just as much embittered as their Protestant neighbours. This was foreign and galling to men of the south, who are friendly and tolerant towards their Protestant countrymen. These have produced many of their national leaders, and their standards of respectability and upright conduct are much admired by us, and made use of too, because they possess a civic spirit which permits them to lead or be led, without bickering, for the common good.

And to-day we southerners, who have fought side by side with the northern men in their own regiments, and who warmly remember their bravery and precious comradeship, heartily damn the righteous ones who earn haloes by fermenting ill blood.

Soul-saving missiles began to fly too, directed mainly at soldiers, who seemed to be fair game for all religion mongers. There were tracts everywhere, the products of a dozen queer sects. There was no dodging them. Our tunic fronts were often stuffed with them, and we found them on our beds on return to barracks. My brother and I studied them inquisitively, not bothering about the Vatican *Index*, if it takes notice of such things. Intimate details of the agony of Our Lord were emblazoned on the cheap broadsheets; and the Day of Judgement, always imminent, only appeared to promise a change-over to worse conditions.

A counter-offensive by the gayer Salvation Army drummed sinners back from the gates of perdition, but their preachers also ranted too openly of God. Uniformed women asked us in the streets if we were saved. We were told that we were on the downward path.

An ancient spinster tried to bribe us to join her prayer meetings by promising us tea and buns in the Soldiers' Home, on the condition of going upstairs to sing hymns. The promise of food once tempted my brother. He muttered something equivocal, and went upstairs with another Catholic boy, in a state of mental reservation, to tea and salvation. They were overheard vainly trying to fit the words of 'God save Ireland' to the tune of 'Shall we gather at the river?' and were ejected. Sometimes all the soldiers declined the invitation to go aloft, and then the sweetly smiling spinster tricked them by starting hymns in the reading-room, which most of them did not mind, though we always bolted. We thought it a dirty trick to open a home for the material comfort of men with few amusements, and then to dope them with a peculiar brand of spiritual discomfort. I do not know if the others wanted that kind of thing. We never inquired. The atmosphere of the hostel and of the squalid north Irish town turned us into religious snobs.

We were young and intolerant.

Chapter Eight

CRACK SQUAD

At the end of six months we were trained recruits, and thanks to the hated physical training our bodies were superbly fit and our spirits high. Repetition of work with which we were already thoroughly acquainted became extremely irksome, but we were prevented from getting stale because we were forced to regard ourselves as members of the first and model squad, in which no excuse at all was accepted for faults. Our movements on parade synchronized to perfection, we drilled as one man, and at attention were as immobile as a row of iron railings. The N.C.O.s, seeing us shaping well, were kinder to us when off duty, but on parade they continued to be adamant.

A mistake by one of the crack squad made them foam and rave, but we were used to that kind of treatment, and talk did not hurt, not even when we were likened to fat women in the family way. We had been called every possible and impossible name in the foulest English, and as far as verbiage went were in

D 49

our boredom only interested in the repertoire of new instructors, when they added anything to our already vast knowledge of bad language.

We could still be, and were, subjected to the degradation of being made to double, or to the award of extra drills for very minor parade faults, and we detested one sergeant who was a seeker of crime and grossly unfair. This sadist was in the habit of shouting to a motionless squad: 'Stop scratching yourself in the rear rank.' The inexperienced recruit invariably turned to see the non-existent scratcher, and was swiftly reminded that he had no business to show curiosity by the rasped injunction: 'Look to your front, you, and take one hour's extra drill this afternoon.' A slight pause, and then the corporal was gingered up: 'Take his name, Corporal.' 'Got it, Sergeant.' 'Don't answer me. Take it again.'

After the first instance of its kind, this sort of thing ceased to be amusing, and at the end of six months it simply angered and bored us.

The N.C.O.s were fed up too with their monotonous work of training, and one afternoon three of them surprised and delighted us by sprinting through the town in gym kit and daringly knocking off the hats of the military policemen on duty in the streets. Their rapid attack and swift retreat confused the policemen, and the culprits remain unrecognized and unpunished to this day.

To dislike Red-caps was part of the accepted code of a soldier. They interfered with the little liberty we enjoyed by accosting us anywhere outside barracks in order to examine our passes, or to order us on in the streets. They had the name of being merciless to any one falling into their clutches, and were therefore our enemies. We saw that some of the prisoners they brought into barracks had been knocked about. We did not then realize that they had a hard job handling the tougher element in the army.

During a break in a lecture on the importance of badges of rank, one instructor stigmatized the military policeman by telling the story of a recruit who passed a staff officer without saluting. On being brought to book for his neglect he replied: 'I thought he was a bloody Red-cap.'

Inexperienced recruits were the butt of all and sundry. Old soldiers generally managed to inveigle them into the canteen on their first night in barracks, and made them spend any money they had on 'wets'. Beer was cheap, plentiful, and popular in those days, and the wet canteens did not present the desolate appearance they have to-day.

The recruit had his leg pulled to the most amazing extent. I once saw a lad ready with pail and brush to go and white-wash the Last Post at the instigation of some old soldier.

Chapter Nine

ENGLAND: FIRST IMPRESSIONS

In due course our squad was drafted from the
depot to the home-service battalion, stationed in England. We were exhorted on a last parade to remember
our pride in arms, and in our regiment, and sensitive
to this teaching we saw ourselves as protectors of the
British Empire and the champions of the courage of
all soldiers of our race.

On our way we passed through London and were
sorely disappointed. We expected goodness knows
what of the capital of the Empire, as, huddled like
a market flock in the corner of the roaring, murky
railway station, we stared avidly at everything around.
We saw Englishmen in large numbers for the first
time, and like the inhabitants of the northern Irish
industrial centre, they looked grim and walked about
with set faces in the roar of their huge city. They
seemed keyed up for some great and serious occasion,
each threading the crowd intently with eyes obscured.
No one looked our way, and we felt our new importance as the bodyguard of these strange people un-
justly neglected.

England : First Impressions

We boarded a train for the south with a feeling of general gloom, and left these grim Londoners to their own devices. Some of us found relief in trying to imitate the Cockney porters and cabbies, and we came to the conclusion that the English were very bad at talking their own language.

Thus the southern Irish. The Belfast Scots were more silent than usual thinking of the heaps of money to be made in London, and the good jobs going there.

Our powers of adaptability suffered a severe strain when we arrived at the battalion, as no great interest was shown towards us, except by some older recruits, who had recently preceded us.

Our new commanding officer, a distinguished taciturn Englishman, suffering from old war wounds, ran us over cursorily with his light-blue eyes and limped away without making any remark that I can recall.

In contrast to him a horsey-looking and loud-voiced young officer, with a swagger enhanced by a tilted cap, a fierce moustache, very wide biscuit-coloured breeches, and a little switch which he continually flicked against his leggings, posed conspicuously in the middle of the parade ground and superintended our dispersal to various companies.

We were thus totally disintegrated, our herd instinct demolished, and our spirits at zero as we were marched off to eight various companies. Luckily my brother and I were posted to the same company.

During our brief march from the parade ground to our new barrack-room an old soldier was in the act

53

of leaving the same room for ever. He was methodically cutting his throat with an old-fashioned razor, and his body had only just been removed when we entered the room. His blood was splashed all over the place, and some of it had squirted into an open cupboard on to the bread ration. There was an amazing quantity of blood spilt about. The poker-faced old soldier comrades of the dead man showed little or no emotion as they busied themselves cleaning up the mess in silence. They ignored our questions. They had lost a chum, and we were young strangers.

In time we got the story. The suicide had gone berserk; drink, monotony, *cafard*, or some mixture of all three had been his undoing. He was a South African war veteran, and a quiet, clean, well-behaved fellow. That morning without warning he had started to curse the Boers. He then fixed his bayonet, and charged madly up and down the long barrack-room, lunging at the doors at either end. Having perforated the doors, he was persuaded to stop, and he then went quietly to his bed, and sat down on it. His comrades, having seen him in similar moods before, let him alone, in the hope that all would come well, but unnoticed he drew out a razor and savagely killed himself.

We were appalled, and very much scared. We hardly slept that night, and looked in questioning wonder at the forms of our sleeping fellows, who seemed to forget the incident at once, and hardly ever referred to it again.

England: First Impressions

We paraded next day to bury the dead man with military honours. A military funeral in peace is always poignant, and stirs the feelings more than any quick burial on the battlefield. It is an affair of great length and studied deliberation, as if the warriors were loath to give up their man.

The pageantry, the slow march, the reversed arms and muffled drums, the farewell musketry volleys, and the 'Last Post' on the bugles or trumpets intensify the occasion with their intentional sadness and grandeur. We youngsters prayed fervently for the soul of the unfortunate soldier, and we had moist eyes under the gaudy plumes of our strapped busbies.

The stiff bearing and masklike faces of the older soldiers pulled us together somewhat, and on the return to barracks a lively air by the band almost dispersed our gloom.

'That's a nice tune,' I said to my front-rank number, a level-eyed old sweat. 'What's the name of it?' He answered without turning his head: 'I dunno, but we call it *We'll buy another Swaddy for a Shilling.*'

Chapter Ten

THE REGIMENT

A battalion is like a little town, and viewed in this way has many attractions. The seven or eight hundred men and the thirty or so officers are not solely and at all times engaged in training for war. Working hours are not long, and holidays are numerous. A duty soldier, that is, one fully trained, may ease his boredom by finding employment in various stores and workshops, by looking after horses, by making himself expert in specialized jobs like machine-gunnery or signalling, or by educating himself in the regimental school. While still in the army he may become, among other things, a cook, a waiter, a valet, a clerk, a butcher, an armourer, or a storekeeper, if he so wishes. He may also compete for promotion.

These opportunities for initiative were, however, closed to us for some further months. To our chagrin we found ourselves still classified as recruits, condemned to further drudgery in gymnasium and on the barrack-square, under new and fiercer instructors—iron-willed old stiffs of exaggerated egotism, whose every thought and action were directed to destroy all vestige of individualism in us and to remould the messy remains into an unshaken loyalty and devotion to the regiment.

We were bitterly disappointed. The top squad in the depot, and of no account in the battalion. We were given to understand, in the usual discouraging mean way, that we were considered the worst calamity that the second battalion had suffered for many years. We were regarded as curios by our various leaders, and were once more urged to pull ourselves together. I suppose they were right, because we did even better, and though naturally tired of living at a fairly high pitch of professional perfection, we made yet one more effort, and gradually earned the greatest prize possible—the respect of the battalion instructors, and consequent peace of mind.

About this time I became a criminal in the military sense of the term. A sergeant 'lifted' me for being late on parade, and I appeared bareheaded before my judge—Captain Thom, our company commander. The sergeant's evidence was short, to the point, and dismally incriminating. After my name had been called for identification purposes by the captain, the following evidence was spat out without pause, in a most impersonal manner by the automatic N.C.O.:

'Sir, this morning, the ninth of July, at 8 a.m., I, acting as company orderly sergeant, called the roll on parade, and found the accused absent. He later appeared on parade. He was three minutes late, sir.'

Captain: 'Anything to say?'

Self: 'I am sorry, sir. I was late through no fault of my own.'

Captain (gruffly): 'What do you mean?'

Self (less self-satisfied): 'I was at the rear,[1] sir.'

Captain: 'Why did you not say so before? Admonished. Next, Sergeant.'

Our station was one of the old southern English Cinque ports, and the barracks were inside a large fort, surrounded by a deep moat. A number of the living-rooms were hollowed out of the ramparts, so that about half the battalion lived underground. The heavy guns of the fort often fired out to sea at towed targets, and once we saw one of the gunners with bleeding ears and nose, the result of concussion from firing the large guns.

In the summer we had bathing parades in the English Channel, and were safeguarded by patrol rowing boats. This precaution did not prevent accidents, and one morning we had the weird experience of finishing our swim minus one of our number, whose clothing lay tragically unclaimed on the beach. He had sunk unnoticed in the midst of a swarming, gambolling mass of men. His body was washed ashore, some miles along the coast, during the next week.

Here in our seaside garrison town we saw at first hand the traditional state of jealousy between regi-

[1] The 'rear' is a military expression, probably coined in old campaigns, to describe the condition and location of any soldier fallen out of the line of march for purposes of nature.

ments which is referred to by Kipling, and which now happily no longer exists.

An English regiment stationed outside the fort was our old and sworn enemy for some obscure reason. This was a great nuisance, as it interfered with one of our few recreations, that of walking out in the town. The heavy leather waist-belts were often used as weapons, when blows were exchanged between our Irishmen and the English. A nasty business, as the buckle end of a belt can cut a man about badly. To make it worse, our people were very pugnacious, and would never accept defeat, and when fights did not go in their favour secret messages arrived quickly in barracks and fetched out reinforcements. The Englishmen in our regiment forgot nationality and beat up their own countrymen in the supposed defence of the honour of their chosen corps.

As a consequence, one was forced to move warily, to avoid lonely places, and never to go out alone.

I know of one regiment which was routed from a football field and chased into its own barracks, where an angry commanding officer turned it out under arms. Its opponents, an Irish regiment armed with belts, stones, and sticks, viewed this move with great contempt, and gave the routed ones a worse name than ever.

There was one other English regiment and one Scottish regarded with scorn by our fellows. The reasons were historical.

The first had to do with an action during the Boer

War, when the English regiment in reserve was supposed to have surrendered while the Irish in front
were still fighting. Both battalions had actually been
surrounded and trapped, but as some of the English
had also sought to retire, they were still known to us
as 'The Flighters', though the rest of the army called
them by their older and more deserved name of 'The
Fighters'. Anyway, flighters or fighters, a fight was
always bound to occur when we met them.

Our difference with the Scotsmen was the result of
their too canny tactics during an army final football
match, in which our regiment was beaten by its more
calculating opponents from Caledonia.

At the end of the summer of 1913 we were dismissed
the square and we took part in battalion training as
proper soldiers of our companies. In the autumn we
marched out of our station to army manœuvres, after
which we were to move to another garrison. The music
of our going, the tune of *The Girl I Left Behind Me*,
may have stirred the emotions of some of the ladies,
but the soldiers left the place with few regrets, and
at the end of manœuvres, during which one wit
said truly that he had been up to both Oxford and
Cambridge, we settled down in a purely garrison station near Salisbury, where the green country and the
wide plains more than compensated us for the dark
fort of the Cinque port, the narrow town streets, the
squabbles, the straw-hatted bluejackets, the pubs, and
fried fish shops.

One queer tale of the town deserves telling: that

of a strange duel between two old soldiers which took place shortly before we changed station.

These two men had an argument in the canteen on marksmanship. They were both excellent shots, and were probably in their cups when deciding the strange conditions of their competition. One of them had charge of the miniature range, and to this he led his companion. They each took a rifle and a supply of ammunition, and separating, began to stalk each other from opposite sides of the barracks. They ended in exchanging shots from behind cover of the corners of the brick barrack-rooms at a range under one hundred yards. No harm was done except to the brickwork near their respective foolish heads by the time an irate N.C.O. arrived to stop the vendetta.

Two neat groups of shots testified to their undoubted skill, also to that half-joking, half-serious attitude towards life which is peculiarly Irish, and which can seldom be explained even by Irishmen themselves.

When next seen together the two old sweats were again gravely discussing marksmanship over their beer pots, in their own special niche in the canteen.

Chapter Eleven

WE SEEK PROMOTION

The usual shoal of hawkers and bagmen descended on us in our new quarters. Shoddy mufti clothing, boots half cardboard and half leather, lewd picture postcards, and weird tattoo designs were produced for our temptation. My brother and I escaped the lures that fascinated some of our fellows. We were now settling down to this business of soldiering, and had begun to view it in serious fashion. On long country walks we found ourselves again, and planned to make the best of the army.

We were country boys and loved nature. The sight of the wild birds nesting in the woods and on the downs in the spring of 1914 gave us pleasure, and in a way inspired us. We found many birds strange to our own countryside. Long-eared owls, nightjars, and willow-wrens were great discoveries, among our old familiar plover, larks, linnets, yellowhammers, and various kinds of finches.

'Promotion', I said to him in the argot of the soldier, 'is my mark.'

We Seek Promotion

I had a queer shame in admitting it. To seek promotion is to lose caste and numerous friends. The idea is scorned by the ordinary, professional, long-service private.

My brother returned the chocolate egg of a meadow pipit to the beautiful nest in the lee of a ragged tuft of grass, and agreed that promotion would be a good thing. No more scrubbing of floors and hiking of heavy coal-boxes. We would not be menials. We would lead men instead.

Thenceforward we devoured regulations, textbooks, and standing orders. My first-class educational certificate helped me to get work as a clerk in the orderly room. Our determination was noticed, and in a short time we were both appointed lance-corporals.

The first step from the ranks is the hardest to bear.

A newly made lance-corporal can be the unhappiest man in the army. He is immediately isolated from his old companions, and his new friends jealously watch him for any faults, while the single chevron which marks his rank usually numbs his brain; the little strip of cloth appears to be of huge dimensions, and its wearer to be the cynosure of all eyes. Every order he has to give to an old friend is a pain.

Time is the only antidote to this frame of mind. Time and experience of a new circle of friends critical and competitive, who have responsibilities, and who make and give orders. At first responsibility is a terrible scourge.

It is an acid test indeed, and personality is developed

and character formed in seeking a nice balance of behaviour impressive both to the men and the senior N.C.O.s.

Work increases, and the young non-commissioned officer is kept busy from morning until night, ordering out routine parties for parades and fatigues, or looking after a barrack-room of soldiers some of whom are old enough to be his father. And his work is often shelved in order that he may answer for some senior temporarily called away.

The long-service old soldiers were his best friends in the old days. They showed him the N.C.O.s he should emulate, and often advised him as to his treatment of the yet young and unsettled soldier. They consoled him in his bitter moments when injustice blackened his outlook, for injustice there was in plenty in a system which allowed of no excuses.

That was the curse of life. No explanations or apologies were expected, and none was ever offered. You were right or you were wrong, and that was all about it. Sufficient time was never given to the young lance-corporal in which to do all that was expected of him, yet no one dared to say that there was no time. That was absolutely tabooed.

Had the organization been good the young N.C.O.s would have fared better, and many would not have thrown up their stripes in disgust. Most of the old private soldiers had been N.C.O.s at one time or another, but had not considered the game worth the candle.

Here is an example of the kind of situation we had to face and make the best of.

One morning, owing to some early parade, my barrack-room had not been cleaned to my satisfaction; my men had dispersed to their various jobs, and in fear and trembling I was trying to clean it up myself before some senior N.C.O. should discover it in a dirty condition. In the middle of my task the cook-sergeant sent for me, and wanted to know why the hell I had not got the dining-room cleaned out after breakfast. I had forgotten it, and now I had no men for the work. While being ticked off, and wondering what to do, the bugle blew, and I had to rush off to draw groceries at the dry canteen. There the battalion orderly sergeant was supervising issues, and was quite prepared as a matter of cold duty to place any late N.C.O. under arrest.

However, I was present in good time, but suddenly remembered that I was answering for the company orderly sergeant, and that I had to call a parade roll at the same time that I was drawing groceries. I was too young to know any way out of this quandary, and was quite hypnotized by the difficulties of life when the battalion orderly sergeant, with face alight with amusement at the misfortunes of others said to me: 'Old Paddy Blastit will tear the guts out of your company orderly sergeant, whoever he is; the bugle call for his presence at orderly room has just gone for the third time.'

This meant that old Paddy Blastit, the terror of the

whole battalion, the gruff and awful regimental sergeant-major in whose hands we were all pawns, was
waiting and fuming in his office, with all his company orderly sergeants collected except one, and for
that one five bugle calls had blown; two general calls,
and three particular, and my inward spirit, already
sickened with despair at the complications of life,
told me that I was the culprit, for I was answering for
the company orderly sergeant, who was absent on
another duty.

With my brain in a pulp I galloped off to the office
of the enraged regimental sergeant-major, and interested eyes from scores of barrack-room windows
watched the agitated lumbering passage of an
N.C.O. for whom the bugle had blown five times.
A rare occasion, a red-letter incident that would be
the talk of the battalion for days.

I only wished that it had been my sole trouble, for
was I not liable to be arrested also for being absent
from my roll-call on the company parade ground, for
neglecting my barrack-room, and for forgetting the
dining-room?

Happily this complex situation eased itself, and my
troubles dissolved, as troubles have the habit of doing
more often than we dare imagine. Two good-hearted
N.C.O.s had come to my rescue by taking my place
with good excuses for my absence.

Chapter Twelve

ON THE OFFICERS;
AND MYSELF AS PEACEMAKER

The company colour-sergeant pinned young N.C.O.s
to their responsibilities in pre-war days. 'What, a man
of the company dirty on parade?' (The dirt may have
been a minute speck on an otherwise brilliant brass
equipment tab.) 'Bring him up, and run in the bli-
thering N.C.O. in charge of the half-wit's section for
neglect of duty. And YOU'—staring fiercely at the
corporal in charge of the parade—'look at your men,
—standing there gaping like two rows of ducks in a
hurricane. WAKE UP, and wake them up. I don't
know what this bloody corps is coming to, nor how
half of you were got.'

This colour-sergeant placed himself in our category
of bugbears. He was a coarse, callous, terrible fellow,
uneducated, and very offensive and filthy in language, and he practically ran the company.

At the same time the officers had more to do with
us in the regiment than those at the depot, yet they
seemed to spend a lot of time at sport and amusement.
We got to know them better, and found them a mixed

collection with various nicknames given by the men
to mark their idiosyncrasies.

We two brothers preferred the Irish officers, who
were more friendly than the English, and who were
more democratic, or at any rate less feudal, in outlook. To all three officers of our company however,
we gave a great deal of affection and loyalty. The
captain (company commander), a big man named
Thom, was greatly respected by the troops. He was a
huge, tanned fellow, with a black moustache, quite
handsome and distinguished looking. He seldom spoke,
but he had a very critical eye, which did more to quell
and hold us. In all matters he was extremely strict and
very just. He was English.

His second-in-command, Lieutenant Lomas, came
from the middle of Ireland. He was a gentle, lovable
man, who, in contrast to the captain made a point of
knowing us all, of asking us intimate questions, and
who also had the unusual and welcome attribute of
praising us warmly when we did well; consequently
we would have died for him, whereas we would have
merely killed for the captain.

The third officer was a small-sized young subaltern
named Cross, a young English public school boy, as
yet of no account, except that he was an officer of
Irishmen who looked up to him in their ancient traditional clannish way, a way charmingly friendly, but
rather pathetic, and perhaps out of date in a matter-
of-fact country of very mixed peoples.

In return this young officer got very fond of us,

and our brogue amused him. He used to imitate us very well at the regimental concerts, in which he figured as no mean comedian, and having his information first-hand, he never once said 'begorra'.

At our Salisbury Plain station we had the good fortune to find the Munster Fusiliers, and although we knew our own regiment was at a high pitch of training, and most spectacular when turned out, we were greatly impressed by the superb show given by the Munsters on their church parade each Sunday.

Their parades attracted men from other regiments, and their proud martial bearing, graceful movements, and smart precision showed the professional Irish soldier at his best in all the panoply of 1914. The Munsters were tall men too.

At this time I was the means of preventing a row between our regiment and the Munsters, and this was the way of it.

One evening, as I was strolling towards the Munster lines, I met one of them, slightly intoxicated, making for our barracks. He had the fixed eye and smiling mouth of an Irishman with a purpose. I stopped him. 'What cheer, Dirty-Shirt. Where are you going?'

His soft Cork accent sounded like music in my ears. 'Yerra, I'm only goin' down to have a look at the Belfast min.' I did not like the look of him, and took the advantage of lapsing into his way of speaking: 'Is it wan of our fellahs yeh know, that yer wanting te see?' 'Ah no. Sure I know nun of 'um, but', and he leaned towards me, whispering, 'is it true dat deres Orangemin in your mob?'

'Divil an Orangemun,' I lied. 'What would we be doin' wid Orangemin in the army?'

'Is dat a fact now, is dat a fact? Well, I heard different from wan of our blokes—young Paddy Flaherty. He's a great scholar, and he said 'twas stinkin' wid 'um, and their masons an' lodges and all.'

'Can they fight?' he shouted abruptly.

Could they fight? I thought, could they not! One of them had just knocked me out. They were as hardy and truculent as any Cork man, and as willing to meet trouble. 'What are ye talkin' about?' I said. 'The only Orangemin I heard tell of are in Belfast. Have sinse like a good man. Yeh wouldn't be creatin' trouble now, would yeh, between two good Irish regiments?'

His sticky hand grasped mine in a vice-like clutch, and while he was still pregnantly silent with heroic emotions I avoided the closer embrace that was threatening, and gently slewed him round and walked him back to his barracks, completely taking his mind off fighting by recalling to his pleased fancy memories of Cork places: Mallow Lane, and the Fair field, and Blackpool, and old hurling matches.

'Ah, God be with the old days,' he said again and again, as if he were an ancient, and then stopping, with that droll, slow deliberation of the sons of Bacchus, he warned me solemnly: 'I'm givin' yeh advice,' said he, 'a nice young fella like you. Keep out o'

70

trouble in the army. Have nottin to do wid de likes of Paddy Flaherty. Mischief-makers they are. Aye, mischief-makers and drunkards, the whole seed an' breed of 'um, and 'tis dat kind dat might have landed me in de clink dis very day.'

A wink and a nod to one of his own corps, and a most earnest refusal of all kinds of hospitality, and he was at last off my hands, his plaintive truculent voice continuing to outline the darker aspects of the family characteristics of the clan O'Flaherty, who by this time had become thoroughly outcaste, in fact shoneens.

Had my Cork friend come challenging to the Belfast men, he would have got more than he bargained for, in spite of the soft fighting light in his eye, and his terrible handclasp—signs that did not auger well for any individual opponent.

He was lucky to be out of it. Any rash act on his part might easily have led to a lasting feud between the regiments.

He did not know, as I did, that though, owing to the mixture of breeding, the northern Irishman is normally as careful as a Scot nursing his career, yet once his blood is up, there is no holding him.

Chapter Thirteen

AUGUST 1914

The summer of 1914 passed peacefully and well. We two brothers, both now N.C.O.s, had quite settled down, and were satisfactorily taking our minor parts in the organization and running of our regiment.

Nothing very exciting happened to us, except a small adventure on my brother's part. While on temporary duty in charge of stores in a nearby Territorial camp he got suddenly bored, and with a few friends borrowed the bicycles of the Territorials, without permission, and careered off on a spree to a village near Salisbury.

The cyclists got regrettably drunk on beer, lost their machines, and were wandering about laden with all kinds of ridiculous purchases and making inquiries of the yokels about their forgotten bicycle park, when finally discovered by the military police, who came to arrest them in answer to an SOS from the village constable.

Too much English beer had bemused the adventurers, and their feelings were quite dull and depressing until they sighted the Red-caps. That sight cheered them up considerably. With one accord they dropped their useless parcels, and whooping with joy sprang to the attack on the common enemy. In five minutes, however, they were *hors de combat*, and handcuffed. Their drunken spree was strangely overlooked, much to my relief, and they behaved well afterwards.

Events outside the army hardly concerned us at all. International affairs were beyond the professional soldier. We were ignorant and uninterested until, at the end of the summer, the war-clouds gathered over Europe. Then there was no reasoning. Our job was to fight. We were well trained and willing to fight any foreigner, and we were delighted at the prospect of war and glory.

The British Army in 1914 was more used to battle than that of any other nation. It possessed the highest and bravest traditions that can be engendered in a fighting force, and its experience of wars was such that our own regiment, though a young one in the army, had so many battle honours that they were difficult to memorize.

Our state of mind was peculiar to our task. We despised all foreigners, and only wanted them at the end, the business end, of our snappy little Lee-Enfields. We had great *élan* and great hopes. At first we could not follow the trend of events on the Continent. Whom were we to fight? French, Russians, Germans? What did it matter? A dose of that rapid fire of ours, followed by an Irish bayonet charge would soon fix things. A prayer maybe, coupled with some captivating slogan, old or new, would warm our hearts in battle—*quis separabit?* or *lámh dearg abú!* What did it matter?

Then we were told that Germany was the enemy, and we were given illustrated textbooks of the German Army with coloured pictures showing the clothing of the various arms—cavalry, infantry, artillery, etc. The field-grey, rather baggy uniforms, comic boots, and helmets amused us. Anything strange or foreign was inferior, to the mind of the common soldier.

Our company buffoon had us in fits of laughter with his witty and vulgar sallies at the expense of the German Imperial Army. His surmises as to the contents of various pouches and knapsacks were unspeakable.

The German cavalry, which certainly looked comic-opera, dressed in plumes, skulls, crossbones, and Austrian knots, came in for most of the chaff. I must say that the natty flat-capped British trooper, on his hardy mount, looked a far more business-like proposition than these gaudy representations in review order.

We began to prepare for war. We sold our own review uniforms to visiting contractors. We also sold our mufti clothing and boots, and the other few possessions we had. Property does not encumber Atkins. All superfluous army peace-time gear was given back to the quartermaster; and ammunition, iron rations, jack-knives, and identity discs were received instead.

We were all inoculated against typhoid, and some of the men fainted under the full shot. Half-injections had not been thought of in those days. We were advised to make our wills in our soldiers' pocket-books, but the pay columns of these little books interested us more than the will forms. We would get higher pay in the field. The married men had any allotment of pay verified and entered in their books.

Our reservists came streaming in to make up our war strength; cheerful, careless fellows of all types, some in bowler hats and smart suitings, others in descending scale down to the garb of tramps. Soon, like us, they were uniformed and equipped with field kits, and the change was remarkable. Smart sergeants and corporals and beribboned veterans of the South African war hatched out of that crowd of nondescript civilians, and took their place and duties as if they had never left the army. They were an excellent lot but their numbers increased our strength to an uncomfortable extent. Our barrack-rooms became overcrowded, and we looked forward to moving out of them.

We had not long to wait. The mobilization scheme of the British Army was a well-oiled affair, and its execution gave the ordinary soldier as little trouble as moving off to another station. We were pleased to believe the rumour that our own commanding officer had played no small part in making the scheme perfect.

August 1914

On the 13th August we said farewell to peace and England.

A thoughtful leave-taking of the sick in hospital, the young soldiers, and the wives and children, and away we went by troop-train. We were cheered on our journey by all who saw us, and we detrained in the docks at Southampton, where we lay about in some large ugly sheds for several hours.

The right-half battalion to which my company belonged embarked towards evening in a Cork cattle steamer, and when night came we put out in the channel for some unknown destination.

The remaining half of the battalion followed us many hours later in another ship.

We were packed tightly in our ship, and my heavy kit and rifle encumbered me. I found a small place in the scuppers and disposed myself to sleep. My thoughts were chaotic. I felt a warm sentiment towards our little Irish ship, which was later sunk by the Germans, and I tried to think what war meant. I remembered with horror an actual photograph of British dead in a trench at Spion Kop, shown me some years before by a curio collector. A vivid picture of corpses with dark faces.

The detail of one dead man's sock stuck in my memory, a grey army sock in which one could see the pattern of the knitting. I was wearing such socks now. A feeling of nausea came over me, and I was seasick for the only time in my life. Feeling much better, I got up and looked about me.

August 1914

Searchlights of battleships were playing on us. We appeared to be steaming through a long lane of warships whose beams passed us on from one to the other. The crews of the nearest vessels cheered us, and we were thrilled to see the navy at its work. It was inspiring to feel that we were being guarded by the sailors. We cheered back. The lilt of a popular song came back to me:

> *The British Navy's a fighting navy,*
> *And the neighbours know that's true;*
> *For it keeps them in their place*
> *When they know they've got to face*
> *The lively little lads in navy blue.*

In the meantime the second half of the battalion was being lectured, in the ship following us, by the major in command, who told the men in melodramatic fashion that the Kaiser had a grasping hand outstretched to seize them, but that the hand was a withered hand. This speech had not quite the effect intended, for it was a source of amusement for the troops for many days, during which we heard humorous and dramatic references to withered hands, until we got thoroughly sick of the idea.

The Irish did not feel that their country had much at stake in this business, and that kind of speech raised only critical or cynical feelings.

Most of them, in the manner of the professional soldier were unconcerned as to who their allies would be, and as to the cause for which they would fight, which was just as well.

77

August 1914

They were quite content to do as their officers told them, and were well pleased, as I have said, at the prospect of war. Already some of them were discussing the kind of medal they would get for fighting.

Chapter Fourteen

FIRST CAMP AT ROUEN—
MY SECTION

The dawn of the 14th August followed a fine night
and a good crossing, and with the dawn came a view
of the fortifications about Le Havre, at the mouth of
the Seine.

Strange-looking soldiers like those in the coloured
prints of 1870 scampered about on shore, gesticulating
wildly at sight of our ship. They were clad in huge
red trousers, dark-blue long-tailed coats, and peaked
caps. The red trousers amused us.

The conspicuous colour was supposed to be looked
on with favour by the French gunners, whose chief
at one time opposed changing it on the grounds that
'the little red backsides gave him a good distinguish-
ing line, beyond which to range his guns in battle'!
It was very cheering to see our comrades-in-arms of
an allied force, though we had some faint idea that
French soldiers were somehow not up to our standard. We cheered them. The tricolour on their fort
dipped in salutation, and our stern flag answered.
Our men sang the *Marseillaise,* and this stirred the

figures on the shore to more active antics than ever.

We steamed in and up the river to Rouen. All who saw us on the way rushed cheering wildly to the river bank, and every flag, public and private, in sight came down at our passing. Our volunteer flag-dipper got so tired of his job that he had to be relieved. It was fun for the rest of us. Every few minutes hundreds of men scanning the shore for flags, or anything that resembled them, shrieked: 'Dip the flag!'

Some rows of intimate articles of feminine washing were inadvertently honoured, and one fat French-woman got a special dip and a great cheer all for herself.

Going to war seemed a light-hearted business. Let us look at some of the excursionists for a moment.

My brother and I left England as section commanders. We each had eight men. I was twenty years old and a full corporal. He was only nineteen. I was the small, dark, nervous Gaelic type, very proud and anxious to work well. He was bigger, golden-haired, careless, and easy, and a very good mixer with the men. Of my eight men four were reservists, older men who were not so easy to command as the serving regulars. They groused rather too much, and offered gratuitous advice on soldiering.

One sallow-faced fellow named Grimes, from Birmingham, was always complaining. He did not look well, and perhaps that had to do with his pessimism. He spoke depressingly of the worst aspects of active service, of which he had had experience in South

Africa, and said our blissful ignorance would soon get a jolt. Another Englishman named Hoskins was the ideal soldier. He was a big-framed, taciturn, simple man, who always did immediately what he was told. He never showed any emotion, and being very dependable I counted on him to a great extent.

Bugler Tymble was a horny-handed, uncouth, pugnacious Irishman given to swearing and blustering. He grumbled too much, always calling attention to his minor misfortunes, but at bottom he was a fearless useful soldier. Our cheerful optimist was a Belfast man named Cordwain. Belfast men are usually neither optimistic nor merry, but here was a very cheerful chap who never knew the meaning of 'mine' and 'thine', though this worked both ways, and he would share anything. He was very superstitious in a peculiar way of his own, seeing signs and portents in the shape of clouds. He was the chief wangler of the section, and he stole a lot of things for us.

Another man, Brown, was a nonentity, willing and clean, and just Brown. Kelly, O'Brien, and Shea were three smart, quiet young soldiers. I looked on them with a possessive eye, and felt confident and good about them.

We had a most embarrassing disembarkation at Rouen. The French overwhelmed us, soldiers, blue-bloused civilians, women, and children charged us *en masse*, and barely gave us room to form up. They pressed chocolates and flowers on us, and the women kissed us with alarming freedom. I took the oppor-

tunity to have a look at the French infantry, their
Lebel rifles, and their triangular bayonets. Their bullets were copper-coated and heavier than ours, and
they referred to their bayonet as 'Rosalie'. This habit
was not confined to the bayonet. Later we saw that
each of their field-guns bore a lady's name.

In turn the Frenchmen inspected our kit, and were
full of frank admiration. I successfully aired my school
French to the satisfaction of the natives and our own
fellows, but I got the French babbling incoherently—
words shot by me like streams of machine-gun bullets, and I ended the conversation as tactfully as I
could. Tymble hunched a shoulder, and, turning his
cropped red head, looked askance at the foreigners;
barbarians who could speak neither English nor Hin-
dustani, and he was later heard to remark that the
only Christian speaking things in this bloody France
were the cocks and the dogs.

At length we formed up and marched through the
historical streets, past the famous cathedral, and up
a fairly steep hill, called, I think, Mount Saint Aignon,
to a camp above the town.

Crowds of people hemmed us in, running beside
us, and even breaking our ranks, and all cheering:
'Vivent les Anglais'—a rousing reception to my mind
from the inhabitants of Rouen, whose saint the English had martyred in the old days.

Our first camp in France was a misery. We were
crowded, thirteen to a tent, and the heavens poured
rain on us for hours on end, until the ground became

a quagmire, through which we sloshed ankle-deep in mud. It was here we heard Kitchener's message to the army. It was read out on a special parade by the commanding officer, and afterwards each soldier received a printed copy.

Kitchener reminded us of the correct attitude to adopt towards the friendly inhabitants of the country in which we would be fighting, and of the British Army traditions. The message ended with the injunction to us to do our duty bravely, to fear God, and to honour the King.

Chapter Fifteen

UNKNOWN DESTINATION

On the morning of the 16th of August we left the rain and mud of Rouen without regret, and entrained for an unknown destination. We only knew that our train moved all day in a north-easterly direction towards the frontier. We had no idea where the Germans were, what they were doing, and where we should meet them.

The French at Rouen gave us a hearty send-off, and implored us to cut the throat of every 'sale boche' we met.

At Rouen, and at every halting station en route to Belgium, the people swarmed around us with greetings and presents. Fear, I supposed, and their national ardour made them expose their feelings to such an extraordinary degree. Their promiscuous kissing, the cut-throat gesticulations, useless presents, mad hatred of the 'dirty Germans', and their petty pilfering of our cap-badges, buttons, and numerals, 'browned' a good many of us off. Our train had its sides scribbled all over in French and English with various notices in chalk: 'To Berlin', 'To Hell with the Kaiser', 'Down with the Germans', and the like.

One Irishman wrote 'À bas les Allemandes' to the amusement of our officers and the undisguised delight of the French. These French civilians were too excitable by far, and rather upsetting. Had we given them all they demanded as souvenirs we should have eventually fought naked at Mons, armed only with flowers and bon-bons.

At intervals in our slow journey our engine driver supplied us with hot water for tea. The soldier loves his tea. Our rations were plentiful and good, and were the envy of the foreigners; indeed, the French soldiers by the way regarded some of our food as luxurious. Even our bully beef, which we were sick of already, without any experience of war, was most welcome to them. They got lots of it. They simply raved about our jam, and would barter anything for it. I made use of their weakness for these things by sending them off to buy exchanges of cigarettes and other comforts. The promise of a tin of jam would send a score of all ages rushing off on any errand. We liked their bread. Their cigarettes were rotten. The most popular brand, 'Caporal', had a nasty stuffy taste, and really hurt one's throat. Their long-dipped matches made a foul stink and acted like damp fireworks before the light came. Their chocolate was good, and the commonest advertisement in the country was that of the back-view of a little girl with plaits, standing on tiptoe writing the name of a well-known brand.

This advertisement was everywhere. One for Michelin tyres and one for the English Sunlight Soap were impressed time and again on the vision of the soldiers.

Every bridge, station, and crossing on our journey was guarded by French Reservists, whose slouching gait was commented on by us all. Spy-fever broke out for the first time on this rail journey. We were warned about spies by our officers. Spies were everywhere, most of them in the guise of French men and women, and many had been arrested by the French. The best rumour said that a very common enamel wall advertisement of German tyres had been purposely made of lasting metal, with a secret pocket at the back of it, containing maps and notes on local information, and that every village in France boasted one of these outfits.

Our freshness and pleasure at being the centre of so many joyful demonstrations gradually dimmed as the day lengthened.

We became tired and bored, and fed-up because we did not know where we were going. Keeping the soldier in ignorance of what he has to do is very bad and demoralizing. I am sure we would all have been content and cheerful had we been given some inkling of what was happening. As it was, the afternoon saw us sick of the situation, collapsed into ourselves, unable to sit and rest properly owing to overcrowding, and our cumbersome kit further impeded movement in our fuggy carriages.

The day had been too exciting. The younger soldiers sat cramped and uncomfortable, nodding in sleep, and holding flowers and sweets in their hands. The older ones, more used to discipline and past waiting, had reserved their energy, and sat smoking composedly, puffing at their clay pipes or talking quietly among themselves.

At length, towards nightfall, we detrained at Landrecies in Nord, some twenty miles south of the Belgian frontier. We were gravitating towards Flanders —the ancient cockpit of Europe. We marched a little way through the dusk along ill-lighted dingy streets to a village outside the town, and there entered our first billet in France—a large factory, where we settled ourselves on the floor in the spaces between the machines and prepared for sleep.

The soldiers were now tired and silent after their protracted journey. They sat or reclined in little circles around the small flames of candles in the large, high shed, through whose tall windows faint lights filtered through dusty panes from the streets outside. The roof was lost in shadows, and the whole scene with its cases of candles and half-lit groups of armed men, set against the massy background of dull machinery, gave the impression of some sombre, spacious etching by Piranesi.

Chapter Sixteen

COUNTRY BILLETS

We marched out in good weather through the harvest fields to the pretty little village of Marbaix, where we were billeted in the cottages and the outlying farms.

The English were once more in France, their armies hosting in Picardy. Although the divisions were scattered in billets over the countryside, from this moment they were compact and ready to march and fight.

Apart from our business there, and our warlike appearance, a deep sense of peace and well-being informed us. Nature in its most beautiful and bountiful aspect vied with a warm kindly people in contributing to the happiness of an army resting before battle, and the small number of us of the old Regiment who still live may recall that blissful period with tenderness and gratitude, unclouded by the vexed memories of the great events that followed. We can recall the mellow sunlight of that autumn, and the perfume of the country lanes; the smoke of camp fires in the still evenings, tall trees at their stateliest, and the red roofs of little homes nestling in the orchards and the yellow fields.

There was a touch of sadness in the happiness that remains in the memory of it. To-day I may not look on any harvest, and see it unconnected with those days.

We stayed two days at Marbaix, and helped the busy, homely people with their work. They in turn gave us eggs and fruit and vegetables at very cheap prices. Here we were paid for the first time in French money. Francs and sous puzzled us for a day or two but we soon got familiar with the strange coinage.

There were spirited attempts at conversation with the peasants in French, and the troops managed to convey a lot by facial expressions and gesticulations. I enjoyed myself butting in as interpreter, and helping all except those who wanted assignations with the young women, though these were generally well able to look after themselves, and to all invitations to walk they smilingly replied: 'Après la guerre', a saying which lasted throughout the war.

The French countrywomen were more lively minded than the men; they were busier too, and the heavy work of the fields was their common lot.

They were frankly amazed when they found we were not conscripts.

'What? Volunteers?'

'Yes, madame. There are no conscripts in the English Army.'

'Truly?'

'Yes, truly.'

'But your age! How old are you?'

'Twenty years.'

'What an age. Poor child.'

These people were ignorant of matters outside their own villages and department, and they disappointed some of us by thinking that Ireland was in some part of England; yet we found traces of Irish descent in the names of some of the French farmers. One such called himself 'O'Breen'. I do not know how he spelt it.

We left them, voting everything 'bon' in their village, and marched to a similar hamlet called Saint Hilaire. This village was not far from Avesnes, whose townspeople expressed a wish to see the British troops. We marched there and round the town for their benefit to the sounds of a bugle march, and they were delighted at the smart appearance of a British infantry battalion marching under arms in their country, this time to assist them. We had a halt in the town, and the people broke our ranks in the usual fashion of their greeting, and showered presents on us.

Here our officers had the unpleasant task of preventing the people from giving us wine. Judging from the large number of bottles that appeared on all sides, the town of Avesnes was determined to make the regiment drunk. We therefore declined the wine graciously but reluctantly, much to the horror of some of the Frenchmen, who could not understand it. One man sadly concluded that we were too young, for there was not a single man amongst us bearded like a poilu. The fresh appearance of our shaven faces was often a cause for comment, though our older men had marvellous waxed moustaches.

An English girl in the crowd, from a local convent, spoke gravely to me about the issue of the war, in sharp contrast to the excitable and happy French. She was a sweet-faced, gentle creature, much concerned for the safety of the British soldiers, her own men, with perhaps some sad intuition as to our fate.

As we were about to move off she came near to me and put a hand on my sleeve. I saw that there were tears in her eyes and that she could not speak. I smiled her a good-bye, and, strangely touched, marched off to the sound of the bugles, under showers of confetti from the shouting French.

Fifty miles to the north the German columns were at that moment marching through the streets of captured Brussels.

Chapter Seventeen

FIELD PUNISHMENT

At Saint Hilaire I was seated on the front steps of my billet in the main street near the Mairie, over which hung a large silken tricolour, fringed in gold and hung with tassels. The flag had been put up in our honour, and also in honour of the mayor and of *la belle France*. The mayor and the *curé* are the most important personages in each village. We found them polite to the point of ceremony, even when addressing private soldiers, very hospitable, and actively interested in our welfare.

My attention was caught by a little dog harnessed to the axle-tree of a handcart pushed by a peasant. The little dog pulled hard and willingly, bearing his right shoulder well into the harness, and I wondered at the uses to which animals were put in this country. One saw strange combinations, oxen and horses yolked together to a plough, big and little dogs under carts, or pulling wheeled boxes all by themselves, and stranger still, men and women, too, working shoulder to shoulder with their animals. Yet the people were not as kind as our people are to dumb animals, and we saw many an overburdened beast.

As I sat thinking, our jolly platoon sergeant came up and detailed me for duty as guard commander. He cheerfully told me that my guard was to mount at six o'clock, and asked me how I was doing. Sergeant Benson was exceptionally kind for a sergeant, and I think a bit sorry for the younger soldiers, whom he always helped in word and deed. He was the most popular sergeant in the company.

So I mounted my first guard in France, and the duty opened my eyes to an entirely new condition caused by the war. This was the dreaded Field Punishment Number One, meted out to our troops. I had in my charge four soldiers who were being punished for drunkenness, and one of them was an old war veteran and an ex-corporal. They were tied up daily to either a tree or a wagon wheel in public for a fixed period, and they loathed it. When loosed they were taken back to the guardroom and handcuffed.

Confinement of any kind is abhorred to an indescribable degree by Irishmen. No words can describe the stigma of being tied in public to a tree or a wheel, and of being handcuffed as well as being imprisoned. The punishment also included pack drill under the provost sergeant. These men bore it with hard set faces which showed no more emotion than the faces of the dead. We were all sorry for them, and the passing troops averted their looks in shame and compassion when passing the bound prisoners.

Field Punishment

My ex-corporal prisoner had had his handcuffs taken off by me to allow him to visit the latrine. He had returned with his escort, and I was purposely slow in replacing the irons, as he had large wrists and was suffering more than was intended. He was a big, easygoing fool, and quite harmless. Unfortunately a peppery officer took it into his head at this moment to pay us a surprise visit, and finding one prisoner without handcuffs he rated me soundly, and harshly lectured me on the stricter discipline of war. He then dismissed me with no great gentleness. He told me contemptuously to go away. He was a rude, proud, and overbearing fellow, who should never have been in charge of troops, particularly Irish troops, whom, to say the simple truth, he knew little about, even though he was an Anglo-Irishman. His lack of good manners and his cruel stupidities made him highly unpopular, although he was a brave man, and later distinguished himself in the campaign.

The pre-war officer, despite his pleasant fancy to the contrary, was not very much in touch with his men, whose temper and habits were better known to the non-commissioned officers. The senior N.C.O.s generally made themselves more felt in the companies than did the officers, yet the officers were extraordinarily gallant, and their displays of valour, often uncalled for, though thought necessary by them, coupled with the respect engendered in the old army for its corps of officers, won the greatest devotion, and very often the affection, of the men.

Field Punishment

Nevertheless, it was only too patent to the men that when approaching a battle, or other crisis in the war, more than one officer, finding himself lacking true knowledge as to their character, lost his head and in an astonishing way resorted to threats and other extreme and annoying methods. Then the troops, with their uncanny flair for truth at the first shot, generally dubbed such a one 'Windy' among themselves.

Chapter Eighteen

MAUBEUGE

On the 21st of August our brigade resumed its march towards the Belgian frontier, moving directly north over the Sambre, which we crossed at Maubeuge.

The woods and mellow fields resounded with our songs. *Tipperary* was a great favourite, as were also *The Long Trail* and *One More Mile to Go*. A favourite bugle march was *Marching Through Georgia*. *Good-bye My Bluebell* and a parody of *The Girl I Left Behind Me* were also sung. The last two lines of the chorus in the parody were: 'And I'll do pack drill in Arbour Hill, for the girl I left behind me.' One or two plantation songs like *Way down yonder in the cotton fields* were adapted to our march time. Irish tunes were of course popular both on the line of march and at billet sing-songs. *The Harp that Once, Oft in the Stilly Night, Where the River Shannon Flows, The Minstrel Boy*, and *Fare Thee Well, Enniskillen* were in great demand, and Scotland was represented by *Loch Lomond* and *Annie Laurie*. Another song I have not heard since then was *The Girl I Loved in Sunny Tennessee*.

Maubeuge

But the refrain which sticks more than all the others from that period is that about the man who went to mow the meadow. There is nothing of what the Americans call 'uplift' in this rather depressing tune, but to my mind it is always woven into the sound and pattern of the marching feet of our soldiers of 1914. One man always led with a line in which the numbers of mowers increased after each refrain. As an example, the sixth effort was 'Six men went to mow, went to mow the meadow,' and the whole company roared the answer: 'Six men, five men, four men, three men, two men, one man and his dog went to mow the meadow.'

Maubeuge was a great fortress with a large garrison, and as we marched through it we had a fleeting impression of massive stone and cement works, of moats and glacis and drawbridges.

French poilus swarmed along the streets and in the roads about the town to watch us pass, and they cheered us to the echo: 'Vivent les Anglais.' For my company I gaily corrected them: 'Nous ne sommes pas Anglais, nous sommes Irlandais.' They liked that and laughed with pleasure, and then shouted: 'Vivent les Irlandais,' and we cheered back at them: 'Vive la France.'

We were glad to see the French Army in such large numbers for the first time, though neither we nor they knew that before long their great fortress of Maubeuge would be fallen, and that most of the men who now cheered us forward would be made prisoners.

Chapter Nineteen

THE 'TAUBE'

The next day, 22nd August, we marched into a small village a few miles south of Mons, and were about to dispose ourselves in billets, when a whistle blew at the head of our column, and we were ordered to get off the street and take shelter from view by the sides of the houses.

Then we had the first sight of our enemy in the shape of a *Taube* which flew high over the village and away to the south. It looked sinister as it passed slowly over us at a good height, and more like a hawk than a dove.

We had sensed our enemy, and strange feelings stirred us as we settled into our billets. We were being spied on from the air. We appreciated uncomfortably the efficiency of the senders of the scouting plane, the seriousness of the situation that faced us, and the possibility of anything happening, even disaster. One puzzled soldier thought that the aeroplane had a bloody cheek to behave like that. Others wondered where the Royal Flying Corps was, and what it was paid for.

The 'Taube'

A parade was called soon afterwards, and our platoon commander, Lieutenant Waters, lectured us in the nearest farmyard to our billet. He was a cheerful and popular officer with the grand manner, and his address was short and pointed, though not very instructive. He hummed and hawed a bit and then politely addressed Sergeant Benson, asking him if the platoon was present. Benson replied: 'All present and correct, sir.' We held our breaths a moment, and then leaned expectantly towards our officer.

He fidgeted a bit in his usual way, stroking his ginger moustache, his most ferocious attribute, and then, turning his good-natured blue eyes on us, he smiled as he always did, just as if he had seen an assembly of friends unexpectedly, and spoke to his soldiers.

'I rather think it is, ahem, incumbent on me. Yes, that is to say, a duty, to inform you fellahs that an action with the enemy is imminent. Yes, rather. Rapidly approaching, I mean to say, and naturally, yes, let me see, quite naturally, you will be expected to conduct yourselves with valour, by gad, I mean to say courage.

'I might add that you are bound to be successful, but do not forget that when blooding your bayonets, yes rather, blooding your bayonets, do not on any account bury them too deeply. Damn nuisance you know, endeavouring to withdraw an unnecessarily deep bayonet. I remember once old Corbett, I mean to say Lieutenant-General Corbett, great friend of mine, a most distinguished officer. Yes, rather, damn

99

fine fellah and all that, by gad, telling me what a sad job some of his men had in a bayonet charge in Africa owing to their burying their bayonets much too deep, by Jove. Awkward you know, and rather waste of time. So let that be a lesson to you fellahs.

'I think that's about all. No. No, by Jove, you might also know that our cavalry is already in touch with the Boche. Yes rather, quite in touch, and we are all to be prepared to move at short notice, any moment I mean to say.' A smile here, and: 'I think that's all, Sergeant. Dismiss the platoon.'

We broke away to our billets in great fettle and elation. This was the stuff to give the troops. A battle any moment. Keen as mustard, we overhauled our fighting gear, cleaning and recleaning our rifles and recently sharpened bayonets, easing up our cartridge clips, and looking forward eagerly to action.

A most depressing incident followed. Another officer sent for the non-commissioned officers, and when we assembled we found him sad and careworn. Conscientiously, he went into all details of the preparation of our men for fighting: arms, ammunition, equipment, clothing, identity discs, iron rations, feet, sickness, treatment of wounds, field-dressings, stretcher-bearers, care of drinking water, and what not. All very good, and all noted already.

Then came the blow. His passionless voice rose and became coloured with irritation or anger. He spoke of malingering; a word the mention of which made us turn pale with angry scorn, and threateningly he warned us of the dire penalties awaiting any non-commissioned officer who checked in the attack. He also promised to deal summary justice in the field to any coward or to any scrimshanker who stepped aside to attend to any wounded soldier. He concluded by warning us to be ready to join battle with the enemy on the morrow.

We saluted him coldly on dismissal, and made off thoroughly dispirited and silent until out of his hearing, when the very discipline he sought to maintain was shattered by his insulted non-commissioned officers, who, junior and senior alike, gave vent to remarks of disgust and resentment.

'Well, my God, did you ever hear such a bloody thing before?' 'The blasted old fool.' 'Well, I'm jiggered.' And the like.

Some of the N.C.O.s whistled in surprise, and some were silent.

An old sergeant curtly warned the talkers to be careful, and to shut up. His acid blasphemy as he did so was not altogether directed towards them. They realized that, and grinning dispersed more quietly.

Towards evening it was learnt that the Germans were nearer than expected, and one of our companies was detached on outpost duty to the nearest village between us, and the line of the enemy advance. It marched out to occupy this position so as to cover our billets, in order that the remainder of the battalion might not be surprised at night.

This occupation of outposts was the first warlike

act of the battalion, and from now on until the armistice there was no peace for those of us who survived.

The three remaining companies lay on their arms in billets ready to move forward if alarmed.

Chapter Twenty

THE RIDERLESS HORSES

At midnight I was aroused from my shakedown on the kitchen floor of our billet by our platoon-sergeant, Benson, shouting: 'Come along, McCarthy, show a leg, and turn out at once with your section.'

We had not taken off our boots and had been sleeping in our greatcoats, on straw, with our packs as pillows. We were quite used to this in peace-time training, and had slept well.

We quickly donned our equipment and paraded in the village street, where the four ammunition carts of the battalion were already drawn up ready to move. The second-in-command of the battalion then rode up out of the darkness and called for the section commander. He said we were to escort the carts to the place occupied by 'B' Company on outpost, and off we went into the night, headed by the mounted officer.

After a while he called me forward to his stirrup, and asked my name, and my probable action in case I was attacked *en route*. Alas, my faculty for command had been numbed by the excitement and possibilities of my job, and I had made no plan for the defence of my little convoy. However I soon made one and made my eight men familiar with it.

We arrived safely, and halted in the main street of a small village. 'B' Company was somewhere near, but we did not see them.

The major had some difficulty in knocking up the inhabitants, who seemed badly frightened. They had been raided within the last hour by a patrol of Uhlans, who had carried off some sheep. They thought the Germans had returned, and they were overjoyed to find us British. They peered at us curiously, and fervently cursed the enemy. We in turn scanned these trembling, cursing civilians with the cold incurious eyes of armed men; the eyes of fatalists ready willy-nilly to die in their protection.

A mounted patrol raiding for rations appeared normal to us, though we all experienced a thrill in missing the Germans by such a narrow margin. The Frenchmen sensed that we had no time for wordy warfare, and one old man in clogs, the most talkative of the lot, who had made a great point of excitedly showing us about four times where the enemy cavalry had tied up their horses, was the first to become sensible. He grasped the meaning of my repeated request in halting French, and buzzed off to fetch us some hot coffee.

Our major, after warning me to be prepared to defend the ammunition carts, left us entirely to our own devices for the rest of the night. We had little to fear. It was obvious that the enemy patrol was but an advanced detachment of their covering mounted troops, and even if they succeeded again in evading our own cavalry screen, which was well forward of our position, we could easily cope with them.

Mounted men are particularly helpless against infantry, and we were quite ready to receive them with our high-powered rifles.

I now thoroughly enjoyed my little isolated command.

I had the carts drawn under cover behind the gable end of a house, and I reconnoitred the village and the roads to the north as best I could in the darkness. I chose positions for my eight men in case of alarm, and mounting double sentries I ordered the remainder of my men to rest by the roadside, but to remain fully clothed and equipped. Our horses were outspanned. The few remaining hours of pregnant darkness were shared with me by my Lance-Corporal Letts, a quiet good-tempered fellow posted to me since our arrival overseas. We took turn about to keep awake and supervise the sentries.

I wondered a lot that night. My mind was too active for deep sleep. I spent long intervals looking into the velvet blackness towards the enemy, my mind questing and trying to anticipate the next move in this very strange game. Whatever shape that move took it was bound to be momentous. That much at least I knew, though my comrades, some of whom were happily and innocently snoring, seemed to be entirely unconcerned.

The German patrol did not return.

In the morning the villagers helped to cook our breakfast, and, refreshed and alert, we stood ready for any coming emergency.

We had not long to wait. The adjutant galloped up from the rear and ordered us forward about a mile to the next village. He there told us to be ready for immediate attack, so, seeing that all roads from the direction of the enemy converged on the village square, I lined the southern edge of it with my eight men. This was Sunday morning, 23rd August 1914.

The devout inhabitants of our hamlet came out at various hours during the morning to attend Mass in the church at the opposite side of the square, and they presented the only movement to our front for some hours. We lay on our stomachs watching them, and from time to time I had to warn them not to group in front of us, and not to converse with the men. They were very anxious and curious, and their women, mostly dressed in black, looked sad and pale-faced in their sombre garments.

Presently our left hands slipped forward to the fore-ends of our rifles at the sight of approaching cavalry.

Their slow careless gait and khaki uniforms soon showed them to be British. These mounted men were only six in number, and they led in other horses beside their own. On approaching them I was surprised to learn that they had been in action, and were all wounded, slight wounds, bullets through arms and muscles, and that kind of thing. They were hussars. We were full of admiration for these heroes. They told us that some of their regiment had been killed, hence the led horses, and we looked on them and the riderless horses with increased respect. There is something poignant in a riderless horse coming out of battle. For the moment we thought them even greater beings than the cavalrymen. The mildness in their eyes and the grace of their bodies as they pawed the ground warmed us towards them. We patted their sleek necks. The wounded troopers were looking for a field dressing-station. Their wounds did not require the rough treatment we were prepared to give. They were already tied up with their own soldiers' bandages.

My questions as to the nature of their encounter, place, time, and the result of the combat only puzzled them. They were simple ignorant troopers, exaggerated and vague in language, and anxious to get on and have their wounds further attended to.

One of them, seated carelessly on his horse, with his cap lying neglected on the back of his head, took his cigarette from his mouth, spat, and offered the remark: 'Pretty hot up there, Mick,' indicating with a back nod the direction whence they had come. All Irishmen are Mick to English soldiers.

A party of nuns from a near-by convent, armed with lotions, clean cloths, scissors, cotton, and hot drinks, fairly swooped down on the wounded, and I have never seen British soldiers surrender so gladly. The coaxing voices of the compassionate and skilful nuns, their deft fingers, their cleanliness and goodness, contrasted strangely with the blood-stained garments, the jingling harness, and the rough jests of the petted troopers. We left the patients in good hands.

Things were certainly stirring. The sight of blood and other signs of battle and sudden death had a stunning effect, which somehow demanded a consultation with one's inner self.

I mused, collected and inspected my feelings, and examined my conscience. I said a few prayers to make up for my missed Mass, and for our protection in any coming ordeal, and then in a proper frame of mind found all well and healthy.

As I was warning my men to continue on the alert, the adjutant reappeared, cursed my dispositions, and ordered us to rejoin the battalion, which was now to be seen moving forward in column of route on a main road half a mile away to our right. Acting on his instructions we did not rejoin our company, but remained as escort to the ammunition, taking our place with it, in rear of the column.

We swapped news with the nearest men in the ranks, and learned that nothing exciting had happened to the battalion in our absence, except that a line of trenches had been dug as a defensive measure about a mile behind, and then abandoned on the orders of a staff officer, who wished the battalion to move forward towards the town of Mons, now visible through the slag heaps of many mines, on the right front of the marching regiment.

This dirty-looking factory town had no particular interest just then for us, until suddenly above the sound of the tread of our marching feet we heard the booming of field-guns.

A queer, thrilling, and menacing sound about which there were many conjectures, the most popular being that they were French seventy-fives, and that they were giving the Germans hell.

This notion greatly depressed us. We should really hurry up now, otherwise we would miss the battle. The French would get all the glory, while we, with our capacity for deadly rifle-fire and dash in the attack, would miss that crowning moment of victory, culminating in a sweeping bayonet charge, relentless and invincible—the grand assault that would drive the enemy off the field.

So we damned the French for not waiting for us. . . .

Chapter Twenty-one

UNDER FIRE

A staff officer came perspiring from behind, and overtook us. He trotted past in a hurry, asking for the commanding officer. A hundred voices answered him: 'At the head of the column, sir,' and eight hundred pairs of eyes viewed him with that feeling of amusement peculiar to a mass of men finding entertainment in the efforts of an isolated individual.

The soldiers criticized his accent, his face, his seat, and his mount in turn, and then they cursed him because of the result of his coming. This was the order to turn about, and go back the road they had come, to the trenches abandoned that morning.

So about we went, and passing back to the rear of the line of trenches took to open country in artillery formation, and thus extended went forward to occupy the earthworks.

The old army was familiar with the siting and digging of trenches, though it was generally trained for open warfare. The type of trench here was called a kneeling trench, as it was roughly only three feet deep, this being considered good enough for temporary occupation by infantry not expected to remain in it for the entire course of a battle. Our motto was 'Attack, or counter-attack', and we had very little time for entrenchments, which, though they might be useful during a short period of temporary defence, were generally despised.

With many jokes the men settled into their defences and cheerfully waited for the enemy, presenting in his direction a line of first-class riflemen, each trained to fire fifteen well-applied shots a minute. Our two machine-guns poked their squat muzzles in support from their emplacements.

A battery of field-guns wheeled away from the main road, and drew up on the back slope of our position about three hundred yards to the rear. The menacing mouths of the eighteen-pounders slewed round in our direction and remained, while the horses were led rapidly away under cover. The activities of the smart-looking gunners slowed down, and the teams became still behind their gun-shields. A young subaltern came forward to our height as observation officer.

All then was ready, as far as we were concerned, for the battle of Mons.

At half-past three in the afternoon, as nearly as I remember, the Germans discovered us before we saw them, and three or four dull thuds to our distant front followed by a whirring noise rapidly approaching us marked the discharge of enemy guns, and our first moment under shell-fire.

The salvo of shells passed over our heads, and burst about eighty yards in rear with a terrific clattering crash.

We were highly interested. More came, and still more, all going over. The heads of our curious men appeared above the trenches looking back to see the bursts. 'Look,' they shouted, 'a black one', or 'One only', or 'Four more whites'. Some laughingly imagined themselves on butt duty on the rifle ranges at home, and shouted advice to the German gunners: 'Washout', 'Another miss', and 'Lower your sights'. One wag, simulating great terror, cried: 'Send for the police, there's going to be a row on here,' and another, in mock despair: 'Oh mother, why did I desert you?'

Then the enemy gunners shortened, and the shells exploded above our trenches, and the men, already taken in hand for exposing themselves, crouched low.

I had been standing about by my ammunition carts on the open road immediately behind and parallel to our trenches, and not far from the commanding officer, who was, with his adjutant, fully exposed on a little rise nearer to the entrenched companies, when fragments of a bursting shell ripped and slashed all round us. Someone shouted: 'Take cover,' and my men and I, leaving the carts to the drivers, took shelter as best we could in the roadside ditch, amateurishly choosing that side of the road farthest from the enemy.

The Germans now ranged well, and their shell-fire seemed to concentrate heavily on the trenches.

Under Fire

The acrid smoke of the explosions blew about us, and screaming pieces of metal and shrapnel balls flew in all directions. One shrapnel bullet hit my pack, and I instinctively moved a little farther along the ditch to a burly sergeant, who laughed at me when I handed him the still hot ball for his inspection. I was too young to discern nervousness in the laugh. A dispatch rider coming towards us on the road from the west fell off his motor bicycle when a shell burst over him. His antics distracted and amused us. The shell-fire became hotter and hotter, and we crouched farther down in our ditch. The commanding officer still remained exposed to all the fire, and his adjutant kept taking messages to the entrenched companies. Two stout fellows. Finally the shelling ceased, and we put up our heads to breathe more freely. Then we heard conch-like sounds—strange bugle calls. The German infantry, which had approached during the shelling, was in sight, and about to attack us.

Not a shot had been fired from our trenches up to now, and the only opposition to the Germans had been made by our field-gun battery, which was heavily engaged behind us, and making almost as much clamour as the enemy shelling. To my mind it seemed that the whole battalion must have been wiped out by that dreadful rain of shells, but apparently not.

In answer to the German bugles or trumpets came the cheerful sounds of our officers' whistles, and the riflemen, casting aside the amazement of their strange trial, sprang to action. A great roar of musketry rent

the air, varying slightly in intensity from minute to
minute as whole companies ceased fire and opened
again. The satisfactory sharp blasts of the directing
whistles showed that our machinery of defence was
working like the drill book, and that the recent shelling had caused no disorganization. The clatter of our
machine-guns added to the din.

For us the battle took the form of well-ordered,
rapid rifle-fire at close range, as the field-grey human
targets appeared, or were struck down. The enemy
infantry advanced, according to one of our men, in
'columns of masses', which withered away under the
galling fire of the well-trained and coolly led Irishmen. The leading Germans fired standing, 'from the
hip', as they came on, but their scattered fire was
ineffective, and ignored. They crumpled up—mown
down as quickly as I tell it, their reinforcing waves
and sections coming on bravely and steadily to fall
over as they reached the front line of slain and
wounded. Behind the death line thicker converging
columns were being blown about by our field-guns.

Our rapid fire was appalling even to us, and the
worst marksman could not miss, as he had only to fire
into the 'brown' of the masses of the unfortunate
enemy, who on the fronts of two of our companies
were continually and uselessly reinforced at the short
range of three hundred yards. Such tactics amazed
us, and after the first shock of seeing men slowly and
helplessly falling down as they were hit, gave us a
great sense of power and pleasure. It was all so easy.

The German survivors began to go back here and there from the line. The attack had been an utter failure. Soon all that remained was the long line of the dead heaped before us, motionless except for the limb movements of some of the wounded. Every battle seems endless to those taking part in it. All sense of time is lost, and the minutes appear to be hours. The sequence of events is lost, and the most unlikely tales are told by survivors. I am hazy as to what happened after the first great attack. I believe the Germans tried to come on again, but I am not sure. At any rate they did not succeed.

We were not without casualties, but for such a terrific lot of shooting they were very few indeed, and were actually the least we had in any battle in the war. Only three or four men were killed and the same number wounded. Most of the German shrapnel shells had burst too high, and their rifle-fire was hopeless.

A German shell burst on one of our machine-gunners, killing him instantly. His place was immediately taken at the gun by a lance-corporal who was shot almost at once through the arm. He, though wounded, continued to fire his gun, but he rather puzzled those near him by weeping at intervals, either with pain or fright. He would not, however, leave his gun until his arm stiffened. One seldom hears a soldier crying, or raising his voice in any way, for that matter, when wounded. A shot through joints like the knee, or through the stomach, often makes a man shout out in great pain, but most wounds are merely numbing for the time being. Most of the pain comes afterwards when the wounds are being dressed in hospital.

Our commanding officer still stood on the high ground overlooking the scene of action. He now had fears for our ammunition supply. I had doled out a large number of boxes, and an officer presently came along and ordered all my carts away to be refilled. The sounds of battle had died down, and all was quiet except for some intermittent shelling from the Germans. I was to take my carts off to a refilling point controlled by the artillery a mile or so away to the south-east. It was getting dark and the lights of enemy camp fires could be seen in the distance. Nearer, their red-cross lanterns appeared here and there on our front, showing that they were attending to their wounded.

A mounted bombardier came to guide my carts, and off we went, passing along a road that appeared to me at times to traverse no-man's-land, for we passed British infantry facing north, on our right hand. They greeted us and joked at us from their trenches.

We had had orders to hurry, and in the rush of our departure no check was made of the total amount of ammunition still in hand. In order to travel lightly we had also been told to leave our packs behind us in our ditch. Having gone some distance in the darkness, I noticed that three of our four carts gave forth the heavy rumble of well-weighted vehicles, and I called a halt to examine them. I found the three almost full, and completing them from the fourth I took matters into my own hands and brought them back at once to the battalion, terrified lest it should be without a reserve of ammunition in case of another enemy attack. The fourth cart I ordered on to the refilling point, with two of my men and the bombardier.

It was after midnight when I rejoined the battalion, and reported my action. The officer who had sent me merely said: 'Good, now go and rejoin the machine-gun section.' I found the section fallen in on the road behind the trenches, and saw that our companies were also evacuating their positions.

All was very still and peaceful. Quiet words of command were passed along: 'Number'; 'Form fours'; 'Right'; 'Keep silence'; 'Quick march'. And off we went stealthily, in columns of fours from the battle-field of Mons.

In the morning the entire British Army was marching south in retreat.

Chapter Twenty-two

RETREAT FROM MONS

Shortly after daybreak we halted and were ordered to cast away our packs. Mine had already been left behind at Mons. I was very much fed up when I remembered leaving a tin of Capstan tobacco and a packet of Zig-zag cigarette papers in it. We were great smokers in the old army.

The men of the regiment hated the idea of abandoning their packs and greatcoats. That alarmed them. They could imagine this gear being discovered by the enemy, and the German exultation at having us on the run. Besides, although the pack was heavy, we preferred it. It kept us upright, and balanced the heavily laden ammunition pouches in front.

Then this retirement business was not very acceptable.

Why did we retire? We had beaten off an enemy calculated on the spot as being from five to seven times our number. We alone had wiped out at least one whole enemy battalion with the loss of a few men. We had beaten our enemy and were full of fight. Now we looked as if we were in flight. What was happening anyway? And why did we not finish the business by assaulting the broken Germans? Marching away like this was very distasteful. In fact, it was not soldiering.

Gloomily the troops salved their mess-tins, the only article allowed to be taken from the cast-away packs.

To add to our misery a morbid-minded machinegunner, tidying up his cart, handed round for inspection the equipment of the man who was killed at his gun the day before. It was all tattered from the shellburst, and was stained with blood.

We handled it with reverence, and a little fear, and we recalled that the owner had been our champion miler, nearly every one commenting on the spectacular finish of his last race two months before, when he won but collapsed exhausted at the tape. He was now behind us on the crest we had defended, clothed in his uniform, and wrapped in a sewn-up army blanket in a shallow grave.

His comrade gunners went into great detail regarding his mutilation and sudden death. I heard with interest that shattered skull bone gleams like mother-of-pearl. I turned away in nausea, and echoed the automatic prayer of an old stiff who said: 'Well, he was one of the first to pass out. His number was on that shell all right. The Lord have mercy on him.'

The general depression in the vicinity of the gun limbers was dispersed by the inevitable comic incident. A conscientious young soldier was noticed engrossed in counting his empty cartridge cases, which he carefully cleaned and put back into their clips. The idiocy of picking up empty cases in battle—an automatic peace-time rifle-range habit—sent a whole company into fits of laughter, and the nonplussed youngster was mercilessly chaffed.

Cordwain, lying near me, leaned over and asked: 'Did ye not hear of Sergeant Sullivan?' I said: 'No, what is it?' 'Well, he was left behind with a bullet in his shoulder. He kicked up bloody hell about it. Said he came out here to work up to a commission. He wanted to march on, and not to go into dock at all.' 'Ambition is a great spur,' I said. 'He had the African D.C.M. too.' 'Ambition, I dunno about that, but he was bloody insubordinate to the major doctor, and his language would rouse the Divil. A hard man, believe me. A hard man.'

Our company commander then sent for the N.C.O.s and he told us to tell the men that the battalion had fought well, and that the colonel was pleased about it. He regretted that we were going back instead of towards the enemy, but explained that though the Germans in great numbers were checked on the British front, other and stronger enemy columns were marching rapidly round our left, unprotected flank, in an unopposed enveloping movement towards the west, and that it behoved us to move without delay, to occupy our next position in rear, lest we should be overwhelmed while marching in the open.

That sounded all right, but we wondered where the

French army was. We had heard it was a large army. Doubtless it would join us later, and fighting in line with us, would give the Germans their *finis*.

Anyway we were relieved, and we had been blooded in a battle in which we had held up the famous German Imperial Army. We were all very proud about it, and had no fear for the future. We would acquit ourselves all right. Never fear. Oh yes. Some of our lads were already swanking as seasoned warriors during this, our first halt of the 24th of August. One boy, aping the lurch of older soldiers when bored, pushed back his hat to show off his quiff, and addressed Nobby Clarke (one of our finest older men, who was quietly smoking his pipe), saying over his lip-hung cigarette: 'Cushy bit of a battle that, Nobby, but it looks as if we were in for a bit of a walk to-day.' 'Aye,' said Nobby, 'and we may have more than a walk, I'm thinkin'.' Not a whit abashed the lad shouted on to the next friend: 'Mornin', Mac, how are yer poor feet. Any news of what we are goin' to have fer breakfast?'

We had now transferred our haversacks to the backs of our equipment in place of the packs, and we strapped our mess-tins below them, and so introduced a new form of field-dress, which was later officially recognized and called 'Fighting Order'.

We donned our gear, fell in, and marched off to a succession of whistle signals, and after a while the rhythm of our going brought songs to our lips. Our popular *Tipperary* and *One Man Went to Mow* marked the pace of our retirement, while, as the morning drew on, the distant thud of guns fell on our ears, and occasional white bursts of shells could be seen against the green and gold of the landscape behind us.

The Germans, slowed down by our covering cavalry screen, were trying to shell our retiring columns.

> *Good-bye, Piccadilly, farewell, Leicester Square;*
> *It's a long, long way to Tipperary,*
> *But my heart's right there.*

So we turned our backs on Mons, and it was a long time before our soldiers sang their songs again thereabouts.

Chapter Twenty-three

'PUSH ON, PUSH ON'

The battalion marched southwards steadily from 2 a.m. until about 10 a.m., when there came a diversion during a halt.

A German aeroplane overtook us from the rear, and we all opened independent fire on sighting it. It crashed as a result, in a long swoop into some fields on our right, disappearing from our view behind a line of trees. We heard that the German pilot, together with a little boy he had with him, had perished. A queer addition the boy, but I tell as I heard.

While we were still resting our officers visited the local shops for food, and amused us by reappearing with bread transfixed on their swords—an ingenious way of carrying half a dozen bulky loaves of French bread.

Then, as we were about to move on again, someone shouted: 'Take cover,' and we slipped into the hedges and froze. We saw a large body of cavalry crossing open country in front of us, about half a mile away, and right across the line of our retreat. The officers, using their field-glasses, said: 'Germans.'

The whole battalion lay low in ditches and behind walls and hedges as the horsemen crossed from right to left without seeing us. This large force, though trotting, took an appreciable time to disappear, and then we continued our march.

Soon after this the men began to feel anxious. Our rapid marching seemed purposeless, and no other regiments were to be seen. It became evident that we had missed our way. Refugees surrounded and obstructed us. They used all kinds of vehicles, from perambulators to farm-carts, and they blocked the roads with their families, their bundles of household goods wrapped in sheets and blankets, their horses, fowls, sheep, dogs, and cattle. They were in a proper mess. Their many garments, their dirt and dullness, were not very admirable. Some showed despair, others were apathetic. One man excitedly told us that we could find Germans back in a village miles away, if we wanted to fight them. On the whole the refugees displayed an air of calm resignation. The women clutched their babies tightly, as if they would never release them. These mothers were the exception. They conveyed the terror showing in their eyes to their children, while their lips moved in supplication to the Almighty. They barely glanced at the troops, so lately warmly welcomed and now so useless to them that they even pushed them aside in the hurry to imagined safety.

We bridled at our own futility, and at the same time were touched and sorry for the homeless women and little ones; but war is war, and the fighting man cannot burden himself and must have right of way.

Another alarm in the afternoon caused the battalion to leave the road, turn about, and take up a position to repulse closely pursuing cavalry. There were cries for ammunition, and the men of my section, leaping up beside the drivers, trotted the carts out to companies and dumped extra boxes behind the riflemen lying in the fields. Then my convoy reassembled on the road and waited for the sounds of battle, but none came.

The German cavalry had just one look, were not fighting, and had sheered off.

I was then ordered to take my carts along to the transport column, which had gone on ahead in retirement, having been told to move south independently, keeping to the roads, while the battalion, now definitely at sea, struck across country in an endeavour to find the rest of the brigade.

Unlucky battalion. It marched and countermarched across the line of retreat, before finally finding the brigade late in the evening, when it enjoyed a long-deferred meal and a short rest.

The next day and the next the battalion formed part of the rear-guard to our division, and time and again it was isolated in positions covering the retirement. It was definitely reported as lost on the morning of the 26th of August.

Meanwhile our transport moved with a disorganized stream of mixed traffic, and our deadly tramp continued.

My section began to feel fagged. We had had to walk and trot after the carts until we were sick and tired of them. No one except the drivers was allowed to ride on vehicles.

The quartermaster—a kindly old soul—lent me his horse at intervals, and I sagged satisfied in the saddle for many miles. We marched well into the night before halting, and had a short sleep. But 'Push on, push on', was the order, and very little sleep we got. We were up and off early out of our billets the next day, and kept going until evening, which brought us to the comfortable-looking town of Caudry.

As we entered a mob of civilians of both sexes gathered, shrieking: 'The Germans are close behind you. Look, there are horsemen!' Drowsily we gazed back the road we had come, and I and those near me could see nothing of what I could only suppose to have been cavalry patrols dogging us, and we cared less than nothing. The Uhlans were afraid of our rifle-fire anyway. Over and over again the enemy cavalry missed great opportunities of inflicting damage on us. They pressed close just in order to mark us down, and then went off without firing on us. Anyway, we were exhausted and uninterested.

If the Germans were close behind, nothing came of it that night.

We looked forward to a hot meal and a sleep, and

we got both, thank God, from our admirable quarter-master. The dinners of the lost battalion became cold once more, and wasted in the field-kitchens.

After my meal I remember looking in a weary way at the religious pictures that adorned the walls of the kitchen of a little shop in the Rue d'Alçace, which had been allotted to my section as a bedroom, and carefully lifting my harness off my chafed shoulders I flopped down and allowed my mind to race over the events of the last few days, before sinking into the most profound sleep on the stone floor. We had marched from near Avesnes up to Mons, and then back in zigzag fashion to Caudry, in line with Cambrai, since the 21st of August. About seventy-five miles in five days, and a battle into the bargain.

Enough for any troop. To hell with it.

I said a prayer, and sank off.

Chapter Twenty-four

LE CATEAU (1)

I was sleeping soundly on the stone floor of my kitchen billet in the Rue d'Alçace at Caudry on the morning of the 26th of August when the rude reveille of a salvo of bursting shells brought me to my feet. These were the opening shots of the battle of Le Cateau.

I went to the front door in time to see the next shells arriving. They exploded in the open fields just beyond the opposite houses. The Germans were in on us, as the troops say.

I found little alarm as I fell in my section outside. Lieutenant Lomas, the transport officer, passed quickly along the street giving out quiet orders to assemble in the town square. We passed a huge army dump of rations on the way there; bags of bread and sugar, tea chests, tinned milk, and piles of carcasses of sheep—the food of a whole division it seemed.

Enemy shells began to slash into the streets, and the rumble of falling masonry was heard between the reverberating reports of the explosions. It sounded exactly like thunder, blinding flashes followed by the rumble of collapsing houses. The townspeople grew afraid and panicked about. They ran into houses, carefully locking their doors, and at the next roar of shells they opened their doors again, and so kept rushing out and in like rabbits, and sometimes grouping for a moment or two in the streets in little staring crowds.

There was no movement in the town square itself except for the arrival of soldiers in odd lots—the details of many regiments. The civilians had cleared away from that open space.

Military cooks, farriers, clerks, transport men, storemen, grooms, and soldier servants were being assembled and handed over to the command of the nearest officers. The brigadier appeared and came over to our bunch of nondescripts, in which I had the only formed section, and told us two things. First, the best news of the day, as he said—that our battalion was safe and sound, and was now marching on Caudry; and secondly that, pending its arrival, we were to rush off to defend the northern end of the town, against which the Germans were preparing to attack. Men of other regiments, French interpreters, and staff officers helped to load us up with extra ammunition, and led by a Major Williams of our own, the quartermaster, and the transport officer, off went our forlorn hope up a street towards the Germans.

We soon came to the end of the small town, and with other small groups of men from different units

we extended into a defensive position in the open
fields covering Caudry.

A machine-gun section of the Royal Irish took post
on our immediate right. A welcome sight. We had
heard that Brigadier Doran's brigade, which included
his own Royal Irish, had had a tough time, and had
done well at Mons, and we were glad to have any of
them near us. We had hardly lain down when four
sharp bangs from our left rear told us that one of our
own batteries had begun to slam its shells towards the
Germans from under cover of the houses of the nearest
street.

We riflemen had a good field of fire—about four
hundred yards to our front and right. Our left was a
bit blind, as we could see nothing beyond 150 yards
in that direction. We strained our eyes in vain, looking for targets, but nothing appeared. The Germans
had already learned their lesson from Mons, and had
become cautious. Instead of men they sent shells in a
steady and intense bombardment of the town behind
us. And from time to time fresh German batteries
arrived and took part in the game. The streets nearer
us began to melt away, and clouds of varied-coloured
smoke from conflagrations, from brick-dust, and from
bursting shells obscured the view behind. Nearer us,
in the rear, blinding flashes of concentrated explosions licked all about our single gallant field battery,
which had been quickly marked down by the enemy,
and which gradually slackened fire until it was ultimately smashed to silence.

Le Cateau (1)

Bullets now began to swish and whistle about us, and low-flying hissing shells skimmed close over our heads, showing that our thin line of infantry had also been observed. Luckily all these shells were overs; a long, white wall at the end of our particular potato field was hit several times, and nosecaps hummed back over us from the bursts.

Things were hotting up. My section took out their entrenching tools, and, pinned low by the skimming bullets and shells, we dug in as best we could in our lying position. We threw up some earth in front, and lying on our sides carefully excavated long holes to fit our bodies, working right and left alternately, until we sank below the surface into the soft earth. Lord, how we appreciated those entrenching tools, which we had hated so much during peace-time training. We were now fairly safe from bullets at any rate. We could hope that the shells would continue to go over us.

Presently the Royal Irish machine-gun opened fire across our front. I looked left but could not see the enemy, who were evidently drawing in on that flank. The gun crew then lost their target, and sent a scout around to my left to pick a better position for firing. He signalled the gun across to a suitable mound, evidently one from which he could observe. The team crossed over, and were pointing the muzzle of their gun carefully over the mound when one of them was shot and rolled down the little slope. The others collected their gun and went back to their old spot on the right, from where they again fired at intervals. They stopped again, and came over to the mound, again drew enemy fire and returned.

They did this three times in all, crawling about under heavy fire during their daring excursions.

Lieutenant Lomas presently reported that the enemy were working round our left flank, and Major Williams passed along the warning: 'Prepare to retire to the nearest cover in the town.'

A whistle blew, and we sprang up, and were about and away as hard as we could pelt, slipping and stumbling on the potato ridges, while an enemy volley scattered around us. The German infantry had got closer in on our flank than we knew, and seeing us suddenly springing from the earth, had shot us up, hastening our breakaway. A bit ruffling that. I felt like a pelleted partridge. We reached the cover of some walls and found that only one bullet had hit us. It grazed Grimes's cap and did him no harm. He complained about it. He would. I have said he was a grouser. He forgot his narrow escape in a lugubrious examination of the damage. We directed our relieved laughter at him.

Excited and winded by the scamper, we stood about leaning on our rifles to recover our breath. The major then joined us with the transport officer, Mr. Lomas, and, shouting something about retiring slowly through the town, led us back to a crossroads, where we lined the streets, ready to shoot the German infantry if they appeared. Shells crashed all about the place.

A few yards to our left front a gunner major crouched dead on one knee against a garden railing. In line with us was the open door of a big house. We could see the mirror and other ornaments in the hall. All the civilians had run away. Incongruously in the din of the bombardment a cock crowed close at hand. I hoped he would not crow three times. I don't know why. Along the street to our left front, towards which the dead major had been going, the silent British battery lay somewhere out of sight in the debris of fallen houses. A gunner walked calmly up and down in that street as if on sentry-go, while houses literally tumbled down around him. Possibly something was being done to get the guns into action again, or to get them away. Anyway there he remained, held by some duty to his stricken battery.

The Germans had too many guns for us.

A shell exploded in the street ahead of us and showered us with fragments of metal and stones. Something hot hit me on the left buttock, and I said to Tymble on my left: 'I think I'm hit.' He looked at me with concern while my hand groped and detached a piece of hot metal from my backside. The falling piece had not even burnt my trousers. Tymble grinned. 'No,' said he, 'your number was not on that.' More shells burst in the street and we were ordered back to the cover of some tall houses at the crossroads. We up and ran for it round the corner, and took cover close against the walls of the protecting houses.

Our major and the quartermaster went away to the right and disappeared, meaning to get into touch with any of our troops on the right. That was the end of them. A shell caught them as they rounded a corner, and they were badly wounded out of our sight.

Then we got it. We were struck down as if by a stroke of lightning. A heavy shell exploded just over our heads, and we were all knocked flat on the pavement, where bricks and pieces of mortar rained on us. I rose slowly and waited for the others to get up. I was dazed slightly. A sergeant went off at the double, leading those who were not injured. All my section except two went with him. He beckoned to me. I thought a moment and looked hard at the scattered khaki forms, dead and dying, from which little streams of blood flowed across the pavement into the gutter, and I turned away too.

I had only gone a few yards when a voice cried in anguish: 'For God's sake, Corporal!' There was no denying that appeal. I turned back slowly and carefully lifted up my wounded Lance-Corporal Letts. Another man of mine, Hoskins, was lying dead near him.

I dressed Letts's wounds as best I could, using my bandages and his own, but I could not cover all his gashes.

He was peppered with bits of metal in both his arms and in his right leg and thigh. He bled profusely and limped badly.

134

Le Cateau (1)

He turned obstinate and would not part with his rifle and ammunition. So we walked slowly back through the town, he trembling and leaning heavily on me. The last to retire. A heavy salvo bursting on our left caused a whole wall of factory windows to vomit their glass.

A young woman came across the street to us with a glass of brandy. One sniff of it, and Letts half fainted. I waved it away and on we staggered. I then wished I had drunk the stuff myself.

Rounding a corner I got another severe shock. About twelve corpses of soldiers of our regiment lay scattered about the street. The sight of the badges and buttons of these dead men of my own corps had a queer effect on me. I became angry with the Germans for the first time. Then my anger turned to anxiety. Was my brother among the slain? Hastily I propped Letts in a doorway, and examined the bodies.

A French civilian who was covering their faces drew aside a cardigan jacket from that of one corpse and disclosed a raw mass in place of a face. I signalled to him to cover up.

The men were not of my company, so my brother was safe I hoped. But evidently they had been fighting behind us in the town. An alarming situation. I collected Letts, told him to stop fingering his wounds, and moved on, but I now watched my front and flanks for Germans, as well as keeping a weather eye to the rear. The woman of the brandy had told me of a new hospital opened up in a street up the third turn to the right.

We found it, marked with a Red Cross flag, up a hilly little street, and went in by a gate to a kind of schoolroom converted to war use, and full of stretchers and beds. Outside, at the gate, an officer's charger was tied to the railings, with a bullet through its barrel. It stood quite calmly there. In the yard was a stack of British rifles discarded by the wounded. Inside the schoolroom all was quiet bustle. No sounds except suppressed groans and hard breathing. The French civilian doctor, a small, bearded, fussy fellow, was adamant in the matter of Letts's rifle and equipment.

'No, no, monsieur. No arms in a hospital. It is forbidden. Put them outside.' And we lost his attention, for he turned away without deigning to look at the pig-headed Letts.

'There you are,' I said. 'Give us your gun.' I got impatient and took it now without parley. I was also anxious. I was detached from my regiment and had lost a lot of time. I laid him on a bed and took off his equipment. I felt the urge to escape. 'So long, chum, you'll be all right. No great damage done.' He was now very weak, and got pessimistic. He raised one of his wounded arms, and held my neck clumsily: 'I won't see you any more.' 'Indeed you will. Good luck now, chum.'

I got away. I drew the bolt of his rifle and chucked it over a wall, and then cast his rifle on the heap outside. Then I drew bolts from three or four other rifles and threw them away. I hated the idea of letting the enemy have any good stuff of ours, apart altogether from my training in dismantling serviceable arms that had to be abandoned. I should have liked to put all the rifles out of action, but I had to be off. I was much too near the enemy. At the gate I halted, and considered killing the wounded horse, but uncertain as to whether I could give it a quick death, I left it alive. It looked contented, and gazed quietly at me.

Then I fled, bearing south, down the shelled and deserted streets.

I reached the town square, which was now badly battered about. One side was ranged with hundreds of cycles left there by some French cyclist corps when they fell back. Our huge food dump lay untouched in the Rue d'Alçace, a present for the enemy. I made off across the square, and getting into a street leading south I saw a soldier walking in front of me in the same direction. This sight relieved me. I had missed the company of Letts, and was more afraid alone in a bombarded town. I overtook him at a run, and hurried him on. He was a ginger lance-corporal, a Dublin fellow named Ryan, with a twinkle in his eye.

The twinkle was still there. Feeling green myself, I looked at him in astonishment. He winked, and drew loot from his bulging haversack; apples and cigarettes and biscuits. I asked no questions. I took his offerings, emptying my haversack of a packet of bulging maps to make room for them. Bad discipline. I held the heavy packet of maps in my hand for a moment. It contained maps of the whole of Belgium, as far as I remember, as well as most of the departments of northern France; a cumbersome bundle. I kept what I considered to be the most useful two and jettisoned the others.

Ryan was full of news. He confirmed my surmise that Germans were inside the town while we were supposed to be defending it. He said that his company, 'B', and some of mine, 'A', had been fighting at close quarters with the Germans near a gasworks. A windy place, as they expected that the gas container would be blown up any moment. He said they gave the Germans gyp, and chased them out of it.

A young officer of 'B' Company had led an assault and had killed a German officer with his sword. The German officer had run him through the thigh in a duel.

As the Lance-Jack spoke a detachment of 'B' Company, led by the limping officer, passed across the end of the street, and we followed them at a distance, giving way to a natural tendency to avoid disciplined formation; the ever-disciplined soldier's weakness. Ryan also told me that one of our two French interpreters had been wounded in the town square and left in a private house.

Still chatting, we quickly got clear of the town and went up a road to a rise in open country, overlooking the southern exits of Caudry, where we found our battalion extended in the harvested corn-fields, with a battery of guns in action in the open country across a road on their right.

Le Cateau (1)

The freebooting Ryan, exuding the air of a warrior last out of battle, reported with a smart salute to the nearest officer of his company, but I would report to no one yet.

I looked for my brother and found him. His face lighted up at sight of me. In our relief at finding each other we then did a silly thing. We gave each other nearly all we had in our respective haversacks, and then, realizing what we had done, we grinned and punched each other.

I got a heart-ache about his being in this slaughter, and foolishly asked him to join my section. Rightly he answered: 'No fear. Don't worry. I must stay with my own section.'

That reminded me of mine. I searched them out and collected them on the road near our ammunition carts. I had now six men instead of eight. The quiet Hoskins was dead. Letts was wounded, and probably a prisoner.

It was now 2 p.m., and we had been in action about eight hours.

Our stomachs cried out, and we sat down to chew bully beef and biscuits, supplemented by apples, and then we began to gobble quickly, glancing furtively to our front, because the battle, having abated in the last hour, had begun to liven up again. The Germans were preparing to debouch from the smoking town of Caudry and their covering shells began to fall again in our vicinity.

Chapter Twenty-five

LE CATEAU (2)

The storm of battle rose steadily, though no enemy infantry came out of the town on our front. There was a rumour that a German officer had ridden out of the town right up to our front line and, wheeling, galloped back to safety, unmolested in the excitement. I did not see him, and I give the story for what it is worth.

The battery on our right was discovered by the enemy, and was outgunned in no time. Artillery men and horses fell down under the shells bursting accurately on the gun positions, and some men stampeded. One flung himself on a horse, and came charging back out of hand. He was checked by our colonel.

Our gunners did gallant work that day, but they had no chance against the apparently limitless resources of the enemy.

Then the German infantry flowed forward round Caudry. West and east of it they came, leaving the town itself isolated and fairly quiet, except for gunfire, luckily for us who were immediately facing it.

Le Cateau (2)

A tense excitement was now shown by our fellows in the course of the battle on our right flank. Things were not well there. Men were coming back, disorganized, some in haste. The Germans had broken through. We still remained, though we knew our right flank had wilted.

The left then claimed attention. An English regiment of our brigade facing the eastern side of Caudry had charged, and charged successfully, driving back the advance troops of the enemy. In the noise of the conflict the victorious cheers of the English charge sounded thin and weak, like the wailing of infants.

Farther to their left the German penetration had succeeded, and enemy troops were working forward behind our left flank. There was increased anxiety and activity at our battalion headquarters, which was situated right up in our front line. Staff officers came and went, and the divisional general visited us more than once, a brave man who always came up to see things for himself.

Our brigade was now in the air, and in great danger of being cut off by the enemy. I was once more ordered to get away with my carts, and I pushed off just as the first companies of our battalion rose and began to retire slowly in good order over the fields.

Down the road I went, and saw a dreadful spectacle. Wagons, guns, and men were breaking in helter-skelter on to the road from the captured lines on the right, enemy shells pursuing them. One regiment had partly panicked. The traffic became chaotic. The drivers in rear under the cracking shells whipped up their horses regardless of rules of the road. Cries of urgency rose on all sides.

Infantrymen mounted every vehicle in sight, while others ran alongside. Some of their wounded were slung on the gun limbers.

A staff officer, his face hot with the shame of it, diverted the fleeing men into a side street in the first village we came to, shouting frantically at them: 'For God's sake men, be British soldiers.'

They swept my carts with them in the confusion, and I halted my convoy opposite to them while they were being marshalled with difficulty by the staff officer. The sight of these soldiers of a regular battalion, stampeding, grumbling, and looking about while they were being reformed was an unforgettable and disgraceful scene. The staff officer, noticing that my section did not belong to that lot, ordered me on. The movement of my convoy to rejoin the main road was the last straw, and the sign of *sauve qui peut* to men already well in flight.

Those farthest down the line from the officer broke away, murmuring, and the whole lot, following suit, streamed off again in an undisciplined mob, leaving the chagrined officer alone and impotent. I thought with pride of our Irishmen, extended and controlled, falling back steadily at the trail across country behind us, protecting that lousy mob, some of whom had even chucked away their weapons. I cursed the nearest, calling them sanguinary specimens of human excreta. They turned angry frightened faces towards me and cursed back, threatening me in spite of my stripes. My lads kept cool and curious about it all, except Cordwain, whose outbursts of critical blasphemy on the general military situation, and on the broken regiment in particular, are unprintable.

Later in the evening officers of the brigade and general staff, making no appeal, sternly sieved the disorganized stream of retreat, collecting men into groups of their own regiments in a wayside field. Thence they marched slowly back at intervals and in good order. Our transport was directed to the outskirts of a village, where we waited and were joined that night by the battalion, and here we had food and some sleep.

So ended in our immediate vicinity that remarkable stand of the single Second British Corps against the whole of the German First Army, and it is said by some that through the course of the entire war never were British troops as heavily outnumbered.

My battalion had lost one hundred officers and men—a small number of casualties in comparison with other regiments. Still, that was a fairly hectic Wednesday.

We were up and fighting again in the small hours of the following day, acting once more as a rear-guard, and we marched all through that day and night, with only two long halts for food, most of which we wangled from the villages *en route*, as our ration supply organization had broken down owing to the rapid pace of our retreat. In passing through Ham we found the inhabitants, men and women, feverishly digging trenches; a vain task, as we simply marched through them, ever onwards to the south.

Still marching, on the morning of the 28th of August we approached the first billet to give us a complete night's rest since the 21st. General Sir Horace Smith-Dorrien inspected us as we marched into it. He did not wear the hard and sometimes haughty look of other generals, and we liked him for it. Calm and kindly-eyed, he gazed from horseback on soldiers weary of marching and fighting. He forbade us to march to attention, and we appreciated his concern for us, though well-trained troops like to salute their leaders in the first proud meeting after battle.

We searched his face, as troops will, for signs of commendation or satisfaction, and saw both there. He had I think a special *grádh* for the Irish. He complimented us.

Many an officer overnurses the spirit of discipline as carefully and in as hidebound a manner as the cold logician his syllogism. That does not always pay. General Smith-Dorrien knew that he viewed a body of men aching in every limb, to whom the smallest action, even that of moving rifles to attention, was an added minor torture, and he excused us—the good old stick. He was our man.

We slept that night in a lovely barn, where we had hay to lie on.

Chapter Twenty-six

SLEEP-MARCHING

Dreams and ideas mingle with the realities that form the broken memories of the following bitter week.

Had we marched for four days on end, or for that matter for a week, the recollection of events in their proper order would be an easier task. Enemy action, physical weariness from mere marching, lack of food, and often of water, did not trouble us much. Our curse was loss of sleep. We stood at bay in retirement, or marched on in a trance, or rather in some idiot nightmare wherein images jostled material things, while the enemy relentlessly pursued us.

Our minds and bodies shrieked for sleep. In a short time our singing army was stricken dumb. Every cell in our bodies craved rest, and that one thought was the most persistent in the vague minds of the marching men.

Snatches of *The Ancient Mariner* came to me and remained, and fascinated me, and time and again I loudly recited the following verse:

Sleep-marching

O sleep it is a gentle thing,
Beloved from pole to pole.
To Mary Queen the praise be given,
She sent the gentle sleep from heaven,
That slid into my soul.

Because of our good discipline very few of the men
gave up and fell out on the line of march. We noted
with wonder that those who did were generally men
of big stature. The smaller men were hardier. Officers rode up and down the ranks encouraging the
soldiers, and one of them actually said that to give in
to fatigue would mean four or five years in a German
fortress, but this true prophecy was ignored by the
most tired. No threat will stir a man in extremity.

The pained look in the troubled eyes of those who
fell by the way will not be easily forgotten by those
who saw it. That look imposed by circumstances on
spent men seemed to demand all forgiveness from
officers and comrades alike, as it conveyed a helpless
and dumb farewell to arms.

This hopeless resignation to utter fatigue was a
thing to wonder at. The pride of the fighting man
was forgotten, and even the threat of immediate capture or death at the hands of the enemy had no power
to change or influence it.

Some who collapsed were rescued by ambulances.
Others were left unconscious in deep sleep by the
roadsides and in the fields, and they passed out of our
ken for years.

This dreadful phenomenon came on us like a creep-

146

ing disease. It develops slowly. I think it was about the tenth day when the frightful agony of sleeplessness began to smite us. Men slept while they marched, and they dreamed as they walked. They talked of their homes, of their wives and mothers, of their simple ambitions, of beer in cosy pubs, and they talked of fantasies. Commonplace sensible remarks turned to inane jibberings. The brains of the soldiers became clouded, while their feet moved automatically.

One sergeant kept up a long dirge for hours on end about his lost pack, yet he was still wearing it, being the only one in his platoon who had stuck to it throughout the retreat.

Another man, whose dreams seemed optimistic, talked confidently and in a fresh voice of being a policeman in Paris, a city whose signboards became more ominously numerous as we went ever south. Our faces and hair became dirtier and dirtier, and lice began to breed rapidly in our underclothing. The smartest men allowed their puttee strings to loosen and trail.

Some, as I have said, did not know if they were waking or dreaming, and they mixed up fact and fancy. This resulted one day in the whole company believing that we were all entraining within an hour. It afterwards transpired that this was all due to the vapourings of a dreamy corporal attached to battalion headquarters, whose persistent phantasm was a waiting convoy of armoured trains.

As the days drew on and my troubles pressed on

me I wondered about my brother, and how he was sticking it, and I sought and found him in the line of march, and walked beside him.

His usually bright face was bony with fatigue and begrimed with perspiration and dirt, but he was cheerful and contented.

His section had had no casualties, but I looked with interest at the men who had fought close to him, mainly because they were my brother's men, and, I knew, his champions too. I found it hard to recognize any of them. They were mostly youngsters, but their faces looked aged and drawn, and more like those of strangers.

One pale-faced lad was delousing himself as he staggered along. They were all very quiet.

My brother told me that most of them had diarrhœa from eating green apples. Some of my men were similarly affected, and that added to their weakness. Neither of us had had the heart to prevent our hungry men from eating them.

We swapped stories of our experiences during the battle of Le Cateau, and strangely he thought me a bit of a hero because I had lost two of my eight men. I then told him of the courage of the commanding officer and the adjutant at Mons, and the tale of the ammunition carts. He grew a bit intense about the ammunition carts, and repeatedly asked me at what time I had returned with them. On realizing that I had nearly missed rejoining the battalion before it moved off from Mons, he cursed the C.O. whom we

had just been praising, the officer who had ordered
me away, and myself. I only smiled my thanks at his
anxiety, and then I sobered down when I felt I had
a brother deeply concerned about my welfare. Hitherto, in peace at any rate, I had done all the concern-
ing. I joked him off the subject after the manner of
uncouth young men who are touched by finer feelings.

I did not like seeing him look so tired, and I made
a habit of paying him short visits like this during the
march.

One day he alarmed me, after a long period of
silence, by remarking casually: 'One more turn to
the left now, at the top of Tawney's Hill, and we're
home, my lad.' As he spoke a halt was called, and he
bumped helplessly into the man in front and woke
up. He stoutly denied having spoken, and then I
knew that he had been asleep on the march, and had
been enthralled by the prospect of rest and refresh-
ment in a farmhouse of our childhood days, where as
little boys we had built forts in the summer meadows
and practised mimic war in the role of Irish chieftains
dealing death and destruction to the Sassenach. My
heart became sore with longing for the warmth and
shelter of the large farm kitchen in Ireland. I could
see its smoky ceiling festooned with huge joints of
meat, and hear the purr of the fire-blowing machine.
So I mused along in worship of my distant Irish shrine
of comfort, food, warmth, and rest, and words of
glowing hospitality from the lips of God's kindliest
people echoed in my strained ears: 'Draw in now,

acushla, draw in and eat up.' 'Oh thank you, thank you. *Maith agat.*' So I dreamed a heavenly rest for all the senses, heavy-lidded eyes, nostrils choked with dust and stale smell of sweating men and horses. I could see rich food and drink for sticky tongue and craving stomach, and a bed, O Lord, an Irish feather bed, beautifully warm and soft and unhygienic for my aching head and back, and feet benumbed by the tramping of countless miles on the hard square-set paving stones of the national roads of France.

' "A" and "C" Companies will take the first turn to the right off the main road, and halt to take up an outpost position for the night, while the rest of the battalion marches on to bivouac.' We obey numbly. We are warned that we may have to fight a covering action to allow our main body to get away, for the Germans are but three miles off. We go back our road a bit, and stumble across country to ground commanding a good field of fire, and await the appearance of the leading enemy cavalry patrols. Nothing comes of it. Some shots away right, and another sleepless night of watching. In the morning we collect ourselves, and on again we go.

The officers at last begin to feel the strain. One captain turns his whole company about and marches back towards the Germans. The commanding officer gallops after him, and the captain tells him he is tired of retreating. It is bad for the morale of the troops, so he prefers to fight and perish if necessary. The unnerved captain is relieved of his command, and his gallantly docile company comes back to us under a junior, and joins the tail of the column.

Our own cheerful platoon commander, he who was so keen on bayonet charges, now limps badly, and commandeers a heavy Belgian cart-horse—a vile animal, a stink factory that gasses the whole platoon and adds to our misery. Another horse, an officer's charger is found by a corporal, who rides it all day, and only late in the evening discovers that the saddle-bags are stuffed with chocolate. There is a scramble for the chocolate, and the artillery come and claim the charger to take the menial place of a draught horse gone lame in a gun team.

Many artillery horses fall out, lame and fatigued. The men outmarch the horses. Some horses have been shot, others stripped of harness and left alive, stand or limp, along the line of the retreat.

One of our signallers stops to repair a puncture, and is left behind. He returns on his bicycle waving the busby of a German Death's Head Hussar, a cavalry point who was closely following us up. He has shot the enemy cavalryman, but what about the horse? He has shot the horse too, in his excitement. He is damned for his stupidity by the officers. There was intense interest in the possibilities of that horse all day. The busby was chucked away.

We enter a forest, and a troop of British cavalry come cantering down a side road, chinstraps down, leading six German horses. They have had a successful skirmish in the rides of the forest. On sighting a

Uhlan patrol they dismounted, quickly opened up rapid fire, and emptied the enemy saddles. Then they led the captured horses back at a hand-gallop, one boisterous trooper gibing at us: 'Want an 'orse, mate? You'll find 'im cushier than the bleedin' road.' We give them a small cheer.

Then we cheer louder at a still more refreshing sight. A whole French regiment of cavalry, the first of the French Army we have seen since before Mons comes riding slowly past us and back towards the Germans. They are cuirassiers, and look resplendent in their breast-plates and brass helmets, from which horse-hair tails hang down their backs. A Cork man bursts into the *Marseillaise,* and our entire battalion sings or hums it. The Frenchmen raise their right arms in acknowledgement, orders snap along their squadrons, and out flash their sabres in salute. Then they in turn break into the refrain of the war-song of the Republic:

> *Aux armes, citoyens,*
> *Formez vos bataillons;*
> *Marchons, marchons, qu'un sang impur*
> *Abreuve nos sillons.*

Their voices die down in the distant aisles of the forest behind us, and we hold a gallant memory of French cavalry riding into battle.

We tramp on through the forest. Night falls, and we lose our way. Some French civilians come to our rescue and guide us out. Hereabouts—or was it far-

ther back?—we see the names and places of battle of
other days—Crecy and Fontenoy.

The turmoil and confusion of the retreat decrease
somewhat as we outmarch the bulk of the refugees,
yet each march succeeding monotonous march be-
comes more and more unbearable. Short rests and
little sleep bring us to such a pass that time and again
we wonder dully if we can last out the next five minutes. No rations arrive. Some of us miss our tobacco
more than our food. We go days without a hot meal,
and as many as a dozen men share one hand-made
cigarette of tobacco dust and pocket fluff. Even the
solace of a good smoke is denied us. We move on day
and night, glad of the change to darkness which
brings a drop in temperature and a respite from perspiring, yet when night falls it increases the numbness
of our bodies and minds, and enhances the regret felt
in passing resting-places and the comfort promised by
the inviting lights of houses and villages by the way.

The stream of refugees thins out at evenings, and
there is some solace in the calm harvest moon, whose
beams deal kindly with forsaken civilian carts and
the cast horses and other debris of our own retreat.

There is a great stillness in the nights, hardly broken
by the dull sounds of marching feet of men and horses,
the rumble of limber wheels, jingle of harness, and the
occasional hoarse rough calls of encouragement to
men and animals. The men get quieter and quieter.
They came to France to fight, not to march away in
torment. They obey, but they do not now bother to

acknowledge orders. Their tongues are a bit swollen, mouths sore and slimy, and their lips dry.

I rate Tymble for lurching out of his section of fours, and he tells me to go to bloody hell. I say: 'Shut up, cover over, and get the step.' He tells me that bastards like me ought to be shot for annoying the troops, and that it would not take him long to do it. I get annoyed, and moving close to him ask him gently what he would suppose I would be doing while he was loading up to shoot me. His comrade nudges him. He titters like a drunkard, wipes his mouth wearily with his sleeve, and says he is sorry. A bad business. Too much on the men when they begin to talk like that.

During one of the nights late in the retreat we saw a curious phenomenon, unique in my experience. The moon was shining over our left shoulders, and the meadows on either side of the causeway of the road were overhung with white night mists, which, viewed through the roadside trees, gave the appearance of long bands of lake or sea water. At one part of the road we came to a clearing in the trees, and the horizontal mists lay closer to us. Gradually between us and the nearest misty belt appeared a white circle, after the manner of a rainbow, except that it was smaller, and as solid-looking as the mists, and was a complete circle, resting not in the sky, but standing upright on the land.

I have since read that a similar sight occurs by day in foggy alpine regions, and that the daylight luminous circle is called the 'Circle of Ulloa', after a Spanish naval officer and scientist, but I have never heard or read of this strange thing happening at night. We all felt rather gloomy and superstitious immediately after seeing this eerie vision, but in time the peaceful lines of mist lying over the long stretching meadows softened our mood and gave a gentle peace to our tired senses, uplifting us with some vague good promise of better things in store.

We forgot our tribulations in the later beauty of that pearly night, and there were some of us who experienced something joyous, supernatural, a blessing perhaps, from those at home, or from above, unconnected with war and fatigue.

Now we had crossed the Oise about Crecy, the Aisne near Vic, and the Marne at Meaux, where we were the last unit to cross the bridge, which was immediately blown up behind us by our sappers. Thereabouts we found ourselves within twenty miles of the environs of Paris, from which the French Government had fled.

We crossed one more river, the Grand Morin on the 5th of September, when the retreat from Mons ended and we went into bivouac, where we were joined by our first reinforcement, a number of fresh officers and men, that more than made up for the hundred we had lost.

We washed and changed our clothes, and slept, and fed, and slept again. We noticed with satisfaction that the soles of our feet had calloused in a thick, hard, healthy skin from our long march. We also derived satisfaction in allowing the members of the new reinforcement to interview us, and in telling them in an affected casual manner what war was really like.

All the same, our explanations were restrained, for we realized that the killing of men cannot be loosely talked about. Too grim anyway, and you never knew when you would get your own bullet.

That same day we heard that the French had halted too, and turned about, and had driven back the advanced German troops away on our right, and that on the morrow we too would turn back facing north again, and start chasing Germans for a change. Now that was to our liking, and we felt braced about it.

Chapter Twenty-seven

COUNTER-OFFENSIVE ON THE MARNE

On the 6th of September the British Army had retired to its limit. It no longer covered Paris. Instead,
it lay in billets and bivouacs to the east and south-
east of the city, and the capital of France was almost
in the hands of the German First Army under von
Kluck. Away to our left some retiring French territorials and another small force, Gallieni's hastily collected Sixth Army, rushed out in taxis from Paris,
barred the ponderous momentum of the enemy, whose
heavy howitzers would soon, no doubt, make dust of
the city's fortifications, as they had made dust of the
concrete and iron fortresses of Belgium. The last of
Sordet's cavalry, who had filled the gap between us
and the French Fifth Army on our right, had now
gone across our line of march to the left to cover Paris
and our left flank. We were rather uncertain about
their movements. The impending doom of Paris dispirited me and others who had a sense of the appalling
situation, and the swift ruthlessness of the enemy. It
seemed a cold surrender.

But now something happened, something historical, which according to the experts immediately and
lastingly altered the course of the war in favour of the
Allies.

The Germans appeared to go crazy. They suddenly
stopped short of Paris, and no longer pursued us. They
went after bigger game, or thought they did. Their
long massive columns wheeled abruptly left and inwards until they headed east instead of south, and
thundered on across the line of our retreat, with the
intention of rolling up the French Army on our right.
Paris and the small British force could wait. The
German staff had already reported the British as no
longer effective.

Thus when we, refreshed and reinforced, turned
back to fight again, the Germans no longer faced us
ready to deploy into battle array, but were doing a
grand march past from left to right with their right
flank exposed. This astounding error was exploited at
once. The French Commander-in-Chief swooped and
hit immediately, sending forward his left armies in
conjunction with the British against the unprotected
enemy flank, and hurled the German hosts over the
Marne, and beyond it to the Aisne, thirty or more
miles to the north.

Our battalion took little part in the battle of the
Marne. We were in reserve throughout the action,
and only once carried out the duties of advanced
guard. This we found to be a ticklish business. We
expected every hedgerow to belch machine-gun bul-

lets at us, and a man of my section hit off our feelings
very accurately by saying that 'it gave you a nasty
wobbly feeling in the blooming stomach'.

We moved rapidly, with trailed rifles and in open
order, across country while thus operating ahead of
our brigade, closing in on towns and villages on our
way, and raking them for signs of the enemy. My
section had the job of leading in the clearing of
one village, and we found it in a strange condition. Tables loaded with wine bottles were set up in
the open street. All the shops were looted, and all
kinds of merchandise were scattered about outside
them.

Overturned chairs showed that the enemy had
retired in haste. We worked slowly through the rav-
aged village, cat-walking in single file, as we hugged
the houses on either side, and, finally making clear,
came on the German bivouac in the fields on the northern side. This deserted bivouac was the strangest I
have ever seen. The German soldiers had taken the
mattresses from the houses of the villagers and made
their beds on them. Those who could not get mattresses had looted clothing of all sorts, men's, women's
and children's, and had made piles of these to sleep
on. On and about this conglomeration of bedding
were heaps of stolen foodstuffs, preserves, and bottles
of wine, and in the narrow spaces between some of
the beds there was fresh human excreta and newly
opened tins of peas and other eatables.

Our force halted when we reached the village, and

my section remained on outpost beyond it until the next morning.

We made light entrenchments on the high ground overlooking the disgusting German bivouac. Here, before dark, I got a job of work I did not relish. I was foolishly sent out alone by our platoon officer to find a railway line, which he swore should be visible from our position, according to his map. It did not happen to be visible for the very good reason that a long, low, continuous wall, about six hundred yards to our front, hid the metals, which ran closely parallel to its other side. Anyway, I set off to find the invisible railway line, and I was moving cautiously through a small wood, on my approach to the wall, when I saw a figure flick under cover of the bole of a tree. The thump my heart gave did not slacken my swoop to similar cover, whence I drew a bead on the bole and waited for the next move. It came in the shape of a rifle muzzle slowly poked round the tree trunk, and then slewed on to me. I saw the peak of a British khaki cap above it, and dropped my own aim, ducked back behind my tree, shouted, and then walked out into the open to greet a British trooper.

He told me I nearly gave him the shits, and that he had left his horse in a copse to have a 'look see' over the wall. We explored it together, and having found our railway line were both glad to clear back and make our respective reports. It is too exciting, and not very great fun, prowling round alone between pursuing and retreating armies.

Counter-offensive on the Marne

That night there was a shoot-up on our left front. We stood to arms, and after a while a lonely figure came in at our post. He was an Irishman from an English regiment in our brigade. and he asked in a pathetically comic way if it was at all possible to get an immediate transfer to our battalion, while on active service. He pleaded ignorance of the King's Regulations on this subject, but hoped there would be no difficulty about it. His reason was that two reconnoitring patrols of his own regiment had bumped into each other in the dark, and had fired into each other, so he had temporarily severed his connection with his dangerous companions and was making his way back alone. This joker left us loudly thanking God that we had a navy somewhere.

The following day the advance continued, and we went again into reserve, keeping some distance behind the forward troops, who this day met with resistance. We heard gun-fire ahead as we dropped into the valley of the Marne, and signs of war and death soon reappeared. Dead Highlanders were seen lying in the fields and on the roadside. Thin, black-japanned German cable ran in all directions across country. If this wire was successful in use, the Germans were ahead of us in signalling. It was so light that one man could carry miles of it.

We marched on behind the fighting troops, and as we entered a village at river level we saw a large number of German prisoners at close quarters for the first time. There must have been about six hundred of them, and some were seated in a churchyard on chairs taken from inside the church to accommodate them. To us this was a cheering sight.

An arrogant German officer, standing apart from his men, folded his arms rather too high on his breast, and surveyed us, cynically we thought, as we marched by. His attitude merely tickled our men, and each company gave him some devastating nickname as they saw him in passing.

These Germans had foolishly entrenched themselves on the forward slope of a hill to fight a rear-guard action against us, but our gunners had neatly trapped them by putting down gun-fire behind them, so that it cut off their retreat over the crest, and the Germans fell into the hands of a Scottish regiment—Royal Scots, it was said—who captured them in a swift assault. When we crossed the bridge we saw the place where this natty job of work was carried out. We also saw several dummy trenches, only about six inches deep, with the earth deceptively spread front and rear, and in each trench a row of German helmets just showing over the top. Our artillery had wasted a good many shells on these. Across the Marne there were many encouraging sights of an army in rapid retreat. Discarded uniform, equipment, and carts lay about along the roads and hedges. We saw ammunition in large quantities. The German bullets, very like our own, came away more easily from their cartridges, and we examined the small, black, square powder flakes with interest. These were very different from the long, thin strands of brown cordite which filled our cartridges. We also picked up a number of saw-backed bayonets, some of them much longer than ours. These were supposed to be more workmanlike than the plain-edged bayonet, as the saw easily cut away any obstruction, on the withdraw, after a thrust. Our fellows joked at this form of frightfulness. The abandoned German transport was the most heartening sight. The British Army was certainly getting its own back. We passed a deserted Red Cross wagon, which was also believed to have carried two machine-guns. I cannot remember having seen the guns. German machine-guns, to our misfortune, had already been connected in our minds with ambulance work, for the reason that the German Maxim was carried in the field by two men, and when covered with a cloth had the appearance of a body on a stretcher. The result had been that our men had more than once held fire, and kindly allowed German machine-guns to get into forward positions, thinking in each case that the gun was a man being succoured.

A reprehensible incident occured about this time.

One evening in billets a man who had already said he was fed up, deliberately shot himself through the left hand. He was in the room below that in which I was billeted, and the bullet came through the floor near my feet, narrowly missing me. The man said that the wound was an accident, and that it

163

occurred while he was cleaning his rifle, but others later confessed unofficially to have known his purpose.

Another man of ours, while scrounging about an empty house, was said to have found a thick wad of French notes hidden under a stair carpet, upon which he promptly reported sick, and was rumoured to have got away back to England with a tidy sum. He might easily have been shot had he been discovered.

There is yet one more peculiar and unsatisfying thing connected with my memory of the Marne. On reaching billets one night I was asked by a soldier: 'Did you see the baby?' I said: 'What baby?' and he replied: 'The bayoneted baby in the front window'. Now I had seen a propped-up figure in the window of an upper room, on the line of march that day, but I took it to be a large doll placed against the inside of the glass, and I said so. However, several stated it was a dead infant, but I cannot believe it was. There was too much colour in the face of the doll-like figure. It still gives me the creeps to think of it.

Such were the incidents that occupied our minds and tongues as we pursued the Germans, but one thought surmounted all others, that being: When will the battalion again go into action? That could happen any moment. The guns of the retiring Germans drummed daily in our ears.

The thought of another battle did not discourage us. We wanted a dig at the enemy, and smarted at the recollection of his having chased us. Our tails were up now, and we were different men—veterans in a way. A good many of us had fought three battles at the age of twenty. Not so dusty.

And we had the Germans on the run.

Chapter Twenty-eight

ACROSS THE AISNE; DEATH ROLL

Our advance continued steadily as the Germans were driven back from the Marne. Their rear-guards showed some resistance every day, and occasionally we picked up stragglers and wounded from the enemy army. Although we took our turn in our brigade at advanced guard and outpost duties, our battalion did not really cross swords with the enemy again until 14th September. On that day, and on the few days preceding it, rain fell, and we were not very comfortable either in bivouac or on the line of march. The weather began to get cold.

On the evening of 13th September, a British aeroplane, one of the few the British Army possessed, approached us from the German side, and, wheeling around, alighted in a field to the right of our marching columns. The flying-officer climbed slowly out of his machine, and, coming stumbling towards us in his heavy kit, did not wait to find an officer, but shouted to us all: 'There they are, waiting for you up there, thousands of them.' And he waved his right arm towards the wooded heights, across the river Aisne, some three miles away. Then he composed himself, and asked for the nearest battalion commander. We showed him the riding figure of our colonel at the head of our unit.

But we did not fight that day. We went into bivouac on the south side of the river, and had a meal before resting for the night.

My brother went early to rest under his groundsheet. This was not his custom and I found he was suffering from a stomach-ache, probably caused from eating green apples. He was in pain and would not report sick, it being the code in the old army not to go sick with minor complaints. I fussed about him, feeling rather miserable myself, and wet and chilly on the first cold night of autumn.

Then I set off to find the medical officer, but seeing him dining I was too shy to disturb him. We had a great respect for the officers' mess. I slouched back to my brother, chatted to him for a bit, and on his saying he was sure he would be all right soon I said 'Good night' to his curly golden head, which was the only part of him visible, and crept under my own damp ground-sheet.

Early next morning a battery of our field-guns came into action near our bivouac. They were camouflaged with green branches of trees, and appeared to be firing across the river at some target in the woods on the other side.

The tone of the orders given us, the close inspection

of our ammunition, and our rapid fall-in showed that there was immediate work ahead. We marched on quickly down the sloping south side of the river valley to the River Aisne, passing close to other guns in action, and making way for the trotting ammunition wagons which were feeding the batteries. I saw my brother for a moment. He was looking cheerful again, and complained only of slight cramp.

It was a fine fresh morning, and we moved on exhilarated by a feeling of the unexpected, down a wet leafy lane, until we came to an open space between the woods and the southern bank of the river, where we shook out into our first deployment.

We gripped our rifles hard. We felt on the edge of a fresh battlefield, with the curtain about to go up, and looked all about our front for the direction of the first threat of danger.

Our shells swished close overhead on their way to the dominating heights on the far bank, and presently enemy shrapnel whipped and cracked above us. A curse or two expressed the nausea which every man with a stomach experiences when he feels helpless under a rain of slivers of steel and bullets hurled at him by an enemy two miles or so out of rifle shot.

My company turned right on gaining the river and moved section by section in single file east along the river bank, and from time to time we halted a moment to crouch or lie flat behind tussocks of grass lining the bank, as the enemy shell-fire increased. We were making for the railway bridge east of Vailly, which at that moment was being recrossed by an English regiment retiring out of action from the northern side of the river. The bridge had been blown up by the Germans, and was now under steady observed shrapnel fire—rather heavy stuff too, judging by the sounds of the bursts and the dense rolling clouds above and about it.

As we approached the bridge we saw that it was completely wrecked; a tangled mass of ironwork, most of which was submerged, with a dead horse held against it by the current, and only a line of single planks, which sagged in the middle, as a means of getting over. This line of single planks was hastily and precariously rigged against what was left of the iron supports of the railway bridge. A nasty proposition.

We did not wait to contemplate it. A fresh English regiment crossed over as we drew nearer, and we 'blondined' across it section by section close under the bursting shells. No casualties occurred near me, but shouts of alarm from behind showed that the following company had caught it. We did not turn to see. We heard that some of those hit had fallen into the river. Our commanding officer, with his usual bravery, stood upon a height on the south bank, just close to the bridge, during the whole time taken by his battalion to cross over.

On gaining the other side we found the regiment which had preceded us disappearing towards our right front, as it worked up the hill through the trees and undergrowth. We deployed rapidly into attack formations. A shrapnel bullet penetrated my haversack, and tore into the middle of a folded towel inside it. I felt startled and angry at the tug it gave, and at my narrow escape, and pushed on with the others. The Germans had seen us cross over, and were now firing salvoes at us. Our company commander was hit in the arm.

Two or three other officers of the following companies were also hit, and a good many men were knocked out, but we did not miss them in the excitement. We went on steadily uphill, seeing nothing of the enemy. We had hardly cleared the shelled area near the bridge when bullets began whistling about us. We must have been within a couple of hundred yards of enemy riflemen but though we looked hard through the undergrowth we could not see them. We cursed them, and relying on the luck of soldiers, we bowed our heads a little, shut our jaws, and went stubbornly on. Quicker we went, on to our toes, and crouching lower. In for a penny, in for a pound, quicker and quicker to get it over. Their rifles cracked sharply now, and the whistle and whine of bullets passing wide changed to the startling bangs of bullets just missing one. The near rattle of machine-guns sent our hearts thumping, until we sounded them on the front of the English on our right. They were getting it hotter. The rifle-fire in front ceased gradually, and we pushed on harder still.

Our own shells were now bursting a short distance

ahead, just beyond a crest line clearly visible to us. This line marked the near edge of a large plateau, and as we made it in a last rush we found this plateau edge forming a small continuous cliff of chalk varying from two to four feet high, giving good protection from bullets, and fair cover from shell-fire. Automatically we halted here, and our officers ordered us to improve the position by digging.

We missed some of our number when we had a look round after taking a breather. They had fallen quietly in battle, almost unnoticed, for in the attack the dead and wounded are soon out of sight behind. On the whole the enemy riflemen had been rotten shots. . . .

We mounted our sentries, straightened the little cliff by digging at it with our entrenching tools, and were soon behind a decent breastwork. My section had suffered no losses in gaining the plateau edge, and I was glad to see my men safely under cover of the little chalk cliff, with their loaded rifles lying on the grass of the plateau, all ready to drive back any attackers. I wished though that we had had a proper trench with a parados. From our feet the ground sloped backwards into little dells and glens, and our backs were consequently exposed to the backlash of any shrapnel fire.

Battalion headquarters erected a tiny tent in one of the open glades immediately behind us, and there the colonel and his adjutant, with their signallers and orderlies, ensconced themselves, rather foolishly I thought. It was much too exposed to any shells that might come over. It is trying for professional soldiers to see their officers exposing themselves in this fashion, and it generally makes the men anxious and irritable. We were always glad in our regiment when we saw an old soldier servant making no bones about chasing his officer under cover.

Our company had been forward in the attack which gained the plateau, and was now called into reserve. Another company took our place in the front, and we went underground into conveniently situated large caves, a little distance in rear of the line. The medical officer had opened up his dressing station at the mouth of one cave, and was already busy attending to the wounded and the dead. He went along the line of those who had been hit, and his preliminary test for life in each lying figure seemed to be a pinch under the jaw. Those he found to be dead he ordered to be taken out into the open, and waved the most dangerously wounded towards his assistants for immediate attention. He wasted no words.

We had hardly entered the caves when the Germans counter-attacked, and we were at once ordered to stand up and fall in ready to go and help our people outside. The sound of the battle heard from the caves was awe-inspiring. Clouds of smoke from bursting shells obscured the already dim light which filtered through the cave mouth. Heavy ground shells crumpled into the earth roof of our shelter and shook us. Projectiles whined and crashed at varying distances, and machine-guns rat-tat-tatted. The indistinct figures of stretcher-bearers collecting dead and wounded moved unceasingly in the cloudy light of the cave mouth. We felt trapped, and wished ourselves outside fighting, instead of standing restless in the semi-darkness. The appalling noise of the conflict outside made us all very anxious as to the progress of the enemy counter-attack. We got nervy and fidgeted and avoided each other's eyes. One interested soldier at the cave mouth morbidly occupied himself by passing in the names of the latest dead and wounded. I did not want to hear them, and though I listened with strained ears my mind could not cope with the situation. Each fresh name bludgeoned my brain. I had hardly envisaged one strong man lifeless and gone when another name followed. The casualties appeared to be very numerous. A great sense of misery and loss began to possess me as the litany of familiar names continued, and I moved over to my brother's platoon to be near him. He appeared to be absolutely calm, and his bearing had the effect of putting me at ease, so I went back to my own section very soon.

The German attack ceased. It had been beaten back with heavy loss, and all became quiet again. On examination we found that the casualties were not at all as bad as we had thought.

The noise of battle is very misleading, and after such an upheaval one wonders if any are left alive. On this occasion lively shouts that the rations were coming up proved that the fighters outside were still in good fettle, and groups of men from the companies in the battle line came along to the outside of the cave to collect hot tea, tepid meat, and broken loaves of bread which had come to pieces in the sacks *en route* to us. This meal was most welcome. We were all very hungry.

It was also the beginning of the regular issue of food to the front line. This food was carried daily for miles, often through heavy fire, by our company colour-sergeants and their devoted ration parties. Its arrival broke the strain of fighting, and cheered us all up. In a short time we developed the habit of eating under any conditions, even the most appalling.

That night we slept on the floor of the caves in our war gear, and again we had to stand to, as the Germans tried a night attack, which was, however, easily beaten back. The next morning the cry went round that the enemy was falling back, and we cleaned and reloaded our rifles and adjusted our equipment in readiness to carry on the pursuit.

Chasing Germans had now become a habit, and we could not envisage any other kind of war operation at this time. We admired these Germans all the same. They had been going hard, and their stand yesterday, and their night attack showed that they were courageous and had kick in them yet.

We were now to learn a bitter lesson.

We were ordered to fall in outside the caves, and out we went, shying a bit at the sight of blood-dripping stretchers propped against the wall of the cave mouth. Outside we saw some of our dead lying in grotesque positions.

A few of these had previously cut their long trousers into shorts during the hot August weather, and now they looked like slain schoolboys. This impression was enhanced by the peaceful and youthful looks on their dead faces. A hollow in the ground about ten yards from the caves was filled with bandaged wounded, with whom we conversed. They did not seem very much distressed; one or two groaned in low voices, others had dilated pupils, and looked surprised in a rather silly fashion, wondering about their wounds, I supposed, while a few unimpressed ones smoked philosophically.

I was looking keenly at this picture of our wounded, and thinking how good and brave they were, and also envying those with slight wounds who would go away back to England, or, with luck, to Ireland, when the scene suddenly changed. A rising tearing noise like that of an approaching train heralded the arrival of a heavy shell. Nearer and nearer it came and we all crouched down where we were. The wounded squirmed lower down in their hollow.

We closed our teeth to the shattering burst, which seemed right on top of us, and then after a pause and a deep breath I slowly raised my head to see that the shell had exploded precisely over the hollow and killed every one of the wounded.

'Lead on "A" Company,' and we moved forward to the front line in answer to the order, glad to get off at once from the immediate scene of that awful tragedy. We halted on familiar ground, under cover of the little cliff of chalk which we had manned yesterday.

An occasional shell burst behind us in the woods, and some very large ones were sighing over our heads, high up, on their way to Vailly a mile below us on the river bank. Just as we came to the little cliff the officer commanding a company on our right came striding towards us; a tall gaunt captain with the light of battle in his eye. A very religious man he was too, always talking about duty, and a great Bible reader. Tall, sinewy, with pale face and pale-blue eyes, colourless hair, and a large, untidy, colourless moustache, he came at us looking for blood. He reminded me of a grisly Don Quixote. 'They have gone,' he cried jubilantly and with certainty, in a cracked voice, 'all the Germans have gone away, except about one platoon, which I have located in that wood to our left front. I intend to capture that enemy platoon with my company, but I want volunteers from 'A' Company to move across the open to support me, while I work forward through the wood, which enters the left of my company line. Now, who will volunteer?'

I suppose he knew very well that the native pride of Irish troops could be depended on. Anyway the whole of 'A' Company immediately volunteered to assist. The officer selected the two nearest platoons, which happened to be mine and my brother's. He then sent Muldoon, one of my platoon, up a tree to look across the plateau at the wood, in order to confirm the presence of the enemy for our edification. Mul, as we called him shinned up, and presently shouted down: 'Yes there they are, I can see them in the woods.'

'Good,' said the officer. ' "A" Company's two platoons will move forward in line from here, keeping parallel to the right edge of the wood, as soon as my company gets going,' and Don Quixote went off rapidly to launch his attack. A rifle shot, aimed at Mul, cut short that lad's curiosity, and he slid grinning and safe to the ground. We fixed our bayonets, as the enemy were close, and sorted ourselves by sections along the plateau edge, searching for easy places to surmount so as to get on to the level of the plateau.

It cannot be said that the operation was very well organized. It was all too rapid, and we got no definite objective, our task being to engage any enemy on our front by advancing to find him and attack him. My brother's platoon suddenly got the order, unheard by me, and up went the men on to the open grassland, led by their officer. Denis went ahead, abreast with this officer, too far in front of his section, I thought. He carried his rifle with the bayonet fixed threateningly at the high port, and presented a good picture of the young leader going into battle. I wished he had not gone so far forward.

Not quite necessary for a lance-corporal. He was exposing himself unnecessarily and would be one of the first to be shot at. I raised myself high over the parapet of our cliff, and shouted to him: 'Take care of yourself', and I blushed at such a display of anxiety in the presence of my comrades. My brother steadied a moment in a stride which was beginning to break into a steady run forward, and looking back over his shoulder, winked reassuringly at me. The beggar would wink.

Forward he went, and out of my sight for ever.

I had to forget him then, because Lieutenant Waters drew his sword and signalled us. We rose from cover and doubled forward over the grass to the right of my brother's platoon. There was an uncanny silence. We could see fairly level wooded country and some cottages to our immediate front, backed by more broken landscape. With a sinking heart I realized that our extended line made an excellent target, as we topped a slight rise, and went on fully exposed across flat country without the slightest cover. The Germans were waiting for us, holding fire. As we cleared the crest, a murderous hail of missiles raked us from an invisible enemy. The line staggered under this ferocious smash of machine-gun, rifle- and shell-fire, and I would say that fully half our men fell over forward on to their faces, either killed or wounded. Some turned over on to their backs, and others churned about convulsively. With hot throats the remainder of us went on, as there is no halt in the attack without an order.

The wood on our left, through which the other company was advancing, seemed on fire, as it sparkled

178

with bursting enemy shells, and then became almost
hidden under a pall of rolling smoke. The wood was a
shell-trap, and the company had 'bought it', as the
troops curtly say. More men fell, but my section still
went strongly. Two men of the nearest section to our
left fell, and both immediately sat up and began to
tear open their First Field Dressings. They had been
hit low, in the legs. A bullet ripped through the sole
of my right boot, as I ran on, and jerked my own leg
aside. For the next few paces I kept stamping my
right foot on the ground, testing it, and half expecting to see blood spurt from the lace holes. This low
fire was a bloody business, and most efficient—the
kind of stuff we were taught ourselves. I believe I
was now beginning to get really afraid of these Germans.

The high rate of concentrated fire continued, and
the men were now advancing in a very thin line,
with most of their numbers scattered on the grass
behind. No officer remained. A sergeant on the left
shouted and the men nearest him got down into the
prone position. We followed suit, and hastily threw
ourselves flat on the grass. Hardly had we done so
when a machine-gun raked the whole line, a weak
and feeble line now, and shot accurately home into
it. Some of the lying men flapped about, others, shot
through the head, jerked their faces forward rapidly
and lay still. I trembled with fear and horror.

This was a holocaust. The relentless spray of the
deadly machine-gun traversed back along the line

from the left towards us. The Catholic soldiers blessed themselves in a final act of resignation. But the curve of the traverse came luckily short as it swept across my section, and it traced the ground in front. Little spurts of earth showed the strike of each group of bullets, a few yards before our faces.

This was more perilous than shots going over our heads, because the bullets ricochetted, shrieking like some infernal cat-fight all about us, but it was better than being hit direct. By lucky chance or instinct I saw the enemy machine-gun. There it was, mounted daringly on the roof of a cottage, close to the left side of a chimney, about six hundred yards away, and directly to my front. With all my strength I shrieked the range, described the target, and ordered five rounds rapid fire. There was a heartening response as we opened fire at the first and only target we had seen in this terrible attack.

In about four seconds some thirty bullets were whistling about that dark spot near the chimney as we slammed in our rapid fire, glad to have work to do, and gloriously, insanely, and incredibly the German gun stopped firing, and then it disappeared as it was quickly withdrawn behind the roof.

'Fire at the roof below the ridge of the house, about three feet down,' I ordered exultantly, and I could have whooped for joy. I was now commanding effectively. Damn the rest of the enemy fire. Their rifle-fire was always poor anyway, and blow the shells. They might hit you and they might not. There was

none of the deadly accuracy of the machine-gun in
these other weapons of the enemy. I breathed a long
breath of relief and looked about me.

I looked right and left at my section to see that all
were firing. Bugler Tymble had been wounded in
the right arm, and having discarded his equipment
was moving away back. The others on the left were
firing well and steadily. On my right, the nearest
figure lay still with his face in the grass. I roared:
'Are you hit?' and he raised his head to show a grinning face. I got angry, and shouted at the scrimshanker: 'Why the hell don't you fire?' and the man
began to laugh. I did not know him well. He had
arrived with the first reinforcement only about ten
days before. He laughed and laughed and dug his
face back in the grass. It was no grim joke, as I then
suspected. The man was hysterical with fear. I did
not know hysteria, and could not understand him.
Some of our wounded had bandaged themselves and
had continued to fight. The sight of them made me
madder, and I edged towards the laugher, swearing
at him, and I struck him twice in the ribs with my
rifle butt. That steadied him, though his grin turned
to a look of terror. I threatened him with a court-
martial, and told him to pull his socks up. This
sounded damn silly in the circumstances, even to myself, so I crept back to my central position to supervise the actions of more useful men. I looked about
for more enemy targets, but could see none. Our
cover was better than we had first thought, and most

of my section were lying accidentally against a tiny ridge, so small as to be almost invisible when standing, yet it provided us with definitely good cover, and probably saved all our lives. Shells and bullets continued to kick up earth and grass in our vicinity. On the left my brother's platoon was suffering badly. Nearly all the men had been hit, and only a few were returning fire. The shell-fire too was much heavier over them.

Muldoon rose some yards to my left with his face covered in blood, which poured down on to his jacket and equipment. He had been shot through the top of the head. He came to me, and asked for the platoon sergeant. I said: 'What for? Go back,' and he said: 'No, got to report first.' And report he did, going down that awful line, under heavy fire, spurred by a most soldierly but ridiculous conscience to ask permission to fall out. He got back safe, with a peculiar wound, not at all fatal, for the bullet had hit him near the top of the head, and had passed under his scalp, and out at the back, without injuring his skull.

The curious behaviour of some bullets, as in this case, puzzled us then and afterwards.

We were still in great jeopardy, losing men every moment. Nine officers of the two companies—all we had—were knocked out. They fell forward in the advance waving their naked swords.

The Germans, aided by the flashes of these out-of-date weapons, had concentrated their fire with success on our leaders. Two officers had been killed and seven wounded. From this date swords went out of fashion. Our attack had been a fiasco.

Without officers, and sorely stricken, we still held on, until a sergeant waved us back, so we rose and returned to where we had started, exhausted and disappointed. Some of the men walked back disgustedly, not deigning to run for it. I found Tymble under cover, and saw he was quite happy with his wounded arm. He was waiting to go back to Vailly. The Germans followed up our short retreat with shells, and worried us with more casualties among the few survivors. This was very harassing, almost the last straw. Our casualties had already amounted to one hundred and fifty, more than half the strength of the two unfortunate companies. A sliver of shell hit the hysterical laugher of the front line and sent him all diddery. It struck him in the foot, and completely out of control he rushed limping for sympathy to me, shouting: 'Oh, oh, Corporal, what shall I do?' Some one seized him, disarmed him, took off his boots, and led him away, still groaning: 'Oh, Corporal, Corporal, Corporal.' My vials of sympathy were emptied, and I was glad to see the last of him.

A young Cork man named Lane came smiling towards me, with his arm in a sling. He was of my brother's platoon. I asked him about Denis, and he gave me the glad news that he too was slightly wounded in the arm, and had gone down to the village of Vailly with some other wounded. I was pleased and relieved.

The next few minutes reminded me of Butler's picture of the Crimean roll-call, when the senior N.C.O.s listed our casualties from information given by the survivors: '08, Corrigan?' 'Dead, Sergeant.' 'I saw him too.' 'Right, killed in action. Any one seen 23, Murphy?' No answer. 'Right. Missing.' 'What about MacRory. Any one see MacRory coming back after he was hit?' No answer. 'Right, wounded and missing,' and the sergeant's stubby pencil scribbled on. The depleted company moved back the short distance to reserve, and grouped in little parties to discuss their experiences. I left them to seek the orderly-room clerk, who verified that my brother's name had been submitted in the list of wounded of his platoon.

The clerk would not tell me the total casualties. He had been forbidden to speak about them.

Actually my brother was lying dead out in front, about three hundred yards away, all this time, and I did not get to know this for days. Only one man of his section had come back alive. That I did not know either. After some days this survivor told me that my brother was killed with the rest of the section by shell-fire. He also confirmed that he had been wounded first.

Volunteers from other companies were called for, and these went out, when darkness fell, to bring in the wounded. They worked all night and suffered casualties themselves.

The company on the left had got a bad hammering. Their wood was now a shambles of wrecked trees and human bodies. Men had fallen in heaps under the intense shell concentration, yet the stout fellows had pushed on, and actually entered and captured a German trench, and brought back several enemy prisoners, among whom were some gunner observers.

These gunners had a knob instead of a spike on the top of their helmets. The strange, enemy field-grey uniforms made some of us feel bitter, but as we continued to look at them, cold reason told us that they were only troops like ourselves, and not so straightbacked either. They looked pale and scared. The warlike commander of the left company, bleeding from several wounds in various parts of his body, and looking more fanatical than ever, would not have any of his hurts dressed until he had interrogated his prisoners. He questioned them in German, and was removed from them with difficulty, and made to lie on a stretcher.

Some of our wounded lying out did not wait for rescue. They crawled and hobbled in of their own accord. One man presented a wild appearance, coming in half naked. He had been peppered with shrapnel, and had stripped himself under fire out there to look at his wounds. A man is always urgently curious about his wounds. Blotches of blood showed up startlingly on the white body of this half-naked fellow, who was the man who had knocked me out with bare fists in what already seemed the far-off days of peace. A ghastly sight, and he was simply full of abuse. He cursed us for not trying harder, and told us we had disgraced ourselves. A hardy fighter indeed, but we had had our bellyful, and were in no mood to listen to his recriminations. He was soundly cursed at in turn, and left us with a bitter twist on his thin lips, still reviling us with the vituperation of Belfast's back streets, while his red hands wandered unconsciously from wound to wound.

He repelled us, and as he looked strong on his legs we left him to his own devices.

An inquisitive corporal from one of the companies that had remained behind approached Cordwain, asking him what the attack was like, and the strength of the opposition we met with.

'Hell's Bells!' said tall Cordwain, as he remembered the intensity and variety of fire we had endured: 'we met the whole of von Kluck's lousy army, and the bloody German navy as well.'

And he spat reflectively over the hot muzzle of his rifle.

Part Two

AND I

Chapter Twenty-nine

CHALK

From the point of view of the man in the ranks, the situation on the evening of the 15th of September was very bad. A swift attack by one and a half companies had been smashed back, and smashed back efficiently. We had lost a good many officers, and lost them for good, because the wounded, with one or two exceptions only, were absorbed at home to train men or to serve on the staff.

The acme of officer leadership seemed to be to expose oneself in the most dangerous positions as an example to the men. All very gallant, but not very practical, and useless to us. We did not require any good example to fight in those days. Some of us resented the implication in such an attitude, and soon, in the still more difficult and more disastrous days to come, we heartily wished that our lost officers had taken more care of themselves. Their presence certainly always did inspire us, but a little more directing, and less examples of studied bravery, would have suited us better.

Chalk

Their responsibility fell too soon on the shoulders of the N.C.O.s, some of whom were young and unfitted to do an officer's job. Their absence from later scenes of valour on the part of their men was a loss and a discouragement, for many stout riflemen died unknown and unsung who would have been decorated for bravery had their deeds been witnessed by officers. Up to the present very few of our regiment had been recommended. Our colonel, admirable in other ways, believed in the policy that every man's best was his least in the way of duty.

Well, we were sorely puzzled men that evening in September. We had all thought we were pretty well invincible in attack, but we did not know what to think now. As professional soldiers we still rather despised the Germans, mainly I think, because they wore such baggy uniforms, and were such bad shots with the rifle. Well, that might be so, but we had to admit that they evidently had a kick in them, and with their masses of guns and machine-guns they were certainly capable of stopping our advance from entrenchments.

Any further attack on them the same day was out of the question. We were therefore put to work digging in and strengthening our defences. Recalled from our cave, we dug like miners. I did as well as I could until I came to a slab of hard chalk, on which I could make no impression with my small entrenching tool, so I sat on it like a sad Buddha, while my delving companions on either side made me a pedestal.

Chalk

I was fatigued, fed-up, and moody with the raw horror of my recent experiences. Officers being scarce, some from other companies were posted to us, and one of these, a Captain Oakes, came along and ticked me off for laziness, and said as a non-commissioned officer I was a bad example to my men. I showed him my hard slab of chalk, and he solved my difficulty by telling me to get down off it and to undermine it, which I did. I had not thought of that. My thoughts were not very coherent, anyway.

Captain Oakes was well liked by us all. He was never without an eyeglass, and he spoke in a very deep rich voice, like a tragic actor. He was genuinely very fond of us, and would, I think, have given his life for the most humble private soldier. He was the grandest type of Englishman.

Except for occasional shelling all was quiet until night came, when there was a general alarm and we stood to arms and fired into the darkness to break up a supposed German attack. Nothing came of it except increased shelling and more casualties; and a German visitor, in the shape of a machine-gunner carrying boxes of ammunition. He had lost himself in the noise and darkness, and had guided himself by its sound to one of our machine-guns, instead of to his own. He was challenged, replied in German, and immediately received a burst of bullets in the chest from the gun he had mistakenly come to serve. The men recounted this incident with glee. A bit tough, I thought, as I was not for unnecessary destruction. They could easily have captured him, but I'm afraid there is a savage streak in the Irish during battle. In thé light of the following morning, they were also far too curious about his poor corpse.

During the next three days the enemy brought up more howitzers and field-guns, and let us know it, and rain fell heavily at intervals, making us despondent. We had neither greatcoats nor blankets, and most of the men had left their waterproof ground-sheets at Mons, or on the road from it.

Letters arrived from home, and some were read in misery, and at a loss to reconcile fond messages, warm and homely, with the bitter conditions surrounding the readers.

On 19th September the German shelling rose to a regular bombardment of our line, and culminated in another enemy attack.

The tide of war had turned again, and with a vengeance; casualties mounted still higher, and large ground-shells, which made huge craters, fell in and about our works. Four more officers, including our gallant colonel and his adjutant, were wounded, one for the second time. Captain Oakes was wounded in the left leg, but he refused to leave us. The colonel was very severely hit and I believe had to have a leg amputated.

This day we found ourselves fighting in defence of our very lives, and there were many anxious moments.

An officer from an English regiment came up offering reinforcements, saying he had a company close

behind us in the woods. This had been sent forward
to support us by strengthening our weakening line,
but he was told they were not wanted. He was shot
down with a bullet through his head, as he was deliv-
ering his message, and he fell and lay still a few yards
from me. He was therefore unable to take back our
answer, and no one bothered about him in the heat
of the fight.

Another English officer of the same regiment came
up in the same way to offer help. Captain Oakes, who
was directing the defence near me looked around
quickly, and, seeing the badge of the officer, thought
it was he who was already dead, and impatiently
shouted at him: 'Not wanted, not wanted.' The officer saluted, and as he withdrew he too fell, also shot
through the head. The Germans had broken through
the regiment on our left, and were firing across at
any one moving directly in rear of our cliff.

I had to look several times at the two corpses lying
near each other to confirm that I was not suffering
from hallucinations.

During this action a young English corporal named
Gedding distinguished himself by standing up to observe the flash of a big German gun which was doing
a lot of damage to the right of our sector, where the
trench went out at almost a right angle to our front.
His 'Here she comes' was answered by 'Good old
George' as he and his mates cowered low to make
themselves as small as possible against the impending
explosion.

This brave chap was killed a few hours later. He had been a noted footballer.

Gradually the attack died down, and quite unexpectedly a cheer rang along the trenches. I have never heard our later soldiers cheer like these professionals did, in such circumstances.

We cleared away our wounded, and buried our dead in the hollows behind, keeping a wary look-out to the left where the Germans had broken through, and whence the dangerous shots had come that killed the two officers. But the gap had been closed again by a counter-attacking company of the broken battalion, and we worked in safety. It was reported that the Germans had approached close to the line of the battalion on our left by a doubtful strategem. They had dressed up in the kit of Highlanders, and had replied in English to our challenge, but their description of themselves, before too many of them got near, gave the game away. They called themselves 'The King's Own Gordon Highlanders', or some such fanciful and incorrect title, and an officer gave the order to fire on these strange Highlanders, and held back most of them.

Three of our men were buried by our 'C' Company in one grave, and hours later they had to be taken up again, under the orders of an irate sergeant, as the burial party had forgotten to remove the identity discs of the dead. The dead were simply buried, as they were, in their uniforms. Their hastily dug graves were often shallow, and time and again we had the uneasy task of reburying some poor chaps who had been blown out of their graves to the surface by ground-shells.

One body puzzled every one. The man was certainly dead and cold, but we could not find the tiniest wound on any part of him. He probably died of concussion, of which we had never heard.

My company's turn of rest in the caves came again on the 20th, but any chance of respite seemed fatal to us, as we had to turn out to repel another German attack that day.

Captain Oakes was again wounded. He called the remains of our once strong company from the caves, and stood on a slight prominence near the outlet. He looked more dramatic than ever. I think he felt dramatic, and enjoyed that feeling. At any rate, there he stood, his monocle still in his now red-rimmed eye, his face drawn and dirty with many days' growth of beard, a revolver in each hand, and a second wound in his left leg.

He waved his left revolver grandly in a magnificent sweep towards the front line, and said in a deep voice: ' "A" Company, man the earthworks.' His strange appearance and weirdly expressed order amused us even then, and seeing us smiling as we went past him his whole manner changed, in a habitual endearing way he had, and he said simply, as if to each man singly: 'The Germans are very fond of my left leg.' This time, however, he received no quarter from his N.C.O.s and men, and he was scolded and bullied into retiring from the firing line, protesting to the last. Sure, we were very fond of old Oakes, with his 'man the earthworks'.

This was our last serious action on the Aisne. It was bad enough, but milder than the German attack of the day before.

Nevertheless we had both machine-guns put out of action by shell-fire. One of our gunners was shot through the hand while repulsing this attack, but he bravely continued to work his gun, until it was knocked out.

We were relieved, and what a relief, on the 22nd of September, and we went back into billets out of range of the enemy guns. On the way we crossed over the main bridge out of Vailly, which had been repaired by the sappers. This bridge was under incessant fire, and large craters pitted the banks on either side of it. We hurried over in small parties between the intervals of the explosions made by large regularly arriving shells, our nostrils offended by the sweet, sickly smell of the bodies of rotting horses, which were strewn all about the place, and happily we marched from the sounds and sights of warfare, southwards into fair country.

A dull rattling sound in the distance behind us, exactly like the sound of a slow-moving country cart on a rough road, told us that the rapid fire of British musketry had broken out again on the heights we had left. We wished the boys luck and forgot them.

Those of us who still live will remember our first

halt on the roadside clear of the battle; how depleted company looked at depleted company; how eased and grateful we all felt at the relief from our first hard experience of modern war; the stories we had for each other, and the whispered inquiries about absentees, and accounts of how chums died; our ghost-like faces dirty white with the shell-pulverized chalk of the Aisne heights; our stiffness of limb, and our lousiness; yet in spite of all, and though we had suffered heavy losses and felt a bit battered, our old spirit lived, if one could judge by the general gust of laughter that passed along the ranks when one of the surviving company commanders, an old curmudgeon of a fellow, came riding up the road through the companies, and in reply to the timid greeting of one of his subalterns said simply and appropriately: 'Good bloody morning.'

We occupied comfortable billets in a village near Braisne, and life became very sweet once more with clean clothing, good food, undisturbed sleep, and exercise in digging a reserve line in safety south of the river. An alarm that the British line was breaking brought us back hurriedly to the very banks of the river, but the line held, and we returned to billets.

We stayed billeted for three or four days, took our turn in a support line without suffering further damage, and then we marched once more, bearing west, until we crossed the Oise, where we entrained and steamed north through Amiens on the way to La Bassée.

The race to the sea had begun.

Chapter Thirty

NORTH TO LA BASSÉE

The battalion detrained at Noyelles late on 6th October, and thence proceeded by route march towards La Bassée. We had one day's journey in buses at the end of which we took up an outpost line near a place called Floringhem, where nothing extraordinary happened except that during the night some French refugees came through our posts. One family group mistook my sentry's challenge for German, and ran to hide themselves in the roadside ditch, with cries of distress. I spoke in French, saying who we were, and in they came, peasants, trembling and voluble with thanks. I noticed now that we were beginning to get callous about the plight of these war refugees. Sterner and more pressing thoughts of our own risks in this instance excluded the performance of our usual little acts of solicitude, as well as that feeling of sympathy roused by the sight of the poor household gods of forsaken homes wrapped up in sheet bundles. We waved them on without much talk. We were their living frontier against the invader, and doubtless soon a number of us would be facing death again, while these civilians went farther back into safety.

We marched again for two days following this; we did not know our destination, nor that enemy cavalry was raiding miles behind our left farther west. We did not bother, but in the way of adventurers lived only for the moment. We sang our old familiar songs again, and trudged cheerily along. We entertained each other with yarns of what we had seen and heard. A whole platoon would keep silent to listen to one story-teller. A weird tale was told about an officer who completely vanished during the Battle of the Aisne. It was thought at first that he had missed his way and had walked into the German trenches. The rumour now was that he had been sent back for reinforcements of our own battalion, who had arrived at Braisne during the battle, and had been blown to pieces on the bridge at Vailly, and further that the only part of him discovered was a large hairy arm, with the sleeve of an officer's shirt attached to it. This was said to have been picked up in a garden near the bridge.

Following my own experience of hearing that my dead brother was alive and only slightly wounded, I found it hard to believe many of the stories bandied about. The troops, I am sure, did not lie deliberately, but their imagination, in the stress of battle often played strange tricks on them.

Another story was about a member of a yeomanry

cavalry patrol. One day while the battalion was in the van during the advance to the Marne one of our forward sections watched with interest while a cavalry screen composed of North Irish Horse reconnoitred a village. The infantry section on high ground could see the village plainly, and all the approaches to it, but the cavalry operating on low ground ahead had no such advantage.

The leading point of the British cavalry patrol rode on well ahead of his comrades towards the crossroads in the centre of the village, and at the same moment our infantry were delighted to see a German Uhlan riding similarly towards the same crossroads along the road running into it at right angles from a flank. No verbal warning could be given by the observers. They were too fascinated to think of firing their rifles. German and Irishman met precisely at the crossroads, and each wheeled a rearing horse and galloped away from each other as hard as they could pelt.

On the 12th of October we were marching through a flat country of many villages about five miles north of La Bassée, and once more found ourselves listening to the sound of field-guns. That roused some of us and depressed others, and there was much speculation as to what was happening in front, and what part we should play. I hoped that we might not suffer as we did on the Aisne. The men became quieter on hearing the booming of the guns, and a pregnant calm pervaded the whole column. The men took hold of themselves, and marched a little quicker, as they will to danger. Did they feel, as I did in my bones, that we were heading for the last round-up? I cannot say. Strong and young and virile, the soldiers moved in unison. My mind embraced my comrades, and my spirit fondly bound them, and swept out protectingly over them in prayer, while my body pulsed to their marching, their inevitable and terrible yet innocent progress to another rendezvous with death.

Enemy shell-fire was concentrating about the village of La Couture, through which the leading battalion of our brigade passed from sight under groups of lethal smoke puffs which expanded gracefully above them and sailed slowly away. Hard on the disappearance of the advanced guard we saw French cavalry come out of the village and fall back towards us. Our battalion drew nearer, broke up in ordered parties of companies, then platoons, and lastly opening out into sections we moved, well organized, and formed up under cover of the houses west of the village, into the centre and farther outskirts of which shells tore and crashed. Some shells came over our heads and burst harmlessly in the open fields, and spent bullets whirred softly through the air.

A French cuirassier came riding towards us, looking calm but disgusted. I hailed him: 'Les Allemands, ou sont-ils?' 'Par là,' he replied laconically, and pointed towards the north-east of the village, where we could discern the blue-cloaked figures of French horsemen lying dead in the fields, and, nearer, some active khaki-clad British infantry hurriedly extending to the left along the line of a ditch or stream.

Things began to boil up. The Germans advanced to attack our front battalion. Houses began to fall in the village and red brick-dust clouds mingled with the yellow and white of the exploding projectiles. The noise of combat rose and surged and charged us for action. All thoughts except the job of fighting were now forgotten, and here was the old army at its best. To get at the enemy was the work in hand, and past feelings of fear or sorrow were completely cut out by the fighting men. No time for that now. Sitting men stood, belts were pulled in, arms stretched, and weapons examined. Members of the various section groups under cover and around us became active and inquisitive, and eyes flashed with interest.

The Divisional Commander, General Hamilton, came right up near to where we were in order to see things for himself. This brave general was always going into danger. He was killed, unfortunately, during this battle when he had come almost into the firing line.

Motor-cycle dispatch riders rode daringly about, and then messages came for our assistance, and we rushed into the village by sections to assist the hard-pressed battalion in front.

I dashed at the head of my men up the main street and over a bridge, and dived under cover on the right of the road.

This was a hot corner. We got all the 'overs'. Shells broke the houses near us and bullets spat into the walls immediately behind. Other sections were directed into the fields on the left of the road. Officers and men began to fall under the hail of metal sweeping the village, and very soon our walking wounded were going back. A famous boxing champion from the Lancashire regiment to our immediate front passed us with a wounded arm and a jest on his lips. My platoon was ordered to keep well down under cover. We could do nothing at the moment.

We were close up in support to a company in front which screened us, and we could neither see the enemy nor fire on him.

The dour old company commander who had given the queer 'Good morning' to his subaltern after the Aisne rode coolly up to the front line, which was only fifty yards from our position, dismounted, and walked off to the left along a line of willows, where his company were in action. He left his horse on the open road, where it was hit by a bullet. Thereupon the animal walked off under cover of a house, and quietly died.

The company commander came back, and raved and blasted up and down the road, looking for his horse. He even swore at the soldier who showed him the dead beast. Then he went off in a high temper to his company, where he himself was wounded. Another company commander, a very popular one, was killed, and was buried near our platoon. Some officers who attended his quick funeral seemed to be feeling his loss deeply.

Two other officers were wounded, but other casualties were not heavy this day. The attack was successfully repulsed and died off, and my platoon was ordered away to the right into ploughed fields, where we lay in extended order all night without firing a shot. The honking of wild geese passing over us against the stars gave my heart a twist, and I longed for my Irish bogs. With food came news that rather shocked us: a deserter from an English regiment had been executed by a firing-squad that day. We were fed up about that, and would not look at it. An execution for cowardice or desertion hits us all too hard, and I doubt if it achieves the effect the authorities aim at. It disgusted the fighting troops, who perhaps are the most merciful of men.

The following dawn saw the British attacking all along the line. We set to work hopefully, opposed only by a weak rifle-fire and the shells of a couple of batteries. The enemy was in no great strength, and as usual his rifle shooting was poor, his bullets whistling high and harmless. One gun battery which was firing shrapnel, however, marked our company closely. We played a good game with these German gunners. As each salvo of shrapnel burst we dashed ahead under the smoke plumes, and moved so rapidly that we gave them no chance to range us accurately. We avoided halting at hedges and lines of trees.

This manœuvre was repeated again and again, and the ruse succeeded, so that at last we got so close to the hostile battery that we could hear them pulling

out their guns one by one and galloping off. Their
covering riflemen cleared out. German signallers or
observers dropped out of trees and surrendered as we
went through. This steady making of ground was good
fun. We had practically no casualties and the Germans were being driven before us. We made good
progress, advancing about two miles before being
held up by machine-gun fire. Then we dug in a bit
on the line won, and were relieved by an English
regiment, which got such a bad hammering that we
had to go back the same day and let them out for a
rest. My platoon took over a nasty piece of ground.
The English had only just begun to dig there when
they were badly cut about by shrapnel. Most of the
men we came to relieve were lying dead in the open
and we took our places in the intervals between the
corpses. These poor chaps, lying head on to the enemy,
had all been shot in the backs by the raining shrapnel while fighting and trying to scrape holes for cover.
Large numbers of black round bullets were scattered
about.

This meant that the enemy had the correct range,
and any repetition of their gun-fire would smash us
about too. Our hand entrenching tools were too small
to make good cover quickly. Even if we had had picks
and shovels it would have taken us over an hour to
make any kind of entrenchment that would protect
us from shells. These reflections did not appear to
occur to Cordwain, whom I was horrified to see
crawling along the line of dead to my left and ghou-

lishly emptying their pockets and haversacks. I asked
him in God's name what he thought he was doing,
and he grinned at me and said: 'Sure, the poor fellows won't be wantin' their tobacco any more, and
'tis after that I am,' and to illustrate his purpose he
showed me a collection of cigarettes, a clay pipe, and
some tins of Capstan Navy Cut. I left it at that.

One or two shrapnel shells swished over and burst
in the air behind us. This looked decidedly unhealthy,
and we were badly frightened men for the next ten
minutes or so, expecting a repetition of the fire that
had so easily destroyed our English comrades, but
the obvious very often does not occur in war, and no
more shells came over. We dug feverishly. We lost
no one of our section that day and night.

We continued to push our attacks against a weakening enemy for five days, and successfully gained about
seven miles in that time, advancing slowly in open
order from our trenches early each morning. One day
we got so near the Germans that we saw a long line
of transport retiring along a low-lying road, only a
mile away. There was the convoy in the open asking
to be blown to bits, and we went nearly mad with
disappointment because we could not get it shelled.
We had advanced too rapidly, and had outstripped
our field-guns.

I met the sole survivor of my brother's section during this show, and I regret to say I completely lost
control, going for him bald-headed and telling him
that he would not be alive had he done his duty and

stuck to his section commander. That sounds non-
sense now, but then I was beside myself with grief
at the loss of my brave young brother. I dreamed of
him at night, and once he appeared to visit me, laying a hand on each of my shoulders and telling
me he was all right. I felt relieved after this curious
dream.

One or two days afterwards the only man of his
section left alive was advancing in line with me
through an orchard. The Germans, making the best
of the cover provided by enclosed country, were giving some resistance, and shot down an occasional
man in our steadily moving line. A shout from my
brother's man told me he had seen some Germans
scuttling away a short distance ahead, and while his
face was turned sideways, talking to me, he got a bullet clean through the nose. He spun round as if he
had been shot dead, and dropped out. He lost a lot
of blood that day, but he managed to get away back,
and eventually he came safe through the whole
war.

At nightfall on 17 October our forward companies
were well up on the western slopes of Aubers Ridge.

'A' Company, one of those leading, halted in a
deep ditch, which we began to strengthen. When
darkness came we were moved farther forward to
command a better field of fire. Tools were issued,
picks and shovels, and we were instructed to dig
proper trenches.

The Germans, closer than we had supposed, heard

the clinking of our tools in the dark, and opened a sudden and very violent burst of rifle-fire along the line. We dropped our tools and hit the earth like one man, feeling completely exposed and caught out before we had turned a sod. Marvellously the long line of men did not have a single casualty, though we all experienced some palpitation of the heart. The German bullets swished and cracked safely over us, and then their shooting stopped altogether as suddenly as it had begun. After an interval we straightened up cautiously, exchanged our rifles for tools again, sent out additional covering patrols, and worked quietly and steadily in the night, until we had made a good kneeling trench, well traversed.

A regiment from another brigade took over these trenches at dawn, but were so heavily punished by the Germans, who were now bringing up large reinforcements, and whose fresh columns were reported as converging towards us on La Bassée, that we had to go back the same night in relief. The tantalizing loss of an interval of safe rest and hot food was expressed in our most blasphemous opinion of that bloody regiment, as we stumbled back, in black disappointment to the old trench.

A soldier hates going back to a place where he has already fought, hates with a kind of bitter desperation.

We were getting fed up with other regiments who could not hold the line. This was the second in a few days which we had to relieve at short notice. Had we

realized that we had merely been very lucky ourselves we would not have been so savagely proud of
the fact.

Our luck held. Attacks by large bodies of fresh
enemy troops were pushed in wide of both our flanks
on 20th October, and the hastily formed British line
was shaken. That night our battalion was withdrawn
to a reserve position. The next day still fiercer and
more extended enemy attacks took place, but we
were retained in reserve, and so avoided casualties.

We were taken out of reserve on 22nd October and
ordered still farther back—to straighten the line, they
said. We did not like it, this going right back to Neuve
Chapelle, around the east side of which the sappers
had been digging a strong entrenchment for days.
Three of our companies occupied these trenches. The
regiments operating in front retired, and came back
through our line, making us the forward fighting
troops in a new defensive position.

Our trenches, engineer-planned, were good, and
clean cut in straight bays and traverses, some of
which had been revetted with sandbags. We mentally thanked the sappers for their work. There were
still some few things to be done to get everything
ship-shape. Some sections of trenches had not been
quite joined up, but they were already taped and
spitlocked, not much work really. We did not like
the look of the fresh earth parapet. We would cover
that with grass and sods. And the communication
trenches, some yards of which had already been dug

backwards from the front line could be extended gradually to the rear of the buildings of the village of Neuve Chapelle, which was only about two hundred yards behind us. A nice village, with a château which the commanding officer and the medical officer occupied, and a nice large school, which was taken over by the lucky reserve company.

The trench system swung round backwards on the left flank to the north of the village so that on this side we were not quite in touch with the next infantry regiment in line, which was écheloned to our left rear. On the right we were cheek by jowl with an English battalion, the nearest members of which got busy at once making machine-gun emplacements.

All looked bright and cheery. A small man could fire standing in the trenches. Given time, even one whole day, any regular battalion could make the place an earthen fortress.

A runner from headquarters reported the existence of a series of four very deep reserve trenches only three hundred yards away to the left rear of our company. All to the good. Ours was the right-hand company in the front line.

All we wanted now was a little time for final improvements to finish off the good work of the sappers, and we would smash anything that came at us. We would give them 'gyp', as the troops said. But we got no time. The following morning the Germans came at us.

It was the beginning of the end of us, for we had

now arrived at the place of our destruction, and our fine battalion, still about seven hundred strong, perished here, almost completely, in the following five days.

Chapter Thirty-one

WHOM I REMEMBER

At Neuve Chapelle the usual preparations and duties were set in hand at once. Patrols were sent out, digging parties told off, sentries posted, ration and ammunition parties dispatched to the rear, and runners sent off to acquaint themselves with the location of battalion and other companies' headquarters.

Non-commissioned officers supervised improvement in their own fire bays, examined the arms and ammunition of their men, made out duty rosters and range cards, and advised as to the best sites for cubby holes in the trench side for use as ammunition caches. Latrines were made, and so on. We were to have no fires or lights, and empty tins were not to be chucked about indiscriminately, to serve as light reflectors to the Germans, and so enable them to locate our lines of trenches.

Both Sergeant Benson and my rascal Cordwain delighted me by bringing along sheaves of straw in the dusk. We made beds of the straw in the damp bottom of our trench.

Benson and Cordwain were two useful chums. Benson was always cheerful, natty, and self-possessed. He was well educated and highly intelligent, and invariably showed a smile on his round red face. He was of small stature, but big-chested, and his breast pockets were neatly squared-off with notebooks, duty rosters, and rolls. He was highly conscientious and full of the joy of living at the same time. He was also one of the most efficient scroungers in the regiment, and extremely kind hearted, dropping his winnings, ill-gotten or otherwise, into the hands of the private soldiers as he moved among them, always saying some little thing; a quip about a battered hat, a smiling injunction, or a reprimand. He joked his men into cheerful efficiency, and held us all in his capable hand. A daring fellow and the model of an infantry sergeant.

In contrast my Cordwain was a bit of a devil; a likeable laconic devil. He was almost illiterate. He dropped his tribute of straw to me without speaking, and then sat on his angular backside, his knees against his bony face; a face wistful and pregnant with some hidden scheme. I generally hated his schemes.

'What do you want now?' I asked.

'Give us ten minutes, Corp.'

'What for?'

'I'm on to a good thing.'

'What is it?'

'Ah now, ask me no questions. You can say I have the shits and that you gave me permission to fall out, if any one asks.'

'No blackguarding now. No pinching stuff?'

'On me solemn oath, Corporal,' and taking my last question for agreement he flitted over the parados like a ghost, and made off to the village.

A quarter of an hour later Cordwain returned to the trench. He had a sucking pig in his pack, which he managed to cook somehow that night with the aid of the commanding officer's batman, who was a pal of his. I heard later that he had distributed four more little pigs to his friends along the line.

Blast the fellow, I thought. He would have us both in trouble some day. Nevertheless the pig was good eating.

To his comrades' ribald questions as to how he won the pig Cordwain gave no answer. He ate greedily. Towards the end of the meal he voiced some regret that he had left the sow behind. There was a gleam in his eye as he went over her points.

I excused myself and drew hurriedly away from his dangerous companionship. I had already acted much too often as unwilling accessory, before and after, to his undiscovered crimes.

Two other sergeants besides Benson were still with the company. There was Sergeant Kelly, a Dublin fellow, whom we all disliked because he was too fond of work. An unattractive fellow, with waxed moustaches and a skin sallowed by foreign service. He was a man-driver with a sarcastic tongue. He was thin and wiry, and a prey to liver and bouts of malaria.

The other, a Sergeant Jones, was an Englishman

on the Cross, that is to say frightfully religious and a
teetotaller. He was almost unbelievably correct in
every detail—manners, speech and turnout, and more
than once he presented the only shaved face in the
entire company. He had a horrible trick, when ticking a man off, of asking a question which condemned
if answered. He was a bit of a plague really, and
though an honest fellow, we avoided him. The troops
called him 'Why and Wherefore'.

Of our officers I only remember three I knew in
these trenches: Lieutenant Barking, quiet, good-
natured, and easygoing; Morton O'Leary, another
Ulster man, of the same disposition, who amused us
by preceding all his orders with the word 'men'; and
in 'B' Company, on our left, young Lieutenant Cross,
English, very boyish, and popular. He was the young
officer who liked copying our brogue, which he did
very well. Lieutenant Lomas, our company second-
in-command, had been taken away to look after the
regimental transport. We missed him badly, our last
Regular officer, and one of the best.

Barking and Morton O'Leary were both Reserve
officers, and had seen little fighting. They were rather
ignorant of their duties, and this and the fact that
we had war experience made them shy of us. Officers
were getting scarce; sergeants and corporals carried
on.

Next in position on my left a Corporal Biganne
commanded his section. He was music-mad, and
could play many instruments. He was now reduced

to a mouth-organ, which he played on every possible occasion when off duty. He played it muted in the trenches. He was a fellow of fine spirit, an optimist, a bit of a swaggerer too, and given to anglicized expressions. Everything was invariably 'Top-hole' with him. He had a variety of accomplishments, and could act well. He was a fencer, and had forgiven me in the past for running a foil button up inside his nose, though he never forgave himself for not deflecting my point. He had not worn a mask, as he should have, but he was like that—a bit of a swanker. A smart fellow, and a good N.C.O. He had now developed the habit of gravely asking me what I thought of the military situation, which was as obscure to me as it was to him, and he generally ended any meeting with some clever funny story, of which he had a fund, most of them improper.

Of my section I still had Cordwain, O'Brien, Grimes, Shea, Brown, and Kelly. We had had few changes. Hoskins killed; Letts wounded and missing, probably a prisoner; Tymble and the hysterical man wounded; and we had been reinforced. We were a very lucky section to be still at a strength of seven.

I had a good look round at the ground about our position before dark. In front was a large level field with a hedge on the far side, bordering a road that ran parallel to our trenches, about three hundred yards away—a good field of fire. There were two haystacks midway between us and the hedge, one half-left from my section front, and one quarter-right. The ground behind us and between us and the village was fairly open also, but had irregular dykes and hedges zigzagging through it.

I was sorry to see that we had not finished our improvements before dark. We had dug and strengthened the front line in places, and had camouflaged our parapet with grass, but nothing had been done to dig back the communication trench. Communication trenches are always left to the last. This did not look good to me. It meant that all movement from rear to front would be over open ground, and ammunition, ration, and water parties, as well as stretcher-bearers and wounded and our ever busy runners, would be exposed in the open should we be attacked. Also, there was no way out, and, although the textbooks ignore it, a good soldier always feels better when he knows he can move back as well as forward.

Twenty yards to my left there still remained a gap in the line of trenches which had not been joined up by digging.

However, we were behind good cover with a splendid field of fire, and we were all set for anything that might come, or we thought we were.

We stood to arms during the first hour of darkness; sent out fresh patrols which returned with negative reports; and, after food, all the troops, except sentries, and others on special duties got down to it, and had a comfortable night.

Chapter Thirty-two

IT BEGINS

We stood to arms again in the morning according to our standing orders, each man grasping his rifle, and looking to his front over his bayonet-point, our machine-gun Numbers 1 crouched behind their weapons. But our patrols came in once more reporting that there would be no attack at dawn, and we set about our routine. A sharp morning made us bustle about. Breakfast was brought up by transport, and rations and water issued for the next twenty-four hours. The carts also brought us plenty of ammunition, which we cached in cubby holes along the trench under the parapet. Men rubbed their faces with cloths or old handkerchiefs made wet from their water-bottles. Some shaved in cold water. A burst of music came from Biganne's mouth-organ in the next bay. Sergeant Benson came inspecting us with a cheery 'Good morning', and passed along the line. Digging parties got started. All looked good.

There came an interval when I had nothing to do. I had already looked at my men's arms, and my section, except the sentry on duty, stood or sat about lazing, having enjoyed a good breakfast, so to complete my toilet I sat down too, and began to clean out my dirty fingernails.

I was not long at ease. A tearing sound, increasing in force, caused us to raise our eyebrows, and petrified us all into watchful stillness. Our minds were fixed on the rumbling noise of an approaching shell, an uncommonly loud gasping kind of noise, as if the projectile was making efforts of its own accord. It was the loudest shell we had heard in transit to date. I leaped up and waited for the explosion, wanting as usual to see where a first shell falls. Would it never come down? It took an unbelievably long time. Then every man in the front line ducked as the thing shrieked raspingly louder and louder down on us. There was a terrific thump which shook the ground, and quite a pause, then a rending crash, so shatteringly loud that each of us believed it to be in his own section of trench. A perceptible wall of air set up by a giant explosion struck our faces. The monster shell had burst well behind us in amongst the houses of the village. A huge black cloud rose slowly up and bits of brick and hot metal kept clattering to the earth, even as far as the trenches, for about half a minute. The tiles flew off a whole row of houses leaving a gaunt skeleton of rafters against the sky, and then, when we thought that was all, one house caved in on itself and slowly collapsed.

There were shouts of 'Good God' and 'What the

hell was that?' from the astonished soldiers, and no
wonder, for these extraordinary Germans were firing
siege howitzers at us, sending twelve- or fifteen-inch
shells at entrenched infantry. Austrian howitzers, we
read later, which had battered the Belgian fortresses
to surrender, and were now released.

'The dirty dogs,' said Grimes. 'Fancy slinging stuff
like that at poor bloody troops.' There was no fancy
about it. It was bitter fact, and the enemy were ranging Neuve Chapelle with their heaviest batteries.
This meant that they regarded the village as the key
of the British position, and we, directly in front of it,
would bear the brunt of any attack. I kept my sus-
picions to myself, and prepared for the warm time
that was coming. It came.

All that long day the heavy shells came slowly
down with thud and crash, their concussion alone
shaking landslides from the back and front of our
trenches, and making the earth rock as in an earth-
quake. Field-guns and smaller howitzers joined in,
punctuated by the nasty stinging crash of five-nines.
The slow ranging fire of all the guns speeded up to
a regular bombardment, as the enemy found our
position, and we crouched wretchedly, shaken by the
blastings, under a lasting hail of metal and displaced
earth and sods, half-blinded and half-choked by poisonous vapours, waiting for the enemy infantry, while
our overworked stretcher-bearers busied themselves
with new dead and wounded.

A 'whizbang' (7.7 shell) came into our trench and

stuck unexploded in the back wall; another blew in the bay on my right, and yet another scattered the sandbags from the top of the traverse on my left, under which I was crouching. I willed myself smaller and smaller, and prayed like the devil. As lulls occurred I shouted the warning, 'Stand by', to my dazed men, and then to the unfortunate sentry on look-out, 'Anything doing?' and each time he answered: 'No, nothing coming.' I would confirm this with a slow and careful look over the top. I took off my cap, and tilted back my head to make it as small a target as possible, looking over the ground in front along my nose. Time seemed to stand still; an hour was a day under this torture. We smoked nervously, lighting up and passing cigarettes with trembling fingers. The battle smoke killed the taste of the nicotine. As the day grew on we felt hungry, but we had no desire to eat. Our mouths were parched by the poisonous vapours, and with the thought that we would have to stand up to the German infantry attack any moment, and we had no saliva. We drank as much water as we dared, not knowing when our quart bottles would again be filled.

Huge craters flicked open in the ground about us, spouting earth and stones, and sending dense clouds up to thicken the pall overhead. Spots of sudden light in the smoke-screen showed where the shrapnel shells were bursting in air, their minor explosions being undiscernable by sound in the turmoil.

The Germans made the most determined efforts to

shell us out. A compliment to our rifle-fire. The regular prolonged bombardment was intensified on well-observed portions of our trenches, where salvo after salvo of ground shells, meant to blow the troops from cover, were immediately followed up by thick groups of shrapnel to catch them in the open if they retired. But the troops held. The village behind us was gradually becoming a rubble heap.

In the afternoon Grimes began to bemoan his fate. Infected by the superstitious Cordwain he had lately taken to seeing signs and portents. He called our attention to some queer cloud shapes in the sky and told us we were finished. I was incensed and shut him up.

We were in a mess anyway. My limbs were trembling. I cursed them. All my bones were singing from the force of the close explosions, and my throbbing head was being jerked by every painful heart-pump. My senses were strained to breaking-point concentrating on the special shell that was to kill or maim me, or trying not to concentrate on it.

Amazingly the troops began to nod and sleep in this inferno. The strain was too much, and they were being bludgeoned into relieving unconsciousness. I threw stones and lumps of earth at them to keep them alert for the coming attack, not caring a bit, even when some of them woke with shouts and anguished faces thinking they were hit by deadlier missiles.

A second shell burst on our trench, hitting the top

of the parados, and filled the trench with smoke. Grimes, who was just then wishing he was drinking beer in a certain pub in Brummagem, gave a terrified yell. He had been hit. I was not much concerned, as a badly hit man never yells. I went to him and found blood on his trousers, and helping him to take them down, saw a small hole in his backside oozing a little blood, a minor wound. I was glad he got it, and hoped it was a blighty, as I wanted to be rid of the Jonah. 'Right,' I said, 'it is not too bad. Can't dress it here. Go back to the dressing station.' And off I packed him during a lull.

The medical officer bandaged him neatly, and sent him back to the line, because men were getting short, and the commanding officer had given orders that any man who could fight should. Grimes returned to us still grousing, and cursing the doctor. I cursed the doctor too.

The bombardment continued, and the shocking sight of dead stretcher-bearers on their own hard-worked stretchers added a further tragic note.

Our guns replied weakly to the Germans'. At this time our shell expenditure was rationed, and only a few rounds could be fired back by each gun at the heavily armed enemy. This was a sad blow to us. It is very heartening to hear one's own shells swishing over in reply. One gets behind them, willing them on urgently to wider and more devastating explosions. But here it seemed no use. We were being overwhelmed in a tornado of hostile shells, through the high storm of which we could only occasionally discern the weak whine of our own few shells going the other way.

Towards evening our strained hearts bounded to the warning words of our watching sentries: 'Here they are, boys. Enemy in sight. STAND TO.' At the same moment the earth hushed. The guns stopped. Thank Christ. Thank Christ. The relief was unspeakable. We stood up, stretching wide and loose, men once more and no longer cannon fodder.

We leaped to the trench front, and up came our heads to see German infantry moving stolidly, diagonally, across our front in small squads between us and the hedge. Their whole attack was aslant—bearing to our left-hand—badly directed, and their men not yet extended in lines. What tactics! A complete give-away. Marching about like that in 'columns of lumps' within two hundred yards of us. . . . Good Lord! And stranger still, a large enemy column marching, if you please, along the road behind the hedge.

We let them have it. We blasted and blew them to death. They fell in scores, in hundreds, the marching column wilting under our rapid fire. The groups melted away, and no man was able to stand in our sight within five minutes. The few survivors panicked, and tried to keep their feet in retreat. We shot them down through the back. A red five minutes. No fire orders were given, as none was needed. Crowds of Germans at close range were plugged easily and rapidly by every one of us. The riflemen shouted as they fired: 'Come on boys. Let 'em have it,' and the attack spluttered out, leaving lines and circles of corpses and wounded, and we heard shrill cries of 'Kamerad' from those still lying alive under the whip of our diminishing rapid fire.

We had cancelled out our shell-tortured day with a vengeance.

One of my men, Brown, had his rifle shattered by an enemy bullet as he was firing, and scores of metal dust splinters penetrated his face, hands, and chest. He looked in a dreadful mess, but he was not badly wounded, and he moved back out of the line quite unconcerned, judging by the way he kept wondering what part of his rifle the enemy had hit.

We thought to rest after this, but the enemy, apparently infuriated, shelled us hotly until night came. Night, but no rest. One of our patrols returning, came in accidentally towards the English regiment on our right, and was wiped out by their rifle-fire.

Shortly after this mishap another patrol rushed in to us, shouting: 'They're coming, they're coming', and we stood up in the dark, seeing nothing, but hearing groans and labouring sounds as we fired round after round low across the level front, and stopped another attack.

The Germans were evidently all out to capture Neuve Chapelle, and our unfortunate battalion, now rapidly diminishing in strength, was their main obstacle.

In the small hours messengers ran about, and there

was a general sense of uneasiness. The higher commanders viewed the strong German attacks with
alarm. Two of our field-guns were brought up in
the darkness, and dug in, right in the front line,
muzzles flush with the parapet, to reinforce our
battalion, by firing case-shot at close range on further attackers.

The next day, 24th October, we suffered another
severe bombardment, worse if anything than that of
the day before. The shelling began early in the morning and we crouched miserably under it all day long.
It was so intense that all movement was impossible,
and we kept our dead and wounded in the trenches,
hoping to evacuate them when night fell. Our numbers became more and more depleted. The paralysing
reverberations of the now well-ranged enemy shells
were interlaced with the staccato rapping of hostile
machine-guns, whose streams of bullets traversed left
and right along our parapet, killing sentries, and
showering us with earth as we huddled there, each
man pinned to his own fire-bay. We saw little of our
two officers, though we passed along messages between
them in the shape of notes stuck into empty cartridge
cases. Our gloom intensified when we became aware
that the enemy shells were hitting accurately on the
left company. Casualties mounted higher and higher.

In the undug gap between us and the left company
corpses of dead runners and stretcher-bearers lay
piled on each other.

It Begins

Farther along we could see the men of the left
company clearing their dead out of the trench, and
laying the bodies in the open on the parados behind.
A bad show that, and an advertisement to the enemy
that their shelling was successful.

Cordwain was sent for to take the place of a dead
runner.

The bravest men were usually chosen for this job,
and I lost his services and his little personal attentions.
He buzzed off cheerfully grousing, leaving behind
him his encumbering pack.

Corporal Biganne, in the next bay, kept his men
heartened and amused by telling them stories. To
relieve my own strain of mind, and as I was curious
too about the character of a man who could tell
stories in such conditions, I ran round the traverse
and visited him. He greeted me with: 'Hello, Old
Thing. How is the bloodsome war in your part of
the world?' I made a grimace, the grimace of one
who knows not what the next minute will bring, and
the stout fellow concluded a yarn of how he won a bet
at the Aisne by wagering that a certain officer would
be hit in the legs. The subject of the bet had the thin-
nest legs I've ever seen, and they were the cause of
many a jibe in the ranks.

There was a pause in the shelling. Biganne said the
Germans were having their tea.

Sergeant Benson came and joined us, and made us
eat a meal of cold bully-beef and stale bread. The
sight of food sickened me, and leaning towards my

sergeant I whispered that I was getting fed up. He said: 'Never mind, lad. You'll be all right.' I told him I thought this was too awful; it was unbearable to sit down to meals with others recalling that I never now seemed to share those furtive meals with the same people, and that a number of those with whom I had recently fed had been knocked out. Biganne listened-in too, biting his lower lip, and the sober look in those two pairs of steady eyes shared my unspoken question: 'Who next?'

Ashamed of adding my own burden to their hidden agony, I said quickly: 'Oh, what the hell does it matter?' Benson poked me in the ribs, and asked me laughingly: 'How about the young British soldier?' Biganne said: 'Yes, how about him?' I had been fond of reciting that ballad. It certainly seemed stupid now. Who wanted to die, die, die like a soldier? 'To blazes with the young British soldier,' I said, and we all laughed.

Cries of alarm from the left brought us to our feet, and scattered us back to our various commands. The Germans had sprung a surprise and actually rushed in on the left company while the men had slackened off, tired out and nodding after the bombardment. Dusk came, and the situation was uncertain and very alarming. We manned our trenches and fired away to the left, raking the shadowy figures of advancing Germans. There was confusion, wild rumours, and delay in getting information. A fool shouted: 'They're in on us.' One of the field-guns in the line fired a single shot. Ominous. It sent us wildly guessing.

A sharp rattle of our own musketry followed after a long interval. That was better. We also heard a cheer.

News came presently that all was well, but the Germans had badly shaken the left company. They had rushed into the trenches, bayoneted several of our men, and had actually fallen-in a platoon of ours and had haled them out of the trench as prisoners. They also captured one of the field-guns, and turning it round had fired the single shell, but our gunners had purposely removed or damaged part of the re-coil action and the gun overturned when the Germans fired it.

The platoon of sleepy prisoners had an amazing adventure. Hardly had they got out of their trench when some of our shells burst over the group, injuring nobody, but the German escort, showing a great res-pect for the British shells, flung themselves flat on the ground. Thereupon our fellows bolted back into their trench, snatched up their rifles, and with a wild cheer started to kill off their late captors.

Early that night the regiment on our right fired again on one of our patrols. They killed nobody, but the men were scared, and showed several bullet holes in their accoutrements.

I got the wind up about these night patrols. It would soon be my turn to lead one, and I did not much relish the idea of being shot up by our own people. Our men said the other regiment was windy.

It Begins

A small group of khaki-clad figures among the field-grey bodies of the Germans to our right front showed where our first patrol had fallen under their bullets. It was 'no *bon*'.

We were by now all very tired, cold, dirty, and ill-nourished. We were living on our nerves. Men detailed to rest gasped and groaned in broken sleep and jumped awake nervously when touched on the shoulder to be detailed for look-out.

We were all on tenterhooks for the night attack which we knew was coming.

Chapter Thirty-three

TWO SERGEANTS

I had a grand dream. Loving friends were about me, a smiling valley held my home, and I stood regarding it, full of my happiness.

I opened my eyes and saw earth, empty cartridge cases, a pair of worn heavy boots, and two mud-caked puttees. I lifted my head from my knees to look at the man who was guilty of waking me.

Sergeant Kelly stood over me.

The night attack had come and gone: we had lined our crumbling trench and fired, and fended it off on our company front, at what hour I do not know, because we were all only half alive. Fatigue had us.

The Germans had again broken the line in the night, and had exploited the gap on our left, between us and the next regiment, and some Germans had stolen in behind us, occupying the ground between us and the village.

Sergeant Kelly stood above me, blue-jawed like a pirate, with blasphemy on his lips. 'Get up and fight,' he said. 'The bloody Germans are all around us, and remove that man. Is he dead?' He indicated O'Brien, who was collapsed forward on the low parapet, at his sentry-post, his dead face in the wet earth, and a hole in the back of his head. He had been shot from behind by the German infantry in rear.

Young Shea and I lifted O'Brien and propped him in the corner of the trench. The body canted, gave way and fell down sideways, the lifeless limbs slowly adjusting themselves to the accidents of the bottom of the trench. I gazed at it stupidly with heavy eyes, wondering if I should sit him up again. It seemed important that he should sit.

'Will you fight?' said Sergeant Kelly bitterly.

'Fight what, Sergeant?' I asked hazily, more and more bemused at my forgetting that one of my own men had been killed.

'Fight them. Look!' he said with a string of oaths, and he clutched me by the shoulder, and pushing me to the parapet showed me the massed corpses of the Germans in front. The field was now simply covered with German bodies, the nearest only a few yards from the parapet and inside our single strand of wire. I thought the sergeant was batty, so humoured him, and looked hard at the motionless slain.

'No,' said the sergeant, 'not there. I'll indicate. Left haystack, two fingers. Three o'clock. Row of eight men. A fresh lot, they're stirring about. On to them quick. Get a move on.'

The miserable German section was lying fully exposed to us on level ground, where they had remained from the moment daylight had caught them, and they were trying to keep still, shamming dead like the masses about them, but small movements and their regular formation had given them away to the keen eyes of Sergeant Kelly.

'Get up,' I shouted to my section, and, firing with them, we put our bullets into the heads of the lying enemy. Two or three of them rose stiffly to their knees to escape, but the bullets caught them and they flopped down again. One man actually managed to rise to his feet and I shot him through the chest. He pivoted sideways, poised a moment, and swung back to his front, then slowly sank down, his head bending towards us, the sun glinting on his helmet badge.

I felt disgusted. We had slaughtered too many already. I was miserable until the German line was still and I prayed for them as I killed them.

There was another bellow from the unwelcome sergeant behind me, and we all saw the reason simultaneously. A single German, a derelict of last night's attack, rose slowly from under our eyes, where he had been lying against our very parapet, and without looking at us he began to limp away, just as the daily bombardment of our line began again. Then an enemy machine-gun whipped the parapet and we ducked. The sergeant, nonplussed by the sudden opening of fire, and enraged at the sight of the German, shouted: 'I'll get that bugger anyway,' and he raked the already wounded German with a bullet through the hips. We could not look at Sergeant Kelly, nor at each other for the shame of it.

Sergeant Benson came into our trench at a run, saying that he had spotted the machine-gun in the right haystack, and had sent a message through to our guns. This was interesting, and in a short time our shells arrived and exploded, but they hit the wrong haystack and set it blazing. The machine-gun stuttered again, and again we popped down as the bullets traversed along the trench top.

'Up,' shouted Benson. 'Rapid fire at the haystack.' We fired hard at the stack, and at its top and sides, but with no effect. That gun was well hidden. We learned afterwards, too late, that the enemy had the habit of cutting a tunnel from the back right through the centre of haystacks, and mounted their guns in the tunnel; a clever ruse, as no one would fire at the blank centre of a stack. Anyway, we failed to put the gun out of action and it killed a good many before we left those trenches.

Sergeant Benson's attention was called to the wounded German, who, persistent in his efforts to escape, had now raised himself on his elbows, and was dragging his maimed body after him like a crocodile.

The kind-hearted Benson rose up, exposed himself to the enemy, and shouted: 'Come on in, Allemand, come on in. Don't be afraid.' The machine-gun gallantly ceased fire. I added my voice in French, knowing no German: 'Venez vous ici. Vite. Venez ici.'

The German turned at that and came crawling towards us with a smile on his pale face.

Seeing this, Benson exposed himself still more and amused us by promising the German tea and bread and jam. The German came on, and in spite of our warnings the sergeant stooped out over the trench to help him. Then there was a loud crack, some one said: 'My God,' and Benson slipped back into the trench on to his feet, staggered a pace or two, and sagged down dead, with a bullet through his pitying mouth.

We forgot the German in our rush to succour our good chum and his, but it was no use. Benson spouted blood and made no sound. The bullet had come out at the back of his head and blown his poll away.

The German was half over the parapet by now, where he stuck and waved his hand despairingly and deprecatingly towards his own treacherous people. We took him in and laid him gently down under cover near Benson, took off his hairy pack, and placed it under his head, and some one dressed his wounds and gave him water. He was very weak and kept his eyes closed. Sergeant Kelly sneered. He stayed near us for some time, and during the lulls in the shelling he kept us up to the mark by making us stand up, time and again, without reason, under the enemy machine-gun bullets, to resist any invasion of our trenches.

During these alarms and excursions he raged at our small numbers.

Then he devoted his terrible energy to organizing us. He made us clear away the dead and place them on the parados like the company on the left. Under his direction we cleared the trench of smashed rifles and other debris, and he made us man our posts more evenly, spreading us out along the trench, so that our small numbers only allowed one or two men to each fire-bay.

He glared at the useless dead as if resenting their inactivity. He wanted more men for his next task of repairing the smashed-in trenches. He was a great man in a way, and a good war leader; a product of the slums of Dublin, and a stout asset to the British Army, though a nasty piece of work from our point of view, just then.

At last he left us, and disappeared round a traverse, whence his rasping voice cut through the explosions, cursing some unfortunate soldier for not cleaning out his rifle breach. The mud of the trenches had entered the chambers of our rifles and had been baked hard inside by the heat of our firing, making many rifles useless.

We had also to resort to using bacon fat instead of rifle oil to grease the action of our bolts, and we pulled pieces of old socks over the metal work of the movable parts to protect them from the rain of earth blown over us by the bursting shells. This earth got in everywhere; into our food, our hair and eyes and noses, and inside our clothing.

Our supply system had broken down, and no rations had come up last night, as the Germans had extended their heavy shelling to the back areas.

In the course of the morning Cordwain had become a known hero. He was already one to his section.

A mate of his, another runner, caught out in the open by the shelling, and wishing to postpone the danger of his next sally back to battalion headquarters, told us the story in the comparative safety of the front line.

Cordwain had found the runner-route between headquarters and the front under fire from Germans behind our line, and had been shot at by them. He scouted about, and eventually located the Germans in a cottage. Then he went berserk. He told no one in authority, but flew back to headquarters, mustered as many of headquarters staff as he could, and some artillery men, and launched an attack all on his own against the occupied cottage behind the lines.

His party beat down the rifle-fire of the Germans, and he himself led a final charge. He leapt in first, through the broken window of the cottage. Inside he found eleven German infantry men lining the walls with their hands up.

Wasting no time he formed his victorious storming party into an execution squad, and was about to shoot down his prisoners, when an irate major of artillery, in pursuit of his missing gunners, entered the room and saved the Germans.

It was said that Cordwain even threatened to shoot

the major for interfering, but we took that with a grain of salt. Cordwain's extravagances needed no embellishments.

The runner's tale was interrupted by the whines and loud crashes of shells, and by the weak cries of 'Mutter', and 'Wasser', from the wounded German

Chapter Thirty-four

TALK OF THE DEAD

My section, now reduced to Kelly, Shea, and the wounded Grimes, fought on. I think we stopped two further attacks, one by day and one by night, but my memory fails me, because dreams and realities became mixed. The two forward companies were taken out of the line on the morning of 26th October for a belated rest, right back through ruined Neuve Chapelle to the village of Richbourg Saint Vaast, about two and a half miles behind. We were silly from lack of sleep and stumbled about like drunken men. We washed, devoured the food produced for us, and dropped down to sleep anywhere in the house allotted to us as billets. A whole platoon of us, now only ten strong, was housed in an attic festooned with strings of onions. The troops picked off one or two and ate them, and the Frenchwoman who owned the house objected violently, and fussed about entirely disapproving of us. A shell burst in the village, and set our worn nerves jangling. Thank God, a single shell only. The woman raised her voice and scolded us, saying she would just as soon have the Germans as the thieving English in her house. I got up, pushed her down the stairs, and told her in French to go to hell, and stay there.

Sergeant-Major Sullivan of the other company paid us a visit. He was looking for men missing from his company. His eyes were red and swollen. We could not help him. He was a tall, gaunt, bony Irishman and a ferocious fighter, but now where there was no fighting he was restless and broken-hearted, and was seen to weep more than once for his lost men. He also blamed himself because so many were killed. He told us that Captain Atkins was dead. This Captain Atkins had been left behind in England, an invalid unfit for active service, but he had stolen out to France to join his men and had lasted only about five minutes in the bombarded trenches. That set all the platoon talking of dead officers and men. I wished to forget it, and I went to sleep, and slept all day.

In the evening we were joined by a reinforcement of one officer, a Captain Jameson, and one hundred men fresh from Ireland, and at the same time we learned the grim news that the two companies who had relieved us in the line in the morning had been beaten out of Neuve Chapelle.

The commanding officer and the medical officer had become casualties, their beautiful château having been blown in on them, and the battalion was now commanded by a captain.

Talk of the Dead

We were turned out, paraded, issued with new bandoliers of fresh ammunition, and told we were to
recapture Neuve Chapelle. We marched back to
do so.

Chapter Thirty-five

WIPED OUT

We halted in the twilight about half a mile from
Neuve Chapelle, which was in flames and under
British gun-fire, and here, joined by the remnants of
the forward companies, we deployed for the attack
across the wintry fields. Mine was the right section
of 'A' Company, and Captain Jameson and his reservists were on my right. We were to attack when night
fell. The Germans were fairly quiet, and had not
pressed beyond the village.

Our Company Sergeant-Major came along the line
of men, and told us we would advance straight on to
the burning village on the blast of the whistle. He
asked us if we were all set, and each section commander replied: 'All set, Major.' He then ordered me to
go and see Captain Jameson, and to keep in touch
with his party throughout the attack. I went off to
the right and was surprised to see the men of the reinforcement digging in. I stopped them, and asked
for their officer, and they told me where to find him. I
found him rather anxious. I told him that his men

were wasting their energy digging cover here, as we
would all be going forward soon. Some of his men
clustered around in a rather undisciplined way while
we talked, and one of them said they were under fire.
They had become jumpy in the fading light, and one
or two bullets, their first weak baptism of fire, were
whistling over the fields. I intentionally laughed at
them, and chased them away to their positions in the
line.

Poor devils, if they called that being under fire.

Captain Jameson wanted to keep me with him,
complaining to me that he had no Regular N.C.O.s
with his hundred men, all going into action for the
first time. I told him I had no orders to stay, and
could not anyway, as I had to go into the attack with
my own section. I left him and went back to my men,
who were now sitting up under cover of the night, and
taking it easy while waiting.

Presently came an order, passed along the line,
and we all fixed bayonets. Then the whistle blast
which sent us stumbling over the uneven fields towards the blazing village, while some machine-guns
of ours, and I believe a pom-pom, added supporting
fire to that of our few field-guns and howitzers already
in action.

Enemy rifles began to splutter ahead, and some
bullets came at us. Then there was a short halt to
straighten the direction of the attack, and the sergeant-major came again to me, asking if everything
was all right, soon after I had lost touch with the

left-hand man of Captain Jameson's party. I told
him we were all right, but that the reinforcement
which had started in line with us had disappeared.
He sent me off to find them, and I explored the right
flank in vain. I came back and reported accordingly,
and the sergeant-major blasted me for a bloody fool,
and sent me back to the rear to find and fetch the
missing men.

I found them about 150 yards behind, where they
had started to dig in again on coming under enemy
rifle-fire, and I was lucky not to be shot by them as I
answered their ferocious challenge. I swore at them,
and shouted as loudly as I could: 'Fall in, the reinforcement.' I was still smarting under the reprimand
of the sergeant-major, and I was fed up hiking rifle
and gear around, and stumbling sideways and backwards in the dark over bullet-swept fields.

I was still angry when I reported to Captain Jameson that the attack had gone on without him. He had
an awful job in the dark with those men, who had to
be persuaded that they were not in the thick of the
battle. He asked my advice, and as I could not imagine them advancing with any kind of cohesion in
extended order, I told him, that to save time, we had
better fall them in, regain the road on the left, and
march up to Neuve Chapelle; so we formed fours, I
trusting to luck, and the captain trusting in me, and
we marched on without mishap right into the village,
which we found occupied by groups of our own men.
They were in good fettle, as they had met only small

opposition in the shape of scattered rifle-fire and the attentions of a few snipers, who were then in the act of coming out of the broken houses to surrender.

The safety enjoyed by the troops in the streets of the blazing village was incredible. This ruin had cost much blood, and was still the prize coveted by both sides, but neither shells nor machine-gun bursts entered it, for the simple reason that the gunners on each side thought their own men were in possession of it, or they were not sure. So we moved about unmolested where we had expected to be blown to pieces.

I halted the reinforcement on the British side of the strongest-looking house I could find at short notice, and directed Captain Jameson to the commanding officer at the crossroads, near the centre of the village. I saluted and retired to a respectful distance to listen-in for any news.

Near me a wayside crucifix hung high, untouched above the debris. I overheard that our advanced platoons had regained the old front line, and that Captain Jameson's party was to strengthen up the weak left flank of the position. One of the few surviving officers approached Captain Jameson with 'Fancy meeting you here, Jimmy!' They talked a moment, their faces lit by the flames around them, and then Captain Jameson shouted: 'Where is my Regular corporal?' and again: 'I want that corporal who brought us up.' But I had had enough of wild-goose chasing with his party, which had no claim on me, and I made off silently to find my own section. On my way I saw a group of soldiers keeping well in to the wall of a house, with one man wandering about in the middle of the street. Burning houses fell down from time to time, and sent up brighter flames and sparks as they crashed.

I drew near the group and asked about the careless fellow.

'That's Corporal Ternaghan,' I was told. 'He's off his bloody nut. He just shot a German prisoner, and he's wearing his cap.' Ternaghan was wearing a soft field-grey cap, and there were tears in his eyes and a happy smile on his lips.

He had no difficulty in recognizing me, and said: 'Hello chum. Only four of us left now. You and me, and Biganne, and Winters.' He was referring to the four surviving corporals of the thirty-two who sailed with the battalion for France just over two months ago. He asked me to admire his little souvenir, pointing to his German cap, and then he burst into tears.

I patted his shoulder, and drew him to the group, and he developed another mood, insisting that I could not part from him until I had shared a Maconochie ration tin of cold pork, beans, and potatoes, which he pulled out of his haversack.

I ate quickly, one man whispering to me the while: 'And Ternaghan is not the only one. There's a dead fusilier down at the village pump. He put himself on duty yesterday as sentry over the pump, and carried on marching up and down, in front of it, with fixed

bayonet, until they shot him. He would not leave it
for any one.'

I said I must be off, and following their instructions I worked forward under cover, giving no sil-
houette against the fires behind me, and eventually
came to the bit of communication trench leading into
'A' Company's old front line, and there in the dark
I found my men, and had to greet them severally,
they were so glad to see me back. Two of them pawed
me to make sure of me, one of them older than myself. I was touched at this unexpected show of feeling
and by the solicitous tone of their questions: 'Is that
the Corp.?' 'You all right, Corp.?'

I gave them all the news I had, and asked what was
doing, and they told me our chaps were back in the
line just in front, and all was well. I got uneasy about
the position of my section, as we could not use our
rifles in a packed communication trench, which was
a shell-trap anyway, and struggling forward to Lieutenant Barking I asked him why we did not go forward the few yards into the front trench, and man
that.

He told me everything was all right, and to go back
to my men. He would call me when wanted. So I
returned, and lay down with my fellows, hating the
crowd in the bit of communication trench, and hating
worse the runners who stumbled back and forwards
all night, treading on our bodies.

That bit of trench became sulphurous with plaintive blasphemy, until a Dublin soldier incongruously

247

checked it by vehemently demanding: 'For the sake of the sufferin' Saviour, can't yez shut yer bloody blasphemy, even in the face of sudden death?'

A Belfast voice said cynically: 'Listen to yon.'

I wished I could smoke, and I also wished that officers would tell us a bit more about the blasted war.

The enemy, unaware of the situation, mounted no counter-attack that night.

On the morning of the 27th of October we once again occupied our old position, moving up from the communication trench and manning our own fire-bays. The trenches were hardly recognizable as such in places where large shells had blown them to ground level. Bodies of British and German dead lay every-where, and shattered rifles, blood-stained equipment, and other debris were scattered about. The smell of the unburied filled our nostrils, and mangled and soiled corpses presented unspeakable sights.

We cleaned up as best we could, clearing the bays for easy movement during action, and ceased only when the dreaded bombardment of our thin line be-gan once more, and pinned us to the trench wall. Dumbly we suffered it. We seemed born for nothing else. And dumbly we saw again our comrades being maimed and massacred.

Once more lines of German infantry, apparently inexhaustible, came over the field of dead, and again those of us still sound stood up to stave them off, but our strong ranks of riflemen were gone, and our weak fire caused alarmingly few casualties. The enemy swarmed everywhere in sight, and wearily, with bloodshot eyes and tired limbs, we destroyed them, shooting at one group, until we saw another threateningly nearer. We shot and shot, and we stopped them once more on our company front, but they got in again on the left, and to some purpose. Fugitives from the left company joined us, saying that the Germans had overrun them and were now in their trench, and presently we were horrified to see large numbers of field-grey soldiers moving steadily forward over the ground behind us, and then we found ourselves once again surrounded, and under German fire from front and rear.

To add to our misery and uncertainty the British guns, getting a message from those who had seen the Germans behind us, thought we had lost our trenches, and spattered us with Lyddite shells, until we did not know which side of the trench we should use for fire and cover.

Additional machine-guns swept the parapet, and their bullets sogged into the bodies of the dead on the parados. Several British shells scored direct hits on our trench, and the poisonous heavy vapour hung about us. I moved left from a coming shell, and found Corporal Biganne, our music-maker, dead in the next bay, his face up with open eyes staring skywards, and all his skin and clothes painted a ghastly yellow by the Lyddite shell that killed him.

Wiped Out

On the left the Germans had not captured all the trench of the other company, for several groups of our men, though surrounded on all sides held out in their own fire-bays.

One man, not waiting to be bayoneted by assaulting Germans got out of his trench to sell his life dearly. He was a noted fencer, and he was reported to have bayoneted six oncoming Germans, and held up the attack in his immediate vicinity, until a seventh German, refusing the challenge of cold steel, checked in his stride, stood back, and shot the Irishman through the forehead.

Our extreme left flank was, however, completely turned by overpowering numbers of the enemy, and the unfortunate Captain Jameson and his men were entirely missing, either killed or captured.

Sergeant Kelly, dutiful and inquisitive, had gone along to the left to see things for himself, and he was struck down, mortally wounded in the stomach by a shell splinter.

Imperturbably he faced this new situation, resigned himself to his fate, and propping himself against the trench wall, he calmly fished out his Rosary beads and began to tell them. He was no longer interested in this life. But the Germans had not finished with him, for a little later, in their wild rushes and counter-rushes to dislodge the stubborn groups of our men, one German soldier got in and bayoneted him with the beads still in his hands.

The trench, now under fire of both friend and foe,

and attacked from front and rear, became a shambles, and untenable. The wounded lay neglected. There was no hope of holding out much longer here, and I said my last prayers. Then battalion headquarters, realizing our plight, somehow got a message through, and ordered us to fall back on the village.

But it was as difficult to withdraw as to hold on, and many of the men hated leaving their fire positions. Others did not care what happened. The Germans in front remained checked, but those behind had gone to ground, and were now working in to us, and others were slowly gaining along our trench to the left.

Lieutenant Barking came and ordered us to close on the right, and we moved along to the head of that hopeless communication trench, whose length was only a few yards. Lieutenant Morton O'Leary lay dying in it, hit, like Sergeant Kelly, in the stomach, and kind and gallant to the end he said: 'Men, you can't go down there, the end is under machine-gun fire.' We could see a heap of khaki bodies of those who had already tried to escape lying about the exit, and at the same moment several bursts of bullets shrieked close over us.

The way of retreat was under observed machine-gun fire.

Lieutenant Barking now said it was the only way. A man said 'I'll chance it', and another took up the cry, and they went crouching to the end, and then up, and out into the open at a run. We queued up for

our turn, our hearts thumping. We groaned for each
lad that fell in the mad scramble. I became too
excited to see if my section was present. I could not
see Grimes anywhere. I remember I missed him then.
Along the trench someone stumbled over Benson's
body, which had fallen in off the parados. The
wounded German was still alive, lying farther along
the trench, where we had placed him days ago.

My eyes lifted off him at the sound of the German
Maxim which opened as three of our fellows broke
cover simultaneously. We tensed ourselves as one fell,
and sighed in relief as he rose again and sprinted on.

From then I kept my eyes on my boots, not daring
to look at any more running the gauntlet. It was a
case of hit or miss. I reflected that it would perhaps,
be better to be killed outright, than to be wounded,
for the wounded fell in the line of fire, and every subsequent burst got them, if they were unable to roll
away.

My turn came. I crept down to the end of the communication trench and I purposely waited for the
sound of the machine-gun. I had observed that the
gun had taken to following up the men ahead as they
went from cover to cover towards the village, and
at the next burst of fire, which I reckoned would
be aimed at them and not at the trench exit, I made
my break into the open, and found myself alive cork-
screwing like a snipe towards a deep shell hole about
fifteen yards in rear. I fairly bounded, my heart in
my mouth, expecting a gun burst in my back any

second, but it came too late, skimming over me as I fell forward into the hole, safe.

Cautiously employing similar tactics, and making each move when I heard the gun firing at some other target, I made the village in short rushes.

A good many were cut down by the machine-gun and also by the enemy behind our line. Sergeant Jones was struck and remained behind. He was last seen in a shell hole attending to men who were worse wounded. I found a small party, including Corporal Ternaghan, in the ruined village, standing under cover, all looking relieved. From time to time a gasping man joined us.

Ternaghan was his old self, his temporary madness ended. I had a splitting headache, made worse by the worry of finding that Grimes had been killed somewhere in the front trench, and that Kelly had disappeared, probably shot down trying to get away. I therefore found myself commanding one man, Shea, though Cordwain joined me later in the morning.

For safety we proceeded by small parties to the rear of the village, into which shells never ceased to fall, and then we formed up and marched for about half a mile west along the road in the direction of Richbourg Saint Vaast.

On the way back Ternaghan described how he had seen Sergeant Kelly and a good few more bayoneted by the Germans. He said he thought the Germans were excited when they entered the trenches, and so were unable to discern the wounded from the fit. I could see that.

He told me too that young Lieutenant Cross was dead, and he mourned his unnecessary loss. It appears that there were a good many wounded in the section of the trench occupied by the corporal and the lieutenant. These could not be got away. There were also a few fit men who preferred to stay, and when the order came to retire the officer was loath to leave them.

Ternaghan got him out of the back of the trench, but half-way to safety he stopped and turned about to go back to the front line. Ternaghan stopped too and grabbed him, urging him to escape, but he shook the corporal off, saying: 'I must go back.' But he did not get as far as the trench. Two Germans rose up just behind it, and, rushing him, killed him with their bayonets.

They kept us on the battlefield, and we fell out on the side of the road for a rest, while waiting further orders.

During this rest the roll of the battalion was called over, and we found that only forty-six of us survived to answer our names. We still had two officers.

We had lost Neuve Chapelle for the second time.

It was rumoured that our generals were not satisfied, but thought that we might have done better.

Chapter Thirty-six

LIFE GOES ON

The battalion was wiped out as far as the authorities were concerned, and, although our forty-six men were kept near the scene of action, we were not called upon to go back into the battle. Yet we knew that the object of keeping us so close up was to use us in case of emergency. The Germans on the immediate front were coming through the gap we left in the line.

Odd lots of various regiments were turned out of transport lines in a great hurry, and went by us to repair the damage caused by our defeat. A private soldier of one of these parties, fed up, as he said, at having to do our fighting, cursed us bitterly as he came through. A roar of fury swept along our small party of battered troops. One of our fellows lost his head and went for the insulter with a bayonet in his hand, but an N.C.O. stepped in and knocked him away, at the same time calling the Englishman a bastard and telling him to get to hell out of it.

A whole Sikh battalion came along with brand-new rifles and halted by us while waiting for orders. We thought them fine-looking fellows, big and bearded, but they seemed to feel the cold intensely, judging by their stamping and hand-clapping. After some preparation they deployed almost on the same ground which had served the launch of our previous counter-attack by night. But this time, in daylight, the extending troops were in view of the Germans, who were now strengthening the captured village, and who immediately started to shell the Indians with heavy shrapnel. This shelling confused the Indians, who were unused to big stuff, and showed it for a passing moment, then they steadied, and went by in good fashion, in several waves.

While this was happening a man of ours was shot by a sniper, whom we could not locate. A passing Sikh was then shot in the hand, and this Indian, guided by some instinct unknown to us, immediately pointed with his good hand to a tree, only about a hundred yards away, and there we saw a German in the branches. The Sikhs nearest the tree rushed, pulled him down, and disarmed him. It was lucky for the German that the Irish did not effect the capture, as our fellows now were in a rather nasty mood, stirred up and wild, and a bit ruthless from hard fighting. After an interval the Sikhs had to go on and the prisoner was handed over to us. The guard that mounted over him took him away round a corner and were manhandling him until I followed and intervened. As I joined them one man was pushing the sniper about with one hand, and shaking a trem-

bling fist in his face, repeating: 'What did yous fellows
do to the poor bloody Belgiums, haw?' I pushed him
aside and spoke to the prisoner, who thanked me
courteously in English. He was a tall bespectacled
German corporal, who admitted coldly and fearlessly
that he was an N.C.O. in charge of a sniper party
behind our lines. He said the English had no hope of
winning the war. He was quite sure of that: the might
of Germany was so great, and our little army was too
small. The French and the Russians were no good,
and the war was bound to end in a German victory
inside three months. In civil life, he said, he was a
schoolmaster, and he spoke better, or at any rate
more concise English than our Irish fellows. The utter
contempt in his voice and his mincing pronunciation
irritated every one, except myself, beyond endurance.
I was highly interested.

One fellow said: 'You should be shot, you bastard.
All bloody snipers should be shot.' The German replied: 'I don't care whether you shoot me or not,
but it is against the laws of war.'

I could not help thinking that if I pushed off without another word he would soon learn something of
the lawlessness of war, but I curbed the temptation,
and said instead to the men, in order to cool them
down:

'All these Germans think they are marvellous.
After all, we think that no army is as good as
ours. This fellow has no intention of being insult-
ing. He is a foreigner, and cannot talk any other way.

He is a brave fellow anyway, so leave him alone.'

The German saluted me as if I held a commission, and our men withdrew growling, but it was some time before any of us quite recovered from the effects of this mingled display of arrogance and sublime faith in an enemy prisoner.

After that we sat about the roadside feeling in our bones that we could not be used again in this battle, and with curiosity we watched the attempt to regain Neuve Chapelle. We saw it fail, and our troops checked and held up on the near side of that dreadful village, where they were getting it hot in the open. As the attack petered out they went to ground in shell holes and ditches.

We fidgeted as a few overs from the German guns came in our direction, but they burst harmlessly in the empty fields.

Now that we were in safety our inner man asserted itself and hunger gnawed at our empty stomachs. The butt ends of cigarettes were passed round, and Cordwain, ever faithful, drew near me and produced a variety of foodstuffs from his haversack, and shared out. A group of soldiers collected around him, and the result was that our appetites were only whetted, as there was not enough to go round. The Regulars always shared as a matter of course.

Cordwain then spied Flannigan, a signaller who was orderly to the transport officer, and scornfully attacked him with his tongue: 'What the hell happened to our rations anyway? A nice bloody lot of transport you bleeders are. Couldn't deliver grub to the blasted fighting troops.'

Flannigan smiled. A bit of an old sweat he was; he walked over to us, quietly puffing an old dudeen, and placed an arm round Cordwain. He had a lovely yarn.

Last night, he told us, he and the transport officer led the ration carts into Neuve Chapelle, turned left at the crossroads, and finding no guides, went right on to the rows of deep reserve trenches behind the left company.

The drivers quickly dumped the food bags at the flank of the trenches, and drove off. Flannigan and the officer then went to the end of the nearest trench in line with them, and Flannigan, seeing no movement in the depths, shouted down: 'Turn out, you fellows, for your rations.'

The two nearest men rose sleepily, and climbed out to them—GERMANS! Flannigan shot them off-hand, and he and the officer bolted. As they ran away they bumped into two more Germans on patrol walking towards them. They were challenged: 'Wer da?' The transport officer kept going straight at them, and shot the challenger with his revolver. Flannigan said the other German disappeared so fast off the road, in the darkness, that he could not get an aim on him.

Then they hared out of Neuve Chapelle, and got away.

There was a brief silence at the end of this story,

followed by loud guffaws of laughter, and passing on of the yarn, until all the grim survivors were spluttering with merriment, which grew into louder whinnies and howls when Cordwain, wearing the only melancholy face in the crowd, remarked sourly: 'Well, my God. Can you believe it? Giving our bloody rations to the Germans. Did you give them any *buckshees*?'

Then we quietened as there came back along the road the walking wounded from the attack, most of them Sikhs. We were a little surprised to see one or two of them with painful wounds weeping as they passed us. Cordwain's opportunist eye rested on them but a moment. He leaned to Shea, whispering, then called: 'Come on!' And both ran to the Indians, Cordwain said ingratiatingly to the nearest: 'Salaam, Ji. Banduk mangta,' and he grasped the new rifle of the wounded man and gave him his own old, dirty, worn one in exchange. The other wounded Indians gave over their little-used rifles without a murmur, and soon every man of us had a lovely new gun.

Cordwain, bucked by his success, remained on the war-path; 'Corp.,' said he to me, 'hear that noise behind us. Hens. D'ye hear 'em? Hens, be the Lord God. I'm after 'em. You take that one.' And he pointed to a little shed, at the same time making off to a similar hen-coop near-by.

I fell from grace and marauded too, and I nearly got my deserts, for as I opened the door of the coop and stuck my head inside a sniper's bullet entered one end and passed out the other, feeling very close to my nose.

Ignoring the fowl, I grabbed the nearest two eggs, and beat it back to the roadside, meeting a Cordwain shaking with insubordinate giggles and displaying three more eggs.

The restless fellow wanted to build a fire at once, but he got no opportunity, because just then a tall major of the Royal Munster Fusiliers came smiling up the road from the rear, and introduced himself as our new commanding officer. Our two officers joined him, and they had an earnest talk which ended abruptly by the major saying: 'I won't have it. Who can expect men to do more? They will not fight again. Not to-day at any rate.'

That was the stuff. We loved that major. We had had our bellyful of war for the time being, and our voices rose loud and jaunty as we numbered off, preparatory to marching still farther away from the battlefield.

This big major watched the men with curiosity and kindness.

He had a large presence in every way. I think he was rather proud of us, and he gave that impression to more than one. Later, when he left us and was killed in battle with his Munsters, we mourned him as one of our own.

We were happy men going back into our old billets at Richbourg, where we fed like hogs, and took off equipment, boots, and puttees. Some stripped right down to the buff to get rid of their itching clothing, and we literally hit the hay in a large warm barn, which housed most of us.

We disappeared like dormice into that hay, sniffing and grunting with satisfaction.

I am almost sorry to record our waking, as it was so similar to countless others at this stage of the war. We were only three miles from the Germans, and they gave us a sudden salvo of shells. One shell sliced the complete end wall from the farmhouse near the barn, exposing the interior of a temporary battalion head-quarters, and the figure of a horrified orderly room clerk, who dutifully grasped a few files and hit the road for safety.

Inside the barn heads popped up everywhere out of the hay, and the memory of the absurd startled faces about me then is still funny. A second salvo which sent a shell right into the farmyard galvanized all to action.

We tore open the large barn door leading out to the fields, and streamed through it, and off like long dogs across country, leaving all our possessions behind.

One man, completely naked, led us well, and we might be still running had not some joker noticing the naked lad taking all in his stride shouted loudly after him in a voice like a view-halloo: 'Hould that fellow.'

This slogan was a shout of encouragement to any one excelling in sports or games in peace-time.

It sobered our pace to a walk, and our grins of terror to smiles, which grew wider when we saw that the naked fellow was not stopping. We were all in a tangle of nerves after Neuve Chapelle.

We collected ourselves, and went back for our kits when the shelling ceased, and then moved off, farther back, to a safer billet. On the road a dismounted cavalry regiment passed us on their way to the muttering battle line, their sabres strapped to their sides, and their spurs still on their boots. They carried their rifles awkwardly at ease, and marched stiffly. A queer sight for infantry.

Chapter Thirty-seven

REORGANIZATION—I BURN
MY DIARY AND GO TO YPRES

Our little party moved back to La Couture on 29th October, arriving there in the twilight: La Couture where this grim battle of La Bassée began seventeen days ago, or was it seventeen years? The battalion transport and riderless chargers, large out of all proportion to our numbers, came behind us. We looked more like its escort than its established unit of one battalion.

On one cart a bundle of swords testified to our missing officers, and to the uselessness of a form of weapon already out of date.

We halted and stood about in the village until the adjutant, an ex-colour-sergeant just commissioned, asked for some one who could speak French. Several men named me, and I volunteered to ask for billets. I made sure I got a comfortable one myself, and I commandeered a large French bed. A bed for a corporal at war was a glorious idea, and it was a glorious bed, a huge four-poster. I had to climb up into it, and I sank into a great billowing feather mattress, and disappeared entirely.

A crusty colour-sergeant, rude of speech and fat of figure, clanked into my den, and insisted on sharing the bed, so I lost it after all, because I hated sleeping with colour-sergeants, and anyway the bed was too soft, so I borrowed some blankets from an obliging Frenchwoman and slept better in solitude on the hard floor.

There were one or two interruptions that night. The colour-sergeant snorted and snored like a war-horse. I knew what he was going through. That bed was trying to smother him. His heavy weight sent him down to suffocation-point, and the mattress rising at the sides billowed over him, creeping over him afresh after each futile movement to adjust himself.

I wished him luck of it, and had composed myself to sleep when a rattle of machine-gun bullets overhead sent some of the tiles slithering down the roof. We both sat up, and quickly appreciating that a strong, high gable wall of the house stood between us and the distant fighting, did not even bother to talk, but went to sleep again, I rather pensively, because I reckoned that the line was four miles away, whereas the distant range of a machine-gun is only about two miles. So what? So what the hell. I was too comfortably bedded to worry.

However, I was not left long in peace. This time two women entered our bedroom. In spite of the suggestive number Cupid had nothing to do with it. Mars was to blame, or rather his sons.

The landlady begged my pardon, and asked me to help her companion, who was weeping. I said I would try anyway, and asked what it was all about. The soldiers had been naughty and had stolen some linen in her house. Would I arrange matters?

I got up and went across the road with her to her house. She showed me upstairs with a lighted candle.

I saw ten men in a large room sleeping peacefully, not a snore, too good to be true. . . . I roused the warriors and demanded a shirt inspection, and found most of the bold fellows wearing frilly night-gowns and chemises under their dirty khaki uniforms.

I asked the woman to leave us, and ordered the men to strip. As I walked downstairs with the rescued garments one soldier who could not find his cast-away shirt hoped to God that the woman would have a good time with his lice. Another, sobbing loudly, wept that he wanted Lizzie, his pet louse, back. She was missing and he was very fond of her.

So I left the ribald rascals, and returned to the musical colour-sergeant.

Next day we marched to Doulieu, and the following day, the last in October, we moved to Merris. Here we got pay and a change of clothing, and I think the first of many comforts sent out by the women of Ulster. We had great sleeps.

A tousle-headed Cordwain, scratching himself ferociously under the left arm-pit, merely from force of habit, said that life was grand.

We marched again on 1st November to Locre. Two hundred more men had now joined us. We did not know most of them, and we were not greatly interested. They were a mixture of Special Reserve and Militia men, with one or two of our own old wounded sent back cured. We made these last tell us all about hospital life, and commiserated with them that they should be sent back to fight again so soon.

In the reorganization following the arrival of these fresh men we lost to a great degree our quality of being old regulars, though the spirit and traditions of the regiment never died. I lost Cordwain and Shea, the last of my section, and had to build again with four new men. These had not the smartness of the Regulars, and I could not take them rapidly to my heart. Their habits were unsoldierly, and repellent to me.

My own morale, by this time not high, ebbed further. I was lonely for many missing friends. Cheerful faces now gone, and the memory of deeds of rough kindness haunted me. In a brief fit of renunciation and despair I burned my diary, the writing of which, though destroyed, helped me to remember most of what I have recorded here. A certain loss of interest dogged me from this time. I offer this in excuse for any errors in dates, or other lapses in the concluding part of my story.

We were four days in Locre, where a rumour

reached us that at a place called Ypres near-by a terrible battle was raging, and the never-ceasing rumble of distant guns, the activity of ambulances, bodies of troops, and trains of war stores on the local roads confirmed it. In this village a priest worried me to teach him English. He would talk English, and mistook my polite slow sentences for good diction. Repressing my respect for the cloth I evaded him. Nothing daunted, he immediately made friends with the nearest group of soldiers, the regimental cooks of the Leinster Regiment, who were cheerfully cutting up fresh meat carcasses on the flat tomb-stones of the churchyard. Their cryptic answers in unintelligible brogue must have worried him a lot. He fished a worn dictionary from his cassock, turned his back to study it, and then returned to his first smiling victim saying: 'What you say? Top of zee mawn. Ees it salutation. Yes?' The brawny cook did not know what a salutation was, and I left them both bogged.

On the 1st of November our newly formed unit (it could hardly be called a battalion) of two hundred and fifty men marched north-west through Dickebusch to Ypres, and thence up the Menin road to Hooge.

Ypres was a pleasant town, busy, with lighted shops, the names over which reminded us that we were again in Flanders. The streets were full of motor cars and other civilian traffic. A prosperous place. The inhabitants, including some nuns, greeted us cheerfully, and did not pay very much attention to a couple of shells which swished overhead, and landed somewhere in the outskirts at the back of the town. At Hooge the people also flocked to their doors, and waved us on.

The noise of conflict was nearer here, and shortly after leaving Hooge we went off the road, and took to the fields on the right, where British batteries were in action, and German shells, searching for the guns, straddled us. In the front line we relieved a battalion, which reported the dismal news that well over half its numbers were *hors de combat*, and that the Germans were attacking ferociously day after day. The old story. Bad that. And we, with new, inexperienced, and untried men.

The trenches were very roughly dug, and had wide, sloping walls, giving very poor cover from shrapnel. They were waterlogged and cold. It was rainy November weather. There was a thin fence of barbed wire all along the front, hurriedly and haphazardly erected, and the shallow trenches were not completed.

Some sections had to take up positions in shell holes.

The Germans tried to attack us next day, but we stopped them easily, and lost only about twenty men.

We had a small local reserve of our battalion, about two hundred yards directly behind us, inside the forward edge of a thick wood. Enemy shells bursting along the edge of the echoing wood made an awful clatter, but our men had avoided the edge, and had dug in among the roots about seventy yards inside the wood, and there was little loss of life. We remained in the trenches for three days, and got a relief of two days on 8th November, which we spent a short distance behind, in reserve trenches.

Occasional shells fell about us, but did no harm, as the reserve trenches were deep and well made.

A British battery in a hollow behind us was getting a pummelling from a German five-nine battery, and stood well up to it. The German salvoes, well observed and directed, raked seemingly under the British gun muzzles every time, but the British most gallantly sent their own shells back with four loud crashes after each enemy salvo. We cheered the return fire again and again. Those gunners were stout fellows. It is a curious fact that gunners have a contempt for enemy shells, while infantry hated them. On the other hand the gunners loathed bullets, which the riflemen took as a matter of course.

We were much amused the next morning to see four tree trunks in the place of the four British guns, and felt great satisfaction when the Germans continued to shell these harmless pieces of timber. And to complete the picture four smart crashes from the British battery, now safely under cover of a hedge to a flank, replied hammer and tongs to the German salvoes. So gunners.

Some French guns were also heard in action farther behind; the famous seventy-fives. They were very heartening. The quick, tinny sound of their rapid fire was clearly discernable as a new noise in battle. They fired faster than the British eighteen-pounders. We were interested and took the first opportunity of seeing them at close quarters, and found each French gun with a woman's Christian name painted on the shield: Suzanne, Marie, and similar names. These deadly ladies performed for our edification. The French gunners appeared to be careless and happy kind of chaps. They did not stand so rigidly to their guns when serving them as our fellows.

One day during this period in reserve the rations came up at an unlucky moment, just as the Germans began an evening hate with heavy shrapnel. My section was gathered round a ground-sheet, on which I had piled the food, just behind the parados, when I noticed with some anxiety that the first shells were bursting at the dangerous angle of forty-five degrees from us, and at the right height to catch us. But it was so bitterly cold that none of us bothered to bestir himself, and get down under cover. Instead we crouched, or threw ourselves flat at each burst of shrapnel, whose black hot marbles hummed around us.

I was keen about this particular issue of rations, for it included some tins of Irish butter packed by Daly's of Cork. Butter was a very rare issue, and I intended to have my full whack of it. I looked affectionately at the nice little tins, experiencing a pleasant feeling of homesickness. I regarded them as a good omen. After the first few dives to earth from the shrapnel my sentimental nostalgia evaporated; a tin of butter was missing.

I said nothing but continued to give out the food. Then on the next burst, white with rage, I alone of the party stood erect to see what was happening to the rations, and I saw one of my men, pretending to take cover like the rest, but falling close to the food pile. His hand slipped over it, and a tin of bully beef disappeared into his greatcoat pocket.

He stood up with a poker face.

Without a word I crouched on to my toes, and stepping across the ground-sheet hit him a right uppercut on the point, as hard as I could. He fell backwards, and dropped over the parados into the bottom of the trench, where he lay on his back, ruefully smiling and rubbing his jaw.

'Come on, you sod. Ante up.'

'Righto, Corporal. Don't get your rag out.'

And the tough blighter who would have pilfered his comrades' food while being closely shelled cheerfully handed back his spoils.

On moving back to our own section of trench a man behind me laughed. 'What's up with you?' I asked gruffly.

'Well,' he said, 'that chap was middle-weight belt-holder of the First Battalion in India.'

I respected the pilferer all the more, as I was no boxing champion, and I had given him a recognized opportunity to retaliate, in ignoring that portion of King's Regulations which outlines the proper conduct of non-commissioned officers towards private soldiers.

Chapter Thirty-eight

THE TWO GOURMANDS

Our orders were to be ready to move forward at a moment's notice, while in reserve, and our task was to counter-attack and recapture any lost front-line trenches.

The enemy smashed the line somewhere or other daily, and the weak British local reserves, held close up to the front along the battle line protecting Ypres, were turned out again and again to retake lost positions. Stragglers from the broken front, including some French Algerians from the left of the British, were collected, reorganized, and sent back again to fight.

The Germans were out to break us, and they would have been even more determined, if that were possible, had they known, as we did in despair, that they were opposed only by a thin line of British, with a few weak isolated companies at wide intervals forming an inadequate local reserve. As far as I know there was no general reserve behind us, no strong body of horse, foot, and guns in a central position, to move when required so as to cover the dangerous breaks. We were all in the fight, and the country behind was empty of troops, as far as we could see. The dwindling Regular battalions faced assault after assault. The fighting was tremendous, and the slaughter such as none had envisaged. Practically every unit had lost three-quarters of its fighting strength, yet fresh German attacks kept coming on, and more and more enemy batteries thickened the circle of guns threatening Ypres, and added their shells to the greatest artillery bombardments ever suffered by any army.

The health of those in the field since August began to fail. Many of us could not now digest bully beef and hard biscuits. Snow fell, and our lower limbs half froze while we slept out in the severest winter for many years. The snow also gave our reserve position away, the tracks made by parties coming and going being visible for miles to the enemy observers, and we gained no respite from being behind in reserve, for the Germans hammered hell out of us with their field-guns, and we suffered as many deaths and wounds as the men in the line, who were often so close to the trenches dug by the Germans that the enemy dared not shell them.

The first great battle of Ypres was drawing to its climax.

Such were the conditions in which I took my small part one afternoon, assisted by a comedian of a militiaman whom I had posted on observation duty. He was put on guard at the forward corner of a wood overlooking the ground between our reserve trench and the weakly held front line. His task was to give the alarm in case of a break-through, so that we might get ready to counter-attack without wasting time.

He deserted his post, and left his sector unobserved.

The adjutant came fuming at me, his section commander. I hurriedly turned out another man, gave him his orders, and showed him the small funk hole I had shown his predecessor, in which to take shelter if shelling became intense near the observation post.

Then I looked for my missing sentry. I searched every hole and cranny near-by for his body, dead or alive. I thought he must have been killed, because the ground about had been ripped and torn by fresh shells and the trees were battered about. There was no body, and no blood. He must have run away. He had.

I quartered the country behind, and as I was doing this a rifle bullet fired at close range spurted earth a few yards from me. Good Lord, I thought, is my sentry turned assassin, or have the Germans broken right through? I automatically hit the ground, rolled into a depression, and released my safety catch. A squealing pig topped a little crest to my front, and bounced about bewildered, flopping its ears.

Another bullet smacked near it, and it bolted.

The mystery was solved, and I got up out of my hole, raging, and accosted a sporting lance-bombardier of artillery at his evening pig-hunt. He met me calmly, and, ignoring my senior rank, said familiarly, as many gunners will: 'What cheer, chum. Any idear of w'ere that bloody pig buggered off to?'

I let him have it; three years condensed experience of the choicest verbiage of two countries. He was quite unconcerned, regarding me as quite normal. So I changed my tactics, and reminded him in an icy voice that a general routine order recently published forbade indiscriminate sporting activities with fire-arms behind the lines, and I ordered him back to his battery. That appealed more to his English mind. He looked respectful and obeyed, but not before request-ing me to keep my hair on.

With frayed nerves I pursued my quest of the missing sentry. God help him, when I got him. Dark-ness fell, and aided me in my search. He was sitting over a large coal fire, in the ruins of a bombarded cottage. The household supply of fuel had caught alight, and the deserter was roasting a plucked fowl, spitted on a stick, over the red coals. Above his head, a second fowl roosted innocently in the branches of a small tree. A peaceful scene.

I sat down on an upturned bucket near my squat-ting man.

'Well,' I opened, 'what have you got to say for yourself?'

'What for?' he countered, cheerfully, giving his chicken a twist.

'Look here, my lad. Are you aware that you have committed an action that amounts to deserting your post in the face of an enemy?' And seeing him looking only slightly bored, I added tersely: 'And now you're looting!'

I looked as savage as I could.

'Ah, come off it, Corporal. What's an ould hen? And I never ran away from the bloody Germans. I saw nobody's face. There wasn't a man of 'em within miles of me. But they smashed up that wood, and that hole you gave me was worse than nottin'.'

'Well, consider yourself under arrest for desertion, and come along.'

'Here,' he said indignantly, 'what's the bloody joke anyway?'

He stood up. I caught him by the collar of his greatcoat with both hands, and backed him against the tree.

'This is the bloody joke,' I said, emphasizing every few words by banging the back of his head against the tree trunk. 'You are now a soldier on active service. You were given a responsible job on which the safety of the regiment depended. You left that job without being properly relieved, and without reason. Do you know I could have you shot?'

'Ah, for God's sake, Corporal, let go, and chuck it. Widout raison indeed! What bloody man would stay there?'

'Anyway, you're for a court martial.' I released him. He simply did not believe me.

'I came out here to fight', he said, 'and not to stand for a bloody cockshy.' And attending to immediate affairs, he picked up his cap, slung his rifle, and carefully collecting his roast chicken, stumped after me.

I was really perturbed, and I lied boldly to cover him when we got back. Without batting an eye I reported in brief military sentences to the adjutant, saying that the man was no deserter. He was found close (I stretched my conscience) to his post near the wood where he had taken up a better observation position when his first post was severely shelled. 'Any action, sir?'

'No action. Tick the blighter off, and look after these new men a bit better yourself. You should visit your posts more often. Do it every hour in future.'

'Very good, sir,' said I, now well used to taking the double responsibility of the non-com., and that ended it.

I got another N.C.O. to prove the army view of his crime to the culprit, and he came later to me, profusely apologizing.

He was really a good chap, but irresponsible and inexperienced. He had had no proper military training.

We went forward into the front line, out of reserve, on the 10th of November, and had a fairly quiet night. Our patrols moved wide and easily in no-man's-land.

Chapter Thirty-nine

WIPED OUT AGAIN; SANCTUARY

Next morning we stood to in the wet shell holes and crumbling trenches under the thunder and blasting flashes of German high explosives. There is no need to describe this bombardment, except to say that it was the worst in my experience.

A few of our fellows broke under it, and one poor chap entirely lost his head and ran back out of his trench. He had not a chance in the open. The earth was vomiting all round us and he tumbled over in a few yards. Better to have kept to the trench. No trained soldier would leave that.

A corporal, a burly fellow, fell near me, with a shrapnel bullet in his head. He lay unconscious all the day, nodding his holed head as if suffering only from some slight irritation, and did not become still until evening. Earlier in the day one youngster said: 'What about putting him out of his misery?' A more experienced man explained that there was no pain. The small stirrings and little moans came from a man who was then already as good as dead.

Another soldier had his belly ripped open, and sat supporting his back against the trench, while he gazed with fascinated eyes at large coils of his own guts, which he held in both hands. This was almost the ghastliest sight I saw. Its sequel was better. The man's entrails had not been penetrated. He got safe out of the trench, was washed, tucked in, and mended well in hospital.

Maimed men passed crouching and crawling behind me, leaving trails of blood on the ground, on their way to a ditch which led back into the woods behind. Some of them were moaning too loud, unlike our old men. One young militiaman in particular came by roaring, and seeking sympathy for a broken arm from every one he met. A lance-corporal told him for God's sake to put a sock in it, and that if he was really badly wounded he would have no breath left to howl. That stopped his hysterics.

I should say that the non-coms. of the old army had the worst time of all, trying in circumstances like these to keep inexperienced men in hand.

Some of these men could not even fire a rifle properly, and at times our hearts quailed for our safety and theirs.

The few officers we had no doubt felt all that we did, but they were free to move about, and this was a great advantage from the point of view of a junior N.C.O. pinned to his sector, to the bit of trench he was given to defend, and always under the close scrutiny of the men he was supposed to lead and encourage.

A runner pushing past me gave me a nasty jar: 'God, are you alive?' he said crudely. 'We heard you were killed, down at headquarters.' 'No hope,' I said, hardly daring a longer sentence lest death should finish it. The trenches were filled with the acrid smell of shell smoke. Heavy shrapnel burst right down on us, its pall of smoke roofing the trench and blotting out the sky. I was flung about by the concussion, and thrown flat against the trench bottom. My whole body sang and trembled. One ear was perforated by the concussion, and I could hardly hear.

The runner came to me, and we held each other with our hands. 'Are you all right?' I nodded, having no talk.

'The message I am taking is: "Stand to," because the enemy is massing just in front of us,' he said. 'Nasty spot, this.' And he hurried along, two more close bursts adding to his speed.

Before the shelling ceased we were ordered to man the trench: 'STAND TO, STAND TO, EVERY ONE,' and our rifles lined our broken parapets. The man of my section on my immediate left kept his head down. I grasped his arm and shook him savagely: 'For Christ's sake, get up, you bloody fool. The Germans are coming.'

He fell over sideways and on to his face when I released him, and exposed a pack covered with blood. He was dead, and my eyes came off him to my shoulder, which was spattered with his brains and tiny slivers of iridescent bone.

281

'A butcher's shop,' I said to myself. 'A butcher's shop. A bloody butcher's shop.' I took my left hand from the fore-end of my ready rifle and hit myself hard on the face, telling myself to be something of a man.

The soldier on my right, wincing like most of us now standing head and shoulders exposed to the fury of the shells, said desperately: 'Mother of God! This is terrible.'

A tall old sweat farther along shouted grimly: 'Ha-ha, me bhoys. Now we're for it.'

Six German army corps were marshalled in the open, advancing like a parade on the weak British Army.

The magnificent Prussian Guards made a review of it. They executed their famous goose-step in the sight of their foe, and the field-grey waves came on. The Kaiser was close behind in some neighbouring town, ready to receive reports of the great break-through.

The left of the Prussian Guard attack caught us. Farther to our left the line broke, mended, broke and mended again. A counter-attacking English regiment went through a temporarily victorious enemy like a knife through butter, and recaptured a lost village with great dash.

We stopped the Germans on our front, and they were the finest troops of Germany, led by the flower of her noblest houses.

That was not all: a weak night attack was repelled.

Wiped out again; Sanctuary

The next morning we found a German alive at our wire. He dropped his wire-cutters and made a friendly motion with his hand, intending surrender. Our desperate fellows covered him with their rifles. I called out: 'No. Save him.' A bitter voice replied: 'No bloody fear. No Sergeant Benson tricks here,' and the brave German was swiftly killed.

We stayed in the line for two more days, easily checking weaker attempts to drive us back, and then once more we went out to reserve. We then ceased to fight as a battalion. We were too weak. We were told off to be ready to relieve the regiments in the line at a moment's notice. A Scottish Territorial regiment with a similar duty twice went up, and twice recaptured trenches and reinstated another battalion. They were unbelievably cheerful.

One young Highlander going back a second time called out: 'Give us a shout if ye want us again.'

The Terriers had arrived. The supposed Saturday-night soldiers. Another regiment of them from London did great work.

We Regulars got just a bit bored at reading their recorded deeds in every newspaper we managed to scrounge.

While in reserve, I was detailed one morning to escort a sick party to Hooge. On the way back I got caught in a barrage and bolted into a dug-out. It was the headquarters of a Regular regiment in reserve. The commanding officer growled: 'Who's that?' I gave my name and regiment, and asked permission to stay a minute until the shells stopped. 'Get out of here,' he ordered, and he sent me out into the shelling.

The next morning some of our men assisted in digging him and his adjutant out of the dug-out, which had been blown in on them. They were both dead.

Now, in a weak moment, I thought I would go sick myself. I had developed hæmorrhoids, and they bled rather badly. A sergeant with a perforated ear like mine said he would join me and go to the field-ambulance to be dressed, hoping to be detained there. We had other minor cuts, and a good many bruises too, and the skin was inclined to go dirty. The knuckles of our left-hand forefingers were cut open from constantly firing our rifles. A calloused knuckle on a left forefinger is the hallmark of the 1914 men.

On the way we had to dodge a good many shells, and in an interval of sheltering behind a house we answered some call we could not resist, and returned feeling ashamed to our reserve trench. On our way we pulled a young frightened lance-corporal from shelter and made him rejoin with us. He later turned out to be the most distinguished soldier in the regiment, and he was four times decorated for valour.

On the 19th of November we were again in the line, because a battalion that had suffered worse than ours had to be given a rest, but that evening the London Territorial Regiment, fresh and strong, came to relieve us; a relief that was to take us away from that battlefield of Ypres, right back to Westoutre.

Wiped out again; Sanctuary

This time only forty men of my regiment were able to march away. The rest were killed or wounded.

Forty . . . forty left out of two hundred and fifty, and only about three weeks ago there were only forty-six left out of an entire battalion. I searched my mind for total figures and roughly reckoned that in three months ninety-six men out of every hundred had been killed or wounded. I was too weary to appreciate my own luck. I was so completely dazed that I lingered in the front line, while a London Territorial congratulated my regiment on giving the Germans 'Denbigh'. He was a cultured man in the uniform of a private soldier. But 'Denbigh . . .'. I did not know the word. I do not yet know its meaning.

The Londoner looked for praise. He liked talking to me, a Regular corporal of the line. He asked if I thought his regiment would, any day, be as good as those of the old army.

I said: 'Yes. Every bit as good.'

My eyes weakened, wandered, and rested on the half-hidden corpses of men and youths. Near and far they looked calm, and even handsome, in death. Their strong young bodies thickly garlanded the edge of a wood in rear, a wood called Sanctuary. A dead sentry, at his post, leaned back in a standing position, against a blasted tree, keeping watch over them.

Proudly and sorrowfully I looked at them, the Macs and the O's, and the hardy Ulster boys joined together in death on a foreign field. My dead chums.

A silence more pregnant than the loudest bombardment stole over the country, the evening silence of the battlefield. A robin sat in a broken bush on the parapet and burst into song.

The Londoner said quietly: 'You'd better hurry up, Corporal. The Irish are falling in on the left.'

Chapter Forty

'VIN ORDINAIRE'

I slung my rifle slowly over the left shoulder. 'So long, chum. Good luck!' 'So long,' said the Londoner, and I left him with our dead. The roll was being called when I joined our small party, but there was no zest in this roll-call. The men stood heavily and answered listlessly. Information about dead and wounded was murmured. Our curiosity now was not for the outnumbering dead but for our few selves, and in a dazed way we inspected each other's faces, because every survivor was a phenomenon in himself. We exchanged half-smiles of appreciation and silent congratulation. Then we slouched off across the cold, barren, wintry fields, without talk, to join the main road at Hooge, and arriving there got into step once more on the hard-paved road. Hooge was wrecked. South of it the Menin road from Ypres was stiff with French cavalry. They were drawn up in long lines on the west of the road, with their horses' heads facing inwards towards the centre of the road—massed in thousands and standing by, mounted, to check the Germans in case the British broke. They were not wanted.

'Vin Ordinaire'

The first battle for Ypres was over, and Ypres was saved.

As we drew nearer to the old walled and moated town we thought it had not been worth defending, for it was already in ruins, and it looked as if every house and building had been destroyed by shell or flame. Half-demolished houses with sandbagged doors and windows covered with sacking were used as the headquarters of engineers, supply services, and other staffs, and office work continued as if conditions were normal. An occasional sentry paced back and forth on sections of footpath cleared of debris before some important office, with funk-hole as sentry box in case of emergency. A fat Red-cap stood very precisely at ease on traffic duty at a ruined crossroads, which had been very heavily shelled. He had little to do during daylight. Some distance from him fatigue parties of oldish men were filling in shell holes.

A halt was called. I could not sit with the remnant of my regiment. I wanted to escape for a few moments, so I went away to rest behind a ruined wall. The air was foul with smells of ruin and decay. I could not escape my own mind. I had to face something—the usual thing for me after battle, a kind of mental survey, and a mental eating and digestion of the most recent experiences. So I absorbed it all again, ending with the dead behind us, the grim French horsemen, battered Ypres, and the small group of living near me, which would again be built into another fighting battalion of a thousand men. Then for the first time fear overwhelmed me, and ate into my vitals. I wished myself away out of this. It seemed that the clouds of war were densest hereabouts, enshrining the mournful spirit of the salient, and I knew that many more and braver men would feel a similar sad fear along this terrible road, on their way to die on the long low ridges. Then the desire to survive this shambles came to me again, and I awoke from the hell of the half-dead, and severed my spirit from the men who had gone west.

I looked at my body objectively and found it dull—very, very tired, chafed, dirty, hungry, and neglected, and I had a terrific thirst. That was good. The latest period of martyrdom was over and I was normal once again. I stood up and breathed freely, and then I fainted from fatigue. This was a great relief. I revived, light-headed and a bit fey, and went back with a light step to join my comrades, who were now falling in.

We all felt better after the short halt, and we hit the road again with livelier feet in anticipation of rest, food, and shelter beyond the range of the torturing guns. Some of our own field-gunners ran to the road flank of their battery to see us pass back. Officers, sergeants, bombardiers, and the bare-armed workers of the guns deserted their gun-shields and, grouping on the roadside, cheered us. We were abashed, and weakly waved our free hands to them in acknowledgement. The tribute from fighting soldiers is hardest to bear. The papers had been full of our deeds, and the supporting artillerymen knew more about our fighting than we did.

Our corps commander had already complimented us for coolness and daring during fierce fighting, and that evening some of us read his citation of our regiment for its stand at Neuve Chapelle. He had written of the splendid feat of the regiment and its great gallantry in repulsing enemy attacks at close quarters, and he directed that every regiment in the 2nd corps should be informed of the fact. About eighty units were paraded and told about us, but most of our own men, having been either killed or wounded in the line, did not know anything about that.

We had now come right back to billets in the village of Westoutre, clear of all fighting, and there we settled down and got cleaned, fed, rested, and re-equipped for further battles.

A large reinforcement of nearly five hundred men joined us, and the forty survivors scattered into various companies. This absorption of the few old Regulars into newly made platoons composed mainly of Reservists was my farewell to the old army of 1914, and to the last formation of the men who were later called 'Old Contemptibles' and 'Mons Angels'. I walked about the outskirts of the village glooming and wondering to what company I would be posted. There were only a few of the original non-coms. left, and no doubt the commanding officer found it difficult to distribute us amongst five hundred new men in order to get the best leavening effect.

'*Vin Ordinaire*'

On my return to billets I got a message that the adjutant wanted me. I reported to him at the orderly-room, and he told me I was being promoted to sergeant. He asked me my age, and smiled when I said 'Twenty-one next January, sir', and he added that he had never seen a sergeant of twenty years before.

Then he gave me a cigarette and told me that the orderly-room clerk (a sergeant) had been given his commission, and he wished to know if I would take on the job. This was double promotion, because the post of battalion clerk was a spot staff job. Henceforth I would be the confidential clerk of the C.O. and adjutant. I would go into action with the battalion, but I would remain a bit behind the front-line fighting troops, under enemy fire, it is true, but no longer in the misery of the front line. I assented eagerly, and the adjutant very handsomely said that there was no other choice, as I was the only non-commissioned officer qualified for the job.

I fetched my rifle, sidearms, equipment, and blankets from my billet, and brought them to a room behind battalion headquarters. In this room my predecessor was checking the contents of two small tin trunks, which constituted the office of a battalion on active service. He had stripped his sleeves of his sergeants' stripes and had mounted the star of the second-lieutenant on each of his shoulder straps. A merry fellow, slightly bald, and looking distinctly old for a 'second loot'. I saluted him punctiliously. Another pal gone. Those stars removed him to higher and more rigid circles. He punched me in the ribs, and delayed the removal by fishing out a bottle of 'Vin ordinaire'.

We sat down on the boxes, and drank to each other and to the future. We got talking, and stayed until the December sun went down and until the darkness swallowed the two little mounds of war gear on the floor of the cold room.

He got up shivering. We shook hands, and he went off to his first officers' mess dinner.

Chapter Forty-one

CLERICAL WORK; THE SOLDIER AND THE FRENCH GIRL

My clerical work kept me very busy. I welcomed it avidly.

There was a lot of writing to be done for a battalion reorganizing. New lists of fresh names and hitherto unknown army numbers formed under my eyes. Most of these men I saw only in name, because when I recorded them the second time they appeared finally in casualty lists.

The new battalion was shiftless, half-baked in every way, and the non-commissioned officers were very poor stuff. I and the few remaining Regular non-coms. were always ticking them off and warning them against familiarity with the men, whom they called by their Christian names. The old army was finished.

The odd familiar name or figure of a professional soldier brought a painful stab of warm recognition, and any killed in action became a great tragedy for the remainder. We remnants stuck to each other in a necessary form of freemasonry which evoked cynical and jealous remarks from the reinforcements. We drew nearer to each other than ever before in our lives, and we got to know and love each other as men never do in peace-time.

Two of my best chums were Belfast Orangemen, and we all shared and suffered together, and made merry too.

We had nothing tangible to hold on to except each other. We backed each other up with great fervour and urgency, and by doing this we preserved and passed on the diluted *esprit de corps* of our regiment.

Trench *tours* had already become a routine in December of 1914. We took over trenches for four days to a week, got relieved by another battalion, and went back to billets in the villages for a similar period all through a severe winter.

We occupied various sectors of the line on the left of the Ypres salient, and hereabouts we dug and made the elaborate trench system in which so many who came after us died without ever seeing open warfare. Existing maps still show the title 'Irish House' applied to more than one farm. These were our battalion headquarters. Others bore the names of our commanding officers.

The reinforcements feared and respected us, and we, already rather shaken, and uncertain of ourselves in the great misfortune, had to take them and their greater terrors under our protection—a heart-rending business, until they took shape.

Their misbehaviour caused through ignorance of the military code brought packs of trouble, and in one

month our court-martial trials ran up to the incredible
figure of thirty-two.

Neglect of duty, absence, drunkenness, and insubordination were the common crimes. The serious
ones were assaulting N.C.O.s, and desertion. We were
dumbfounded. Army headquarters grimly counte-
nanced the shooting of deserters. Luckily we had no
executions, though once we had a narrow shave. One
man of ours slept with a French girl instead of going
into the trenches. He was tried by the commanding
officer and had no defence, and was put back for a
field general court-martial, charged with 'desertion
in the face of the enemy, in that he, on a certain day,
having been duly warned, failed to parade for the
trenches'. I had to do with the preparation of the
documents and the sorting of witnesses for the trial. I
learned a lot about military law, and particularly of
the laws of evidence during this period. The evidence
in this case was complete and damning. The soldier
had been warned personally by his sergeant to parade
for the line, and two independent witnesses, his own
friends, supported that evidence. His section corporal
testified that he never arrived in the trenches during
the whole *tour* of duty of the battalion, and two more
comrades corroborated that. Two further witnesses,
military policemen, swore that they arrested the man
in the house of the woman miles behind the sector of
trenches then occupied by the battalion. Some other
witnesses recognized the accused by name, number,
and appearance as the soldier absent then and pre-

sent now on trial. After the first trial by the commanding officer and the sworn summary of evidence, a very agitated adjutant visited me in the deserted orderly-room—a French dining-room full of metal-work and glass. We groaned at our own enforced efficiency in hounding this man to death.

'This must be stopped,' the adjutant suddenly shouted, his eyes staring in painful wonder. I agreed hastily. It would never do to have one of our Irish shot for desertion. The room began to look like a coffin. I still loathe that room.

We sat down and thought out a plan together, and the adjutant went off. The confined man, now thoroughly alarmed, was visited several times, and he was then rapidly shifted off to some hospital to be placed under medical observation. He was found to be insane, and the adjutant winked at me.

While confined the man had developed the unhealthy habit of swallowing indigestible matter, like bits of his boots, and he spent long periods seriously writing or tracing his name upside down on the walls of his prison. He did many other strange things, and at the same time he vehemently declared he was quite well in every way, and that he was certainly guilty of desertion.

At this time a good many men of other regiments were being executed for cowardice and desertion, and I think one or two were shot for rape. Their names, crimes, and punishments were read out on parade. The troops became morbidly curious, and details of the executions were discussed. Our regiment found one firing party. The young sergeant in charge came back bewildered, and his black hair became quite grey in the following few months.

It was rumoured that some men stood up well to be shot. Others had to be tied to chairs and brought out to be executed in a sitting position. After the rifle volley a revolver bullet was generally fired into the head by the supervising officer.

One of our old sweats said it wasn't too bad, because anyway they were all doped and only half-alive when brought out to be shot. The military authorities took every advantage of these occasions to enforce discipline, and firing parties were made up of bad or indifferent characters to show them what to expect themselves in certain contingencies.

Thus cowardice was curtailed by the fear of a greater horror. Executed men were reported as 'Died' and not as 'Killed in action', which is an honour.

These aspects of the military mind rather disturbed me, while I was trying hard to integrate myself physically and mentally, and for the sake of self-preservation I disobeyed the teachings of my religion, which takes count of all things good and bad, and I began to inhibit the 'unwanted' rapidly. My eyes opened less than before, and I held my heart to a steady callous beat. My character is still affected. Some glory and a lot of loveliness had passed away before I was twenty-one. I turned also from the lesser inner vision that young men hold about this time of life—the picture of some waiting ideal life companion, the secret promise of the yet unknown woman, graceful, beautiful, and constant, to bring serenity and comfort and all else that a chap tired but hopeful wants in that way.

I accepted my lot, and I accepted the poor half-trained soldiers about me. In the limitless wilderness of war I pledged myself as much as possible in kindness to them, and swore to help them in every possible way.

Sometimes I failed, through my fault, and sometimes because such attributes do not always become a war leader, however minor.

Chapter Forty-two

SIGNALLERS' SNUGGERY

Trench warfare was a new game, but the technique remained the same, though there were always new tricks to learn if one was to survive. Having pulled the blind on unwanted memories, I developed this technique of life and death by thinking, planning and moving with circumspection in and about the line.

I gave the impression of being a cool hand. When shells fell in my vicinity I stopped a moment to talk to some one near-by, and I kept my eyes and ears open. I judged the direction of the enemy guns, the strike on hard or soft ground, the timing of the salvoes, and I managed to walk past the danger spot keeping nearer to the parapet than the parados, moving swifter through the open bays, checking at revetments which gave lateral cover, and often adding to my chances of safety by stooping at the most dangerous place to pick up a cartridge or wind a puttee, thus keeping myself well down without giving the impression that I was doing so. The safety catch of my rifle was always forward, and anything I carried was slung clear of my hands so that I could shoot quickly. I avoided batteries, mortars, and machine-gun posts like poison, and kept away from strong points in our own line. All these places got more than the ordinary dose of shelling. I never put my head over the top in the same place twice, and when I moved alone before nightfall I used the ground, trees, bushes and ditches like a redskin. I went unconcernedly when bullets whistled, and got a move on when they smacked in the air near my head. I always hurried into and out of the line, and I never loitered in communication trenches, postponing my halts until I reached the greater safety of reserve or front line trenches. I skipped past trench junctions, and I never delayed at any crossroads, even though it were miles behind the front. My cartridges were always loosened in their clips, my iron ration intact, and my water-bottle full. I ate automatically, and well, and I functioned properly except under prolonged shelling, when I got constipated like most others. I selected the best cover from shell-fire when I wanted to go to sleep, I slept with my rifle handy, and day or night I never took off my equipment or boots in the danger zones. The pocket holding my first field-dressing was pinned instead of stitched, so that I could get at it quickly, and I valued my entrenching tool as much as my rifle, in case we ever had to retire and dig in in the open. I made friends with the quartermaster-sergeants, who gave me good rations, and I chummed in with the signallers, who always cooked well.

Signallers' Snuggery

The signallers' dug-out was generally the best one on any battalion front. Its primary use was as a signal office, connected by land wires with the brigade head-quarters behind, with the supporting guns, with the unit in immediate reserve, and with the battalions on either flank. The signallers lived and slept in it. It was usually a grand, roomy, deep, safe, and warm place, built with intention into the front wall of a deep trench or the near side of a low slope, and generally proof against all shelling except a direct hit. The signallers made a point of living a comfortable, full life. They were all old sweats, gay and adventurous. They possessed a very high morale, and they preserved the romantic aspect of the war. They were the news-wallahs, and the men with the extra rations of rum. They had large possessions. I took to them.

They could be seen in pairs under the heaviest shell-fire, clothed and muffled to the ears with goat-skins, neck wraps, and extra wearing apparel they had wangled, repairing their land wires in the most casual way—talking, whistling, and even laughing at one of their number nearest to a shell burst. Grand chaps, whose first duty was to retain communications by patrolling and maintaining their wires in all cir-cumstances, and their wires were cut by shell-fire nearly every day.

They regarded themselves as privileged because their job was important, and they took advantage of this. They 'won' hand-carts and perambulators to take their kit to the front line, and they moved inde-

pendently like gypsies. They carried all kinds of kit
forbidden to the ordinary troops, and built up a fine
comfort service for themselves. The greatest martinet
turned a blind eye on any outrageous vehicle packed
with musical instruments, braziers, civilian kettles,
pots, and blankets moving impudently and unofficially in the rear of any battalion going into the line.
They shared everything with me. They were first in
action and last out of battle, and they 'drummed up'
the first and the last cup of rich hot tea in any position. With them I also shared all the rumours of the
British Army and the secret information and messages
that directed the moves and war operations of the
battalion. We were the oracle, and anxious-faced
officers and N.C.O.s hung about in our vicinity in
the vain hope of picking up information beforehand.

But we were bound to secrecy, and we could pass a
platoon, and exchange greetings cheerfully, at the
same time knowing that they would probably die
next dawn in a trench raid, and the signallers, gone
on out of earshot, might murmur to each other,
'Poor buggers.' Then forgetting all but the job in
hand they would take over their dug-out in the line,
unpack, connect, and test their own instruments, prepare hot food, and loll back smoking and drinking
tea, while Shorty, one of their number, strummed out
some plaintive negro spiritual on his mandolin pinched
from some music shop on the retreat from Mons.

Happy memories these. My eye still sees the head-
phoned signaller on duty, back to us, silhouetted

against a bottled candle, left elbow on the greasy rickety table, while his right hand played with his buzzer, or his 'In' and 'Out' pads, and my ear can hear the first test morse signals of a unit just arrived in the trenches. Three letter i's in rapid succession, dot-dot, dot-dot, dot-dot ('Are you in and O.K.?') and the long acknowledging 'd-a-a-a-sh' (O.K.) in reply.

It is probably raining outside. Laughter comes through from the platoon in support near our battalion headquarters, perhaps from the men who will hang on the wire in no-man's-land to-morrow. A German shell thumps into the ground in the middle hearing distance, explodes, and crumps its reverberations, which causes the earth to fall off in little lumps from the walls of the dug-out. The air displacement shakes the candle flame. The jumped light shows little runnels of smaller particles of earth forming tiny screes about the fallen off bigger bits.

Shorty, engrossed in musical pictures of the cotton fields, gets the biggest start, 'Where did that one go?' and the lively mind of the operator on duty formulates the assuring reply. 'Oh, a long way away. Front trenches.'

Life and time and my good companions are precious to me.

I stick there waiting until my first take-over situation report is tapped out on the buzzer, repeated, and timed 18.40 hours. This I note for the adjutant, and I leave the earth hole for my office overground, maybe wishing that the darkness and the threatening outside would change into the homely seven o'clock lights of Cork city viewed across the River Lee from the northern slopes of Montenotte.

Chapter Forty-three

KEMMEL

In early 1915 our battalion again took over positions in front of Ypres.

The ruined town attracted me, and on the way back from the trenches I used to explore the debris of the most famous buildings. One day I saw men of an Irish cavalry regiment poking about in the broken Cloth Hall. They were collecting pieces of stained glass from the rubble. I fished about too, and I found a fine old two-handed sword with a crest on the hilt. I packed it in one of our limbers, and later handed it over to our quartermaster to keep along with my other war souvenirs—a variety of objects which I wished to take home to Ireland, including a shrapnel bullet which hit my pack at Mons, and another which penetrated my haversack at the Aisne. I also had German and French rifles, bayonets, shell cases, rifle cartridges, and helmets.

Unfortunately, the friendly quartermaster went on leave, his relief dumped the lot one day on a change of bivouac, and I lost my souvenirs.

Kemmel

I was offered leave myself in February, and I refused to go home, because I was afraid to go back without my younger brother. I think I created a record, for I surely must be the only soldier who refused leave from France during the war. My father blamed me indirectly for having taken my brother away to enlist, and I preferred not to face him.

My work engrossed me. Out of the trenches I spent quite a pleasant time in the huts, billets, and tents south and west of Dickebusch. I sorted all my office files carefully, and collected every duplicate message sent by the battalion since its arrival in France. I made a second collection of every message received, and I got my two bundles smuggled home to our depot.

These valuable records would have been unique as a supplement to the usually sparse war diary kept by every regiment, had they been preserved, but they got mislaid in the depot shortly after arriving there and were never seen again.

The normal dull round of billets and trenches, relieved sharply on each change-over by the recurring sense of impending danger when we went into the line, or the sense of escape when we went back into billets, was coloured also by various incidents, minor maybe, but unforgettable.

One winter night I was the last to leave battle-headquarters in front of Kemmel Hill. The battalion had gone on back to billets, and I overtook a straggler —a corporal who was crying in pain. He was hobbling

along, and he sat down on the roadside as I came up
with him. His feet were swollen to an extraordinary
degree, and were jammed in his boots. I cut off his
boots with my jack-knife, and ripped away his socks
from feet which resembled clubs, they were so massive
and misshapen.

'This must be what they call trench feet,' I said to
him. 'Why didn't you use whale oil?' He said he could
not be bothered with it, as he had not believed in
trench feet. 'Well, you can believe in them now,' I
told him, 'and you can whistle or sing until I send
back a stretcher-bearer.' He sighed. He was a great
singer, whose favourite tune was 'The Girl I Left in
Sunny Tennessee'.

I told him he was a sure case for Blighty, and could
not entirely repress a feeling of envy of his good luck.
I had to assure him more than once that he would get
a stretcher in record time.

Our field dressing-station was located in Kemmel
village, about half a mile back, and it would not shift
until I passed through and reported that all our men
were clear of the front trenches. I left the corporal in
a sitting position, nursing his feet and groaning, on
the roadside opposite Kemmel Château—a lovely
building surrounded by a moat in which a pair of
swans lived, and continued to live, though several
shells had fallen in the waters of the moat.

Hurrying into Kemmel I knocked at the door of
the dressing-station. No answer. The door was loose.
I pushed it and it fell over inwards and seesawed on

the breast of a dead man lying on a stretcher on the floor. I looked at him, and could not recognize him as any one I knew, and I went out shouting for Sergeant Flynn, the medical officer's orderly. Flynn came round a corner smoking, told me the dead man was one of our new chaps with a chest wound, and, asking me to wait a moment, doubled off to dispatch a stretcher for the trench-foot case.

He came back and went for me as if I had insulted him. I knew his grouse of old. It was constantly cropping up. He did not want further promotion, and last night a quartermaster-sergeant with three pals had gassed themselves by sleeping in a dug-out with a charcoal brazier. They were hours unconscious, and suffered from agonizing head pains when they recovered. The quartermaster-sergeant, according to Flynn would be sent home, or at least down the line for a period, and he Flynn would be asked to step up a rank. Flynn preferred his more dangerous job of tending wounded, and I was potentially inimical to his interests because I regulated the promotion lists and I would deprive him of his job.

I promised him I would not interfere. I would speak to the adjutant, and anyway the medical officer would not part with him, which was true. Some shell-bursts round the charcoal-burners' fires on the slopes of Kemmel Hill reminded me we were still within range of the German light guns, and cutting short his loudly expressed thanks I got his assistance to remove the unseemly door from the dead man. Flynn covered

the face, and told me the poor chap would be all
right as a couple of bearers were coming back for him
that night, to take him away for burial.

The loud-voiced and volatile Flynn was a marvel
to me. Back along that road he entertained me with
comic stories in an absurd way until we were both
laughing. We were old pals. I have seen him covered
from head to foot in the blood of the dead and
wounded. He had heard the last words of hundreds
of his old comrades and had buried most of them. He
was very devout and very conscientious. His badly
drawn plans of graves always required to be related
to an official map, a job which gave me a lot of
trouble, because he valued the shape of the actual
grave more than any map reference, and thought
that was enough. He prayed for all his dead and
dying, and retained a compassionate heart in all that
gruesome work, the minor details of which must
remain unwritten.

He was a Dubliner, short-sized, cheerful, and confident to an astonishing degree, and he had an endless
stock of stories, most of which centred round the
comic or valiant way in which his cases behaved.

Kemmel was a fairly cushy part of the line, and
nothing very warlike ever happened there. The Germans were in Wytschaete opposite to us, and our gunners amused themselves by shelling a tower behind
the enemy lines.

On our left front was a slope up which French
infantry had charged, and their strewn bodies still

held some suggestion of the momentum of their assault. We pitied them until we discovered two of their rotting corpses upstream in the brook from which we drank.

In this position, one of our men left his trench one morning in the half-light to fill his water-bottle from a shell hole. He was struck down by a sniper's bullet at the hole. There was an order that no man could leave his trench, and all were forbidden to drink from shell holes. This did not deter a rescuer, who went out and was also shot down. A third man then went out and brought both back, one of them dead. The third man was unwounded. He was casually tried and punished for disobeying trench standing orders.

At this period an extraordinary figure passed forward through our battalion headquarters. He was a sapper officer, very curiously dressed. He wore gum boots to his thighs, a cardigan, and a cap comforter, and he looked unshaven.

He remained closeted with our commanding officer for half an hour or so, and then went forward in the darkness through our front line, and disappeared towards the Germans.

This scene was enacted on two occasions. None of us ever saw him coming back; no senior would speak of him, and we inferred that he was a spy.

Chapter Forty-four

THE NEW WARFARE

To the few remaining old soldiers trench warfare was somehow unreal as if a halt had been called in the conflict.

We were used to aggressive tactics carried across open country, where the combined movements of active rifle formations, the quick aim, rapid shooting, and a good sense of cover appealed to us. We had been trained for that. That was our final remark in war, and our order was 'Move forward'. We were stultified in trenches, and wretchedly restless in any quiet sector of the line. We walked about like cats on hot bricks.

We thought the newcomers were no warriors, because they knew no fighting overground. They even died without seeing their enemy, and they had not our perpetual curiosity about their rivals. The idea that the enemy remained unassaulted a few hundred yards away puzzled us. We knew very well what an assault would now cost in lives even if carried out by seasoned troops, and we somehow could not see our untried new comrades working up to the required degree of dash in any attack. They were not proved, because winter was no time for operations.

War therefore became repugnant—a thoroughly miserable, half-hearted business, a rotten dangerous kind of routine.

Our new men did not take too well to trench conditions. Casualties were frequent, and sometimes as many as half a dozen men were hit daily without anything to show for it. Army headquarters called it 'wastage'.

The intense cold of the winter of 1914 numbed the troops, and the carelessness of the Irish, so useful in active operations, was accounted bad soldiering, in position warfare. The number of avoidable deaths in our battalion caused comment. The men flouted death by recklessly walking in the open and by taking dangerous short cuts. The Australians later showed the same characteristic. It drove any English officer or N.C.O. half mad, and it made every professional wild.

Safety first until a job of work was the proper way to play the game, but when the youngsters were warned they simply went off muttering 'windy', and time and again we saw many of these poor lads outlined dead in their blankets when they might have listened and lived.

The pity of it was that these were not demoralized men in any way. In fact they were so high-spirited that their domestic quarrels about rations, or rifle oil, or some other trifle led to blows between themselves even in the front line.

They seemed to be unable to curb displays of unnecessary bravado, and experienced leaders who might have put them wise were lacking, so discipline suffered.

Officers became very scarce. About March 1915 I was asked to consider taking a commission, and I refused it on the grounds that I did not feel sufficiently fresh. At the time seven months of modern war had more the effect of qualifying me for entry to a sanatorium.

In April the Germans used gas for the first time. This happened in the salient somewhere in the Saint Julien direction, and the Canadian division caught it.

One of our runners said that the four miles of railway from the Canadian right flank to Hell-fire corner was covered with dead and dying. He described the dying as black or blue in the face, frothing at the mouth, and gasping for breath. He said they lay as thick as flies along that railway track, which was the line of their retreat. We were outraged. A boot slung at the stomach shut up a hare-brained raconteur who was making matters worse by saying he had heard that some of the dying Canadians had asked to be shot to end their misery.

We were in bivouac about eight miles from the gassing, and we stood to arms in case we were wanted. Other units mended the broken line, and we were 'stood down'.

The New Warfare

Instruction in protection against poison gas was given to us. We were told to urinate on our handkerchiefs or socks, or any kind of cloth, and hold this over our mouths and noses if ever we saw a low yellow cloud creeping at ground level from the German lines. We were also warned to listen for the hiss of the gas as it escaped from the containers. Then washing soda was said to be efficacious.

In a short time we were all issued with flannel sacks made of grey army shirting. They were fitted with a long oblong window of mica for both eyes, and they stank of some chemical solution which crystallized in little ridges along the folds of the shirting. We had to tuck the bottom loose end of these head bags inside our jackets around the neck, and button up our collars over them to keep out the gas. It was most distressing trying to breathe in these, as they had no outlet valve of any kind. We officially reported on them as being a washout. Then an improved pattern —the first real gas mask—came into being. It had a valve and separate eye pieces made of glass. I imagine that none of these P.H. helmets, as they were called, would have been of any earthly use except against tear gas, but the fact of having some gadget gave us a spurious confidence, which was maintained by the repeated publication of Army Orders extolling the efficacy of the masks.

I am grateful that we never had to test the masks in battle.

In the trenches we erected little wind-vanes,

and were always ready to put the bags over our heads when the wind blew from the German side. We also rigged up lengths of railway line or empty shell cases to act as alarm gongs on the first sign of gas.

Air action had not developed very much early in 1915, and we rather despised all hostile aeroplanes. We took little notice of them except near the line, when they could spot us for their guns.

A sunny morning in the huts near Dickebusch changed our views. An enemy aeroplane came over so high that it looked like a pretty silver moth. Moving slowly it circled gracefully above us in the sunlight, its distant drone hardly discernible. We looked at it lazily and then saw three or four streamers dropping from it and coming down gently directly above us. Some one suddenly said 'Bombs!' and a number of us moved out from the line of huts. I thought the slow-moving streamers could only be some form of signal to guns, or perhaps a message from a British machine, but being doubtful, I doubled away from the huts and lay down in the grass. Most of the troops stayed sitting or loafing about in the warm sun until the swish of the descending missiles warned them too late of an unexpected speed and weight.

The bombs cracked sharp on impact with very little smoke, and small pieces of metal hummed and twanged far in all directions—high explosives.

Nine men were killed and twenty-one wounded. Thereafter we vanished like rabbits into trenches or ditches on the approach of any kind of aeroplane, low or high.

We considered this kind of attack unfair. Then the German night bombers started on our camps at night, and gave us the most helpless feeling as they swooped and circled close over our tents. We used to lie on our backs in the open, holding both hands over our stomachs, and we could easily see the moving shapes of the bombers as they eclipsed the stars. Some of the German planes carried red wing-tip lights.

Their bombs generally missed us at night, and fell in open fields. This dud kind of bombing made our chaps careless and sergeant-majors had to swear hard and loudly to get all tent lights extinguished on the approach of night planes. Men playing cards kept their candles burning until the very last moment. Good gamblers, but not good enough for the rest of us whose lives they endangered.

One moonlight night a German airship sailed over our heads, making, we thought, for Bailleul. Its huge size and apparently slow motion tempted every man with a rifle behind the lines, and we all emptied our magazines at it independently, until the spent bullets of men of other corps dropped about us and sent us indoors for protection.

The Zeppelin sailed on, and a succession of distant dull reports disappointingly informed us that our scattered rifle-fire was ineffective.

Chapter Forty-five

IRISH INTERLUDE

I was offered ninety-six hours' leave from the front in
April, and I went home to Cork, complete with arms
and equipment. The attitude of the English people
astonished me. I met with tender and sympathetic
glances everywhere. My weather-stained, ill-fitting
uniform and the dried mud on my unpolished boots
showed that I was home from the front. Men and
women made way for me, and they talked to me
affectionately, as the English public never before
talked to their soldiers. Questions were showered on
me, and one question was put by all: 'Would we win?'
I had no doubt about that, and my answers pleased
them.

I forgot the English when I landed at Rosslare, and
I devoured every Irish field from there to Cork. I
hurried out of the railway station, mounted a side-
car, and was driven with thumping heart to the home
of my relations at Montenotte. Their fervent welcomes
made me dumb and emotionally upset. Their studied
cheerful greetings collapsed into surreptitious tear-
wiping behind doors and in other rooms. The ghost

of my dead brother had come home with me. However willingly they tried, our family could not easily sacrifice for a cause not directly connected with Ireland. To stave off any disturbing expression of that sentiment I said things light-heartedly to defend the Allies.

I spoke with caution of the fighting, and withheld most of the horrors. Anyway, I wanted to forget them, in this heavenly change to home life, so soft, so easy, and so peaceful. Gardens, flowers, regular habits, good food, books, papers, arm-chairs, talk, and drinks were riches rediscovered. I found I could not stomach the rich dishes provided for me after seven months of army rations, and I secretly slept most snugly on the bedroom floor, because I could not rest in a soft bed.

I flew round to visit old pals, and surprisingly could not say all I wanted to. The division between the civilian and the man-at-arms was too sharp in thought and values. A disconcerting change for all.

Cynically I fled them, and sought peace in the country, where I walked free and lightly across the open fields, and found my temporary solace. For a brief spell I drank in the stillness of Ireland under blue sky and white standing clouds. I escaped back into my boyhood by going bird-nesting in these few days of spring. I fondled the startling blue eggs of the thrush and the speckled olive eggs of early blackbirds. I found anchorage in the undisturbed activities of the birds, and came to regard the non-singers with affection—the pies, rooks, and sparrows.

Irish Interlude

Francis Thompson's verses throbbed to my pulse beats at this time. He had superceded Kipling, and here, in the fields near Blarney, the verses of 'Daisy' entranced me with their mingled mood of sweetness and sadness and beauty that must always be.

Kipling had faded out because romance and glory had but little to do with war. Only one line of his came hammering back unsought: 'You can't get away from the guns.' It was impossible to forget their dread assault, and peace would never be mine again to keep until their discord of death stilled to silence.

At the end of each of those few precious days of leave from the front it was luxurious to lie down to sleep and to feel, for the first time in eight months, that I was not likely to be blown to bits before I woke. Leave also gave me some opportunity to cast my simple account with fate.

My chief asset was that I was alive, young, and hopeful, but I could not enjoy life. I had no right to breathe freely and savour the bewitching sights and scents of spring while death sneered in the offing above the rough graves of an incredible number of soldier friends freshly killed and rotting in France. My mind was slightly troubled, because I would have preferred to have pledged my body to the cause of Ireland, still in thraldom. It was her's by every right and every tradition, yet I felt bound in honour to England too, for I had attested on oath, and I was a British soldier as well as being an Irishman and a Catholic.

319

I disliked compromise on such big issues, and wished myself free of such complications. Blarney Castle stirred me strangely, and the clansman in me leaped back three hundred years to another John Lucy, who had fought for McCarthy, the Prince of Munster, and the owner of the stronghold in the days of Elizabeth. The castle was lost. A member of the class we mockingly dubbed 'descendancy' still held it, and McCarthy was no more. Lucy had been given the right to live, and he appears in the *Feants* of that time as a forgiven rebel subjected to a minor fine for his disaffection. The thought of my old kinsman put me out of humour with myself, and I wished that England had been kinder to my countrymen down the ages. It would have made things easier for me and my like.

Then the English war propaganda worried me a lot, and ended by leaving me stone cold. I did not hate the Germans, but neither did I like them, and I still had the boyish wish to admire my enemy. Seriousness was my key-note. The war held me to it, and deprived me at the age of twenty-one of any desire for amusement or time-killing joys, and I had no taste at all for women, or wine, or song. My only true love was Ireland—that lovely and tyrannical one, who made full claim on all my being, although I did not own a single acre of her green fields. More imperious than any empire, she is always demanding, always insistent, now, and even then when blood and life were already forfeited.

Irish Interlude

I had to turn away, and before leaving again for France I allotted most of my meagre pay to a poor relation. I felt richer after that.

I boarded the train from Cork laden with presents. Quietly other war bound soldiers got aboard. There was only one exception—a recruit who had just joined up, and was going off for his first training to some local camp. His mother filled the railway station with her lamentations. Her voice rose in a keen. She tore her hair, hid her face in her shawl, and then raised open arms invoking the protection of heaven on her poor Paddy. The men for France stirred uneasily, and our sorrow-stilled relations made quicker nervous gestures. No one commented on the emotional drama. I wished myself out of it. The train breathed and we disappeared from sight into the dark mouth of the tunnel.

My lips were bruised from the quick hard kisses of my own women folk.

At Waterloo I could not bear to look at the English partings. Before going aboard at Folkestone, I dumped most of my parting gifts—cakes, sandwiches, heavy pots of home-made jam, woollies, books, and what not, keeping only such practical things as cigars, cigarettes, a flask of whisky, biscuits, an electric torch, and sticks of chocolate.

On the ship there was talk of a spring offensive on the Western Front. Some listeners reacted with nervous coughings.

Wearing lifebelts as a precaution against the submarine menace we stood about on the wet decks, not grouping as soldiers will, but each alone in cold discomfort, individually trying to reconcile the immediate bright past with a more urgent future phase of dull loss and destruction.

Chapter Forty-six

REPORTING FOR DUTY

The battalion was in the trenches when I returned, and I waited in the transport lines until the ration party went up that night.

My best pal, Q.M.S. Winters, got a hot meal going for me. I gave him some of my presents, and he swore at me for leaving the cake and jam behind. He lolled back in a Roorkee chair, the property of some dead officer, as he entertained me in his comfortable outsize bivouac. The quartermaster-sergeants led a dormant kind of life during the day, and rested and slept most of the time. They became full of energy in the late afternoon, collecting and apportioning rations in sacks for each section of their companies in the line. In addition they wangled extra comforts for their officers and men, and many mysterious bundles and packages went into the trenches. The service of a good Q.M.S. was a most valuable asset to any company, and raised the morale of the front-line men to an incredible degree, because warm and well-fed men fight well.

Winters had a proud record. No matter how heavy the shelling at night he never failed to get his rations into the line, and he laughed gleefully with satisfaction when a particularly dangerous delivery was carried out. I liked him well. We called each other most offensive pet names. He was fair-haired, short, cheerful, and well muscled. Later, as an officer, he lost one of his athletic legs.

When I arrived he had a visitor, an H.A.C. corporal, who was on the point of going. The corporal was of gentle birth.

The H.A.C. was a corps of professional men, incongruously fighting in the ranks of the infantry. It was reported that one member of their sanitary squad was a scientist, and another a professor. They were nice chaps and they loved our Irish regiment. They initiated the habit of coming up part of the way to meet us whenever we came out of the line—a dangerous proof of friendship, and one which no other corps ever practised.

They were good fighters, and we admired them for that and for their fine friendship. The corporal was depressed because news had come through that the H.A.C. men were all to be commissioned. He hated that and said they would make rotten officers. I was interested in his views, which were similar to mine— that they had fought in the ranks too long, and were now too stale to make satisfactory officers. All the same he was wrong, and the H.A.C. privates became in time some of the outstanding officers in the war.

The corporal left us, rather shyly asking us would we come to tea, and we agreed. He left a parcel on his seat.

Winters grinned at it. 'He is always doing that,' he said. 'Open it.' Inside was a small plum cake and packets of chocolate. Alone, we rushed at each other and banged and clouted one another in the clumsy affectionate way of chums. Then he set me laughing by imitating the polite invitation of our corporal pal: 'Yes, rather, you chaps, do drop over and have some tea.'

'Well, anyway,' said Winters, 'I, for one, wouldn't mind soldiering under an H.A.C. officer. They understand the troops at any rate.' He put a finger to his lips as his batman entered.

The batman seemed very quiet, and when he had gone out again Winters told me that he had been upset by the death of two horses. The batman was transport driver too, and his two horses were killed a few nights before, when the ration party was shelled on the way up to the line. The other carts crashed on through the shell-fire, but the batman would not leave his dead horses. No one had any great sympathy for him. Hours after the shelling he was found draped in the retrieved harness, and weeping bitterly. He was still sniffy, so we said nothing.

I did not like hearing that the ration parties were being caught out on the night roads. War talk and war scenes were already blurring the memory of my leave. Outside the bivouac dumps of rations, sandbags, fodder, barbed wire, and S.A.A. boxes lay about on a muddy field. Winters handed me some out-of-date letters, which I put away in my pockets, unopened, and I looked at him. He understood and at once commenced to give me the precious news automatically given to a chum coming into a new part of the line.

'Cushy part of the line. Everybody happy. Battalion due out in two days. I was to go up at once—the adjutant and the old man wanted me about some returns that were puzzling them. Roads at night were nasty. Germans started shelling about seven o'clock. A bit of sniping at one trench junction, and a rifle battery firing down a communication trench. Battalion headquarters in a small house. Odd shelling around that. No hits.'

A map was pulled out and we studied the road up, the trench sector, and the location of headquarters.

'How are the old stiffs?' I asked.

'Ticketyboo,' said Winters, 'except Shorty, of course. That happened while you were away.'

And then he told me that Shorty the signaller had gone on a binge the last time the battalion was out at rest, and had wandered inebriated along a narrow-gauge railway line. A slow-moving train had run him down, but he was alive and all right.

He sent the Q.M.S. a letter from hospital, saying he was for Blighty, and would the Q.M.S. be so kind as to send him the name and address of the obliging engine-driver, as he would like to send him comforts.

We guffawed at this, as we were meant to. We would miss Shorty and his music.

Shorty had won the Distinguished Conduct Medal for rescuing two artillery observation officers whom he had warned against moving in daylight in a spot just behind the front line. They thanked him, moved to the spot, and were sniped. Shorty looked comically at their fallen bodies from the safe cover of a trench and said, 'I suppose I'll have to get the buggers now.' So he did, and also got the D.C.M. He regarded his decoration for bravery in the most light-hearted way. He told us we ought to collect bloody medals and become heroes like himself. A fine idea. He was going to make a big collection himself for an imaginary grandson whose parents were yet unborn. He regaled us with the most fantastic tales of valour attaching to the deeds yet to be done. These stories were told as if addressing the grandson.

Simulating very old age Shorty would lift a finger and address the imaginary boy in a quavering voice: 'Well might you ask Granddaddy what he did in the great war,' and louder: 'Do you see that glass case?' (Pause.) Then in a strong stage whisper: 'That glass case contains the Kaiser's penis.'

Then a rough note: 'Here. Take those medals. Wear 'em on Sundays, and never forget your brave old Granddad.'

Winters told me he had had a narrow escape himself. All the Q.M.S.s had gone off to have a quiet drink in an estaminet at Dickebusche. The pub was a corner house, and as they were sitting inside a shell came through one wall and passed out through another before exploding.

Winters said the next round was a sprint.

I tramped up behind the transport limbers that night, and near the front line a stretcher passed us carrying back a dead man of 'C' Company. The bearers murmured his name as they went by, carrying him shoulder high, and the only comment of the Q.M.S. of 'C' Company was: 'One extra ration for company headquarters.'

The limbers halted near the silent, waiting groups of the ration-carrying parties, and I struck away across the mud.

I found the armourer-sergeant forward in my office at battalion headquarters, and I asked him what he was doing there. He was a specialist, and should not have been under fire at all. He said dolefully that the commanding officer had put him in charge of snipers. He was a crack shot and had in his new capacity done in several Germans with a special rifle fitted with telescopic sights. He was very indignant, as his job was to repair rifles, not to fire them. He was a bit frightened too. He had lost one of his snipers, and had had a narrow shave himself. The Germans had discovered and shelled his hide in a ruined house overlooking their front line, and he could not escape from the house during daylight for a whole day. He had never been shot at before and he stuttered with rage.

He showed me a complaint to his ordnance officer addressed through the offending commanding officer, and I told him that, though irregular, it would result in his being taken out of the line. Then professional pride seized him, and he gave me a demonstration of a little stove he had invented. It was good—a burner with three wicks of flannelette fed by rifle oil. We drummed up on it and had tea.

I reported for duty to the adjutant, who was in an inner room with the C.O. and the O.C. 'A' Company. They were talking about a sow. A man of 'A' Company had shot a stray sow, and had the body in the trenches. O.C. 'A' Company was all for taking the sow back on the transport limbers and cooking it up. The adjutant told him to bury the sow, and the C.O. was annoyed by the incident.

The second-in-command—a big, fat, jolly major—came in from a trench inspection, and set them all laughing. He was wet to the waist, and told them his runner had let him down by guiding him into a shell hole full of water. He got his revenge crossing a water-logged old trench on the way back. Darkness had fallen and the major told the runner he would lead across the bridging duckboard, which he removed as he stepped to the other side. The runner, told to step lively, fell into the trench, and the officer cried 'Quits'.

The major then fished his pet from the pocket of his British 'Warm'—a tiny, mewing kitten. This kitten accompanied him everywhere and was always in a blown-up condition from drinking too much milk.

The little animal was a minor nuisance to all except its master, who held up the war in his vicinity whenever the kitten wanted to feed or relieve itself.

This major was a popular and gallant officer, and his many decorations included the Order of St. Michael and St. George. In the previous August he had made a spectacular escape from a German African possession, where he had been employed as British military attaché. He got the news of the outbreak of war by secret messenger while he was dining as a guest with the Germans, and was said to have taken to horse in Mess kit and to have reached the nearest British frontier ahead of his pursuing fellow diners.

He was transferred from us to another battalion, and in a very short time he was shot dead leading an attack.

His death was an occasion of outstanding sadness and loss to us all, and those of us who believed in a heavenly host hoped that he had joined the bright company of the angels. We got no news about his little kitten.

Chapter Forty-seven

SPRING OFFENSIVE, 1915

The spring offensive of 1915 came and went without affecting us. Our sister battalion, however, suffered badly at Neuve Chapelle. It had come home from India, and up to March 1915 had lost only about one hundred men, a number of whom had become casualties from exposure and trench feet. Some of the units from India had foolishly continued to wear the thin tropical khaki drill during a severe winter in France.

Our first battalion (the County of Dublin Regiment) acted as the forward left battalion on a narrow brigade front of five hundred yards, and advanced and captured the village of Neuve Chapelle in good style, with little loss. Then the British plan broke down; friendly artillery support weakened, and on trying to push on the second day for the Aubers Ridge the battalion was nearly wiped out by the reinforced enemy. Four hundred officers and men fell round and about the very trenches where we had been decimated in October—an unhappy coincidence. Survivors told me that the bodies of the men of our battalion had been blown out of the ground after five months, and their corpses, bearing the same buttons and badges, lay mingled with those of the newly killed men from India. It was eerie to think that possible kinsmen came out of their graves to lie beside their brother Irishmen. The first battalion did all that we expected, as a matter of course, and in this, their first big battle, won a name for gallantry and dash in the attack. Some of our own Mons veterans, recovered from their wounds, had fought and died with them.

Neuve Chapelle set the bad example of heavy infantry attacks against positions made almost impregnable with machine-guns and barbed wire. This and other battles of 1915 were futile and wasteful of good man-power. The Higher Command seemed to think that because they had brave men at their disposal those men were bullet-proof.

Even the old soldiers began to lose faith. They said a gamble was good enough—a fight with a chance of winning—but useless sacrifice dismayed us all. We got our first touch of this kind of fighting in the following June. Our battalion, supporting an attack on the Ballewarde salient near Hooge, went into battle six hundred and fifty strong and lost half that number.

I was busy for days before the attack copying maps of the intricate German trench system for issue to officers commanding companies and platoons. On the morning of the attack, 15th June, our guns bombarded the German front line for an hour and a half, and at a quarter-past four in the morning the 9th Brigade, which we supported, advanced, captured the enemy line, and ploughed forward through the mud on to their second objective. Our job was to consolidate the front line of captured trenches, but our men lost their heads, and two high-spirited companies went forward beyond the line with the leading troops of the 9th Brigade. They were recalled with difficulty and set to the less warlike task of improving the captured first line, which they worked at all day under heavy shell-fire, until about half-past three in the afternoon, when the futile order reached them to resume the attack in daylight. The Ballewarde Salient was now an inferno on which every British and German gun in the vicinity concentrated its fire. There was great confusion. The German front line occupied by us was filling with the dead and wounded of about eight regiments, and our men, weakened by casualties and hard manual labour, had to drop picks and shovels and go forward without direct artillery support, over muddy ground spurting shell explosions every few yards and raked by enemy machine-guns from an unprotected left flank. As their waves moved forward patiently and dauntlessly to death and mutilation our officers at battalion headquarters stiffened to pale despair. The companies had just been committed when the signal came through from brigade to postpone the attack. Horror seized every one. The attack petered out, and the survivors fell back to the German front line exhausted and defeated. The German fire was so heavy that a third company failed altogether to come into action. The morning German barrage had broken it before it could extend into fighting formation.

Our smashed battalion was relieved. Comment was impossible. Bleary-eyed, loose-lipped, and muddied, the battered men went back to rest. The machine-gunners, late in leaving their positions, fell in well behind the front to number off and march away. A stray bullet caught the left hand man of the front rank and he fell dead. His comrades placed his corpse on top of the rear gun limber, and brought him back to bivouac like that—a careless emblem of defeat.

Eight days later, a similar force of infantry attacked the same position, and the operation was a complete failure. Something was very wrong, and though our defeat was somehow justified, we all groaned. Strange and unwanted doubts assailed the older soldiers. We began to look askance at the staff, and in shame some of us avoided the direct glances of inspecting officers of the higher commands.

The following month was passed in positions which were subjected to new German activities—liquid fire and mining. A regiment which relieved us near Hooge lost the front line in a liquid fire attack. In the mining area we were lucky also, and no mines went up under our men.

After this there was little doing for a couple of months, and then came another holocaust—the Battle of Loos.

Spring Offensive, 1915

The Battle of Loos was subsidiary to the big French offensive in Champaigne and Artois, which took place the same day—25th September, in a mighty effort to break through the great defence system of the enemy. The heaviest concentration of artillery fire was now realized as indispensable as a prelude to any attack. The battle fronts would be wider, and troops were no longer to be sent forward converging on narrow frontages. The preliminary bombardments were to smash down the barbed wire entanglements and blot out machine-gun nests, and gun-fire was to be sustained forward of the attacking waves as they moved through the enemy positions.

It sounded well in theory.

Our battalion was again unlucky, because we were used as a forlorn hope. We were intentionally chosen to contain German guns and infantry up north by hopelessly attacking them, while the main British action took place about Loos.

Worse still, and incredibly stupid as it may seem, our battalion was picked to attack over the very same ground as in June, and once more we tried to capture the Ballewarde position. It was said that the reason we were chosen was that we knew the ground. No psychological effect was attached to the possible reaction of men fighting on the scene of a past defeat over ground which all our officers and N.C.O.s knew was a death trap. My feelings were indescribable as I said farewell to friends I would never see again—men who knew what they were in for. I did not go forward to battle headquarters that day. My final task was to take last letters and mementoes for relations from my comrades. I would not post them until the battle was over.

On the morning of the attack our sappers sprang mines, and the gunners put down a heavy preliminary bombardment for an hour. Then our two leading companies went forward in the first light of dawn through mud and shell holes, and were met by machine-gun fire which the guns did not subdue. They gained the front German line at great cost, and those that remained went on gallantly to the German second line, where they were simply absorbed. The supporting company, stirred to anger and compassion at sight of the mechanical slaughter of their comrades in the open, rose up from the safety of their trenches without orders, and struggled forward to help.

A few of them managed to get as far as the second German line. The rest were annihilated. Up to two hours after the start of the assault some of our men were seen moving about and signalling from the enemy second line of defence. After that there was no sign of them.

Our fourth company still remained, and that was not committed. For a week afterwards I was busy reporting casualties. Most of these had occurred in the first hour of the attack, and they amounted to over three hundred, a large proportion of which I had to list as 'Missing, believed killed'.

The men were officially reported as having fought

like tigers once they got to grips with the Germans, yet I never saw them look so sad going into battle, or survivors look so stricken coming out. A large number got drunk the day they were relieved. Once in they fought, and more than fought, for again was witnessed the indomitable spirit of Irish soldiers breaking away from safety without orders to fight forward in the thick of battle beside their comrades in distress. By God, it was terrible! I know no braver men than these. A large number, perhaps the greater proportion were Ulster men. All epics of old heroes pale before their straightforward gallantry and simple self-sacrifice. I feel unfit to write of them.

One, a Belfast company sergeant-major, said to me before the battle, 'It's death or the V.C. this time, John.' He led his men right up to the second line, and a German stickbomb broke open his chest. The men said he died saying 'Mother'.

Away to the south the main battle of Loos also failed, and the total British casualties amounted to nearly fifty thousand men.

The following two months were spent by us in holding various parts of the shell-swept salient of Ypres, then our old division was broken up in the scheme to allot Regular battalions to the New Army brigades.

Chapter Forty-eight

ARMENTIÈRES

In November 1915 we went into the line near Armentières, and relieved a battalion of our New Army brigade lately come to France. Their officer and N.C.O. staff were very glum. We wondered what was up, and we feared that the new trenches were no catch, somehow. I was sorely puzzled, and did not like to ask why they were all so sorrowful. The trenches were a dream—all square-cut, dry, and intact. Hardly a shell had fallen in them, and they cut through grassy, unscarred fields.

This made the mood of the New Army battalion more mysterious, and finally one of our signallers asked, 'What's the bloody catch anyway? This place looks like a proper soldier's home. What's up with you fellows?'

A pale-faced corporal clerk answered him mournfully, 'Well, you see, we had some awful losses recently. We had three good men killed in the last two weeks, and our adjutant was wounded by a grenade yesterday.' We were dumbfounded, and stood about stiffly

in various attitudes of sudden catalepsy. We could
not believe our ears. The New Army corporal went
on solemnly, 'One of the men killed was a married
man, with a wife and four——'

The signallers broke down at that. They bayed
with laughter, interspersing their mirth with gibber-
ing excuses, 'Sorry, chum!'

They stuttered questions: 'What kind were the
enemy. Did they patrol?' We were gravely told that
the Germans facing us were marines, and did not
patrol, but they were good snipers.

This was too much for me—non-patrolling marines
who were good snipers! and I broke into a short irre-
pressible chuckle. The poor corporal looked pained.
The signalling sergeant patted his shoulder comfort-
ingly and said, 'Ah, you don't want us here at all,
me lad. What you want is a couple of boats, and the
Royal Naval Reserve with a few duck guns.'

We were a bad lot to bring into that peaceful scene.
Incredibly we listened to stories of flat-capped enemy
troops who showed themselves at dawn and wished
the British 'Good morning'. Now we knew why the
Regulars were broken up, and we automatically did
what was expected. There was no choice anyway.
The morning greeters were shockingly killed off.

Our patrols got busy at night, and the boom of
bombs broke the weird stillness. Our raiding parties
went over and brought back prisoners. Our first raid
was a kind of picnic, and our men wandered about
the enemy lines entirely unmolested, looking for loot,

and were called back with difficulty. The garrison had fled in dismay at their approach. After that the Germans woke up and developed ordinary wartime behaviour. They brought up additional guns to shell us as a reprisal, but their second-rate troops dared not attack or raid us. They identified us by some of our dead left behind in a raid on them, and told us they knew we were one of the old Irish battalions. They shouted flatteries or taunted our men as the mood took them, but our chaps kept silent in stationary warfare, according to the laws of an unwritten code. We had a lovely time in those trenches, and we despised our opposite numbers.

Throwing my customary caution to the winds I rode a bicycle from billets right up to battalion headquarters in daylight, and arrived breathless but unscathed. Time and again the battalion completed a full tour of trench duty with only one or two casualties. Our patrols and snipers kept fairly busy all the time, and retained the initiative for our side without any great effort. The New Army battalions got used to the more warlike atmosphere we brought with us, and shortly took it very much for granted. One of these new battalions took part in a brilliant night raid soon after our arrival. They were reputed to have been very ferocious in the use of clubs, knives, and other hand weapons unknown to us—a Cheshire battalion, as far as I remember. These battalions got over their awe of us when they discovered they could do some things as well or better than we could, and they were far keener in the main than we were, because they had a tradition to build up, whereas we had become used to ours, and did not exert ourselves in any outstanding way simply to maintain it.

Chapter Forty-nine

THE NEW ARMY

Towards the end of 1915 there was no professional army in France. The British civilian had taken over the war. Many of the straight-spined old soldiers looked askance at the civilian warrior, and, indeed the civilian under arms presented many a strange sight to our conservative eyes.

He was undersized. He slouched. He was bespectacled. He wore uniform in a careless way, and he had a deadly earnestness, which effectively took the place of our cold-willed *esprit de corps*. He saluted awkwardly, and was very clumsy with his weapons. His marching was a pain to look at, and the talkative methods of his officers and N.C.O.s made us blush. His childish admiration for what was left of the old army was very disarming.

The old army was distinctly queasy about the future. One consolation was the sight of recently captured German prisoners, whose poor physique filled us with satisfaction and the hope that the New Army might be able to cope with them somehow.

The New Army did, and when we learned that they could fight we forgave them everything and allowed our prejudices to slide away.

Some of those prejudices were pushed roughly aside by the New Army leaders, a large number of whom were practical business men with no time for obsolete customs. These, showing an unexpected flair for fighting, brought critical and well-trained minds to bear on every aspect of the war, and won not only our respect, but our admiration. They made hay of our turgid old textbooks, and produced clear-cut and concise printed instructions on every conceivable military subject, for the first time in the history of the British Army. The war was their show now, and they knew it, and yet they were never too foolish or too proud to consult the older soldiers. They picked our brains and selected what they thought was good. Often they stood aside, saying humbly, 'You've done this before. We know nothing about it. Carry on', and in this manner we gladly passed on our experience, the knowledge of methods proved useful, and some of the old army spirit as well.

We had an easy time around Armentières—safe billets, good food, few casualties, a cushy trench life, regular baths, laundry, and games, and the women of Ulster continued to send us more comforts than we could use. In the front line the signallers amused themselves by telephoning the arrival of heavy shells to brigade headquarters, three or four miles behind us in Armentières. The Germans used a massive howitzer to shell the town, and each time we heard the deep cough of the distant gun, our signaller on duty tapped out a rapid morse warning.

Our trenches were directly below the shell's trajectory, and the tense impression remains of a heavy air-trembling soughing sound as the monster shell approached us in flight, tore over us, and faded gradually to silence on its way into the distance behind us. Then the terrific reverberations of the explosion would spread outwards from Armentières, over the whole night sky of the north-western front, eclipsing the rumbling and crashing of the hateful salient, whose ever sparkling crescent could be viewed from behind, or from a flank, for miles.

More suspense, and a real concern for our English chums of the New Army brigade headquarters. We sit up stiffly to the sound of the buzzer, and listen breathlessly to the strangulated but dispelling cockney voice coming cheerfully over. 'That you, Irish?' 'Yes, Bill.' 'That was a near one. Only two hundred yards away. Blotted an estaminet and three houses.' 'Any killed?' 'Don't know. They say some civilians, but Mamselle is still alive.' Change of tone: 'Are you there, Bill?' 'Yes.' 'Any papers?' 'Yes. We'll send some up to-morrow with Sergeant Jones. He's going up to inspect the new line.' 'What have you got?' 'Oh, bags of stuff. *Sketch, Tatler, Sphere*, dailies, and a couple of books too.' 'Grand. What's the latest news from home?' 'Oh, we're still winning the war. Nice to know, isn't it?' 'Kiss me posterior, Bill.' 'Thanks, Spud, I'll think about it.'

The signalling sergeant turns grumpy at the prolonged talk. 'Here, chuck it, Spud. If any inquisitive officer happens to overhear your blasted conversations you may end up in a bombing section.' The croaking voice of Murphy's friend still comes over, easily distinguishable, and Spud, now taken to task, and suddenly all regimental, cuts in tersely: 'Hallo. That you, brigade?' The other, quick as lightning, suspects the presence of some unwanted supervisor in the advanced Irish battle headquarters, and invents a smart inquiry: 'Repeat last two words of your C.49.' We all laugh.

Distinguished visitors came out from England to inspect the front. Some came up as far as our shelled billets. The King arrived near the forward area towards the end of the year and we sent a small party to represent our battalion. Unfortunately, the King fell from a restive horse, and this marred the occasion. About this time the Prince of Wales was serving with a Guards battalion in France. He had a good name with the troops, and was a popular and brave officer, who was always being forbidden, much against his will, to go into danger spots.

John Redmond inspected our battalion late in the year, and every one—Orangemen as well as nationalists—gave him a cheer. We buried the hatchet of bigotry during the war. In our battalion we had fewer southern men now, and the Ulster men began to predominate.

In December there was a sudden flare-up on our quiet sector. We had asked for it, because every day, from our billets, we had the habit of sending large parties forward with picks and shovels to improve the communication trenches to the front line. The men marched up and back in daylight over open flat country, and worked under sapper officers more in the manner of civilians in peace-time than of troops under enemy observation. One morning the Germans let them have salvo after salvo. The medical officer, called from mess, left his breakfast and rushed away to tend the wounded. He was killed. Sergeant Ryan, his orderly, then took his place, tended the wounded, and brought back his officer's body to billets. The working party was then withdrawn for some hours. Ryan laid out his officer on a stretcher in his little dressing-station, and asked me to come and look at him.

Ryan was very much put out, and mourned as if he had lost a dear relation. He cleaned the dead officer's face, combed his hair, and arranged his tie, and then he asked me to kneel with him and say a prayer for the dead. I did so, though my prayers for the dead had lately taken the brief form of a muttered 'Pax vobiscum' or 'Lord have mercy on you' to any corpse.

We came away, I comforting Ryan, but he was distressed and fitful in his actions, his face fallen too sadly, and he kept repeating 'O God help us. O God help us. To see him there on his own stretcher. Oh what a shame! I'll have to go back to him,' and back he went, like a dog who will not leave a grave.

Outside, a relief working party was falling in, in bitter weather, and it marched off to repair the blown-in communication trench. Hardly had this party arrived when the Germans shelled again, and up went Ryan to see to the wounded. Ryan was killed by shrapnel almost at once, and his body was brought back and placed on another stretcher beside his medical officer. Each had been killed in the act of binding men's wounds. Ryan's patient had been killed with him.

I went in slowly again to visit the dead Ryan and his officer. I prayed for them both. These devoted men had died directly to save their fellows. There was something Christlike about them—the young English public-school Protestant and the Dublin Catholic. The red compassionate lips of Ryan were white-grey. His discoloured teeth showed between them. I patted his cheek in farewell. Then I stood up, and I could not move away. The world turned over. My manhood seeped from me. Ryan's death had hammered the congealed nail of grief deeper into my heart, and a long suppressed tide of sorrow rose and flowed about me. I heard strange sobs coming from my lips, and felt my spirit fainting.

In the little dressing-station I missed all my dead friends again.

Thoroughly shaken I went back to my work. The adjutant, one of those gallant, reckless, and cheerful chaps who would go anywhere and do anything as a matter of course in war, sat rather closer to me than usual and gave his routine instructions in a particularly kind way. He was of the cream of the fighting men, and I always admired him. He took a pride in never dodging shells. He marched upright about the trenches, and was admirably slow and supervising in the middle of the worst attacks. He was decorated for bravery, and his adventurous spirit, surviving the war, led him later to join the French Foreign Legion, where he won further distinction and a commission for gallantry against the Tuaregs. He put his left hand on my right, which I now noticed was trembling, and said, 'Look here, you are beginning to look rocky. Hadn't you better go sick? You have been looking seedy for weeks you know. What's up?' I said, 'I don't know. I have lost Ryan.' He asked: 'You feel that?' and I answered, 'Yes, very much.' I said I did not want to go sick. He then urged me to go home for a spot of leave, and to forget the war for a bit. I accepted gladly.

The new year, 1916, was due in a few days.

Chapter Fifty

I GET MY COMMISSION

My leave from the front in the last days of 1915 was
a nightmare. My sleep was broken and full of voices
and the noises of war. The voices were those of officers
and men who were dead. My people at home found
me very strange. One morning I was discovered
standing up in bed facing a wall ready to repel an
imaginary dawn attack. In my nervous condition I
took gifts and returned them at once. I did not want
belongings. I wanted nothing. I had a real physical
pain in my heart, and there was no lustre in my eyes.
I had loved many men and lost them. My womenfolk
cherished me, but they stood outside my great grief,
and their warm sympathy tragically failed to alleviate
a pain they had not shared.

Ryan's startling end had bowled me over.

My relatives changed their tactics, and regarded
me critically in an objective way. I liked that less.

A doctor was called in to see me. He was very
gentle and very certain. I was quiet, but my voice
trembled because my breathing was all wrong. I des-

349

pised myself and told him that I did. He comforted me by telling me that there were thousands like me, and he stopped my return to France and put me into a country hospital where twenty soldiers were recovering from wounds. My case sheet showed that my disease was 'neurasthenia'. This was very unfashionable and rather demoralizing. I also had to have a minor operation, because my inside had gone wrong from eating war rations continuously for sixteen months.

The operation was a bit messy, slightly painful in its after-effects, but very successful. I returned to the normal slowly and surely and my nerves became easy in the soothing green country, as my thoughts slid out of their war groove.

I took a delight again in the simple and natural things about me, aided by healthy diet, regular habits, and the call of the woods and fields.

I rambled and fished and shot. I found the otter's trail and two nests of the water-ouzel. The nests were a great joy, and were built like the wren's nest but much larger. They were set in the crevices underneath the damp arches of bridges over purling streams, along whose banks I saw the flash of kingfishers, though I never found their burrows. I tickled trout.

One day from a hill-top I saw a hunt. Horses and hounds moved in gay pageantry across the brown and green of the opposite slopes of a long valley. Colour and music and motion all sang together— chestnut and white, pink and chocolate; the winding of the hunting horn, and the belling of the hounds.

Up early one hard April morning I saw a beautiful hare loping from the corner of a wood. I was on my way to the wood for pigeons, which had become numerous and a pest to the farmers, and I carried a miniature rifle. I marked the line of the hare, and ran under cover down wind to cut him off. He stopped and sat down in the open twenty yards from me and I shot him through the head. He was a monster, and his head bumped the ground as I walked back, carrying him by the hind legs. A few days later a deputation of young country men representing the local harriers called to see me, and warned me not to shoot hares in the breeding season, or for that matter at any time. The hares were theirs according to custom, and not mine. I doubted their claim and said so, and pointed out that the hare had actually come through land belonging to a relation of mine. I said too that I and my rifle had as much claim as they and their harriers. They disagreed, with high good humour, and gave me to understand in an indirect way that they would give me trouble if I were not more amenable. I appeased them by being really sorry for killing in the breeding season, and ultimately seeing that hunting the hare was their only sport I agreed not to interfere. I really did not want to kill anything for the sake of killing, but the big hare had been too great a temptation.

At Easter news came of a surprising rebellion in Dublin. I had learned my first military drill as one of

I Get My Commission

Countess Markievicz's boys scouts in the Assembly Rooms at Cork, while still a pupil of the Christian Brothers, who always made a strong point of keeping our national tradition alive, and taught us, as a matter of course, that Irishmen should run their own affairs according to their own ideas. My fellow soldiers had no great sympathy with the rebels, but they got fed up when they heard of the executions of the leaders. I experienced a cold fury, because I would see the whole British Empire damned sooner than hear of an Irishman being killed in his own country by any intruding stranger.

In the second half of 1916 I was found fit for light duty, and was sent to our depot, where I got a clerking job. About this time my relations, shocked by the wartime conditions I had described to them, determined that I should not go back to the front in the ranks. Many of my school friends were officers, who visited us while I was on sick leave from hospital. From force of long habit I found myself calling them 'sir' at tea or drinks, and this too annoyed my relations.

I was called home from the depot to interview a general, who disposed of me very rapidly. He asked me why I enlisted. I didn't know. Did I find the life rough? Yes, sir, rather rough, but many others found the same. Would I like a commission? I should. Why? Mainly from the comforts point of view. I had been at Mons? Yes, and I remembered his regiment there. I looked pretty fit. Was I all right now? Yes, quite all

352

right thanks. Well, he'd see about it. He shook hands with me, and I saluted and left.

In May 1917 the commanding officer of the Reserve battalion sent for me and told me I was due for promotion to quartermaster sergeant, but asked that I might waive that in favour of another sergeant, as my commission was due, and I agreed.

One of the colonels commanding a battalion of Munster Fusiliers knew of me, and asked if I would come to his regiment. The temptation was great. The Munsters were a splendid regiment and were southerners like myself, but I learned that if I did not go to them I would remain in my own regiment. This was a great honour at any time, and in war a commission in one's own regiment is a distinction.

I did not want to break old association with the Ulster men, who were my friends and whose ways I knew, so I experienced a keen delight, in the month of June, when I was dined into the officers' mess at a table I had helped to clean and lay in a menial capacity five years before.

My reception was openly warm. Men who had officered me in peace and war rose to meet me and bring me in. My late title of sergeant evaporated in the first breath of an atmosphere easier and more congenial, though not perhaps as openly intimate as that of the troops. 'Come on, old John. Here you are at last. The first one's on me.' Some one said: 'No. On the mess.' They drank my health in sherry. They each recommended their own tailors—good tailors, who would let you run a long account. I was given the choice of four good batmen and the offer of the loan of any article of kit or equipment I temporarily lacked.

I sat at table on the right hand of the commanding officer, who was very gracious and astonishingly chatty. I noticed at once that in the officers' mess talk was like family talk. The jokes and gibes at table had a homely touch, and my diffidence faded completely when I heard a cheeky subaltern trying to pull the leg of a hitherto terrifying major, who gave tit for tat and laughed merrily with the youngster. All the same, an unwritten code was rigidly observed. It was simple to grasp, for it was simply based on a genuine respect for one's elders, and for the customs and traditions of the regiment. The subjects of religion, politics, and women were taboo. An out-of-date method of dropping visiting cards (paying calls) had to be read up and practised. Uniform had to be meticulously correct, and cranks in the form of senior officers watched one narrowly for faults in dress. As a young officer one felt accused of something like murder when the condemning finger of a senior pointed to a necktie slightly of the wrong shade. Alone in my room I saw these matters against the dark background of the war, and laughed at the incongruity. One other thing riled me, and that was the over-use of the possessive pronoun by members of the mess. In the ranks one had few possessions, and one had the habit of looking on all things as more or less common property. I suppose this was because we had very little individuality and were common property ourselves.

That was now over, and life promised to be more individual, more easy and more pleasant in every way, and I looked forward hopefully once more to the future.

After my first officers' mess dinner I went back to say good-bye to the sergeants' mess, and to take away some small personal objects from a bunk which I had shared with a big Welsh sergeant. He was a very fine fellow, decorated with the D.C.M. and bar. His body had been raked by bullets in reorganizing an attack checked by close enemy fire. His manner was cold and unusually taciturn, and he was a strict disciplinarian feared and respected by his juniors. There were no half-measures with him in anything concerned with the duties of a soldier. His smallest physical movements were consciously deliberated, and his self-control was proverbial. His messmates used to bet successfully on the consistency of his behaviour with visiting N.C.O.s from other units. Big Jim, as he was called would come into a crowded mess, order a beer, stand stiffly, drink slowly with a quiet smile on his face, and answer any questions with a polite grunt. He was a lonely man.

With me he expanded, but only in our shared room. He liked my books, my poetry, and my pictures, and he was entertained by my way of talking of the war. Perhaps the war was puzzling him. He never talked out his own experiences, and had not digested them. For instance, I would not have dared to have asked him how he won his decorations. I had to read up old gazettes to find that out. We became close pals, and we could sit together, or walk long walks without talking, and we thoroughly enjoyed this strange but loyal friendship.

One day Jim introduced me to a natty little English sergeant, a pert, talkative chap with waxed moustaches. Jim, following his usual habit, merely said: 'This chap had something to do with your countrymen in the rebellion last year.' I cocked my ears, and the smart little sergeant spoke: 'Yes. I was there. As a matter of fact I had the job of seeing them off.' My heart pounded. Sickeningly I looked at the Irish harp of his cap-badge, and I stared bitterly at his brown beady eyes.

He was restless, and wanted to talk. Knowing my sympathies by hearsay, he had come to me somehow like a man coming back to the scene of some doubtful act to attempt reconciliation. He was the first of a number of unhappy Englishmen who tried, and tried vainly, to square their acts against Ireland with me.

My shocked silence was mistaken for attention, and he talked on while we walked along one side of the barrack-square. Jim had politely disappeared.

This sergeant of the firing-squad told me of the executions following Easter Week. He described in detail the way the leaders met their death. I cannot remember them all because my blood was racing.

McBride evoked the greatest admiration. He refused to be blindfolded. He smiled at his nervous executioners, and told them he had looked down the wrong end of the barrels of rifles before. McBride left a terrific impression of contemptuous invincibility. He was a great man. The sergeant did not like that job.

He then told of young Plunkett, whose fate was to me the most tragic of the lot, because the others gave the impression of having been seasoned soldiers, at any rate in mind, and Plunkett seemed so young and fragile. The sergeant stopped and took some rosary beads from his pocket. 'See these. They were his. Souvenir. Want 'em?'

I touched them for a reason he would never understand, and said: 'No. Keep the beads. I hope they will do you good,' but really I did not hope that, because mentally I was wishing him and his like nonexistent. He was astonished at my refusal, and hurt because I also refused to drink with him.

I left him abruptly and went back to my Welsh pal. 'Jim,' I said, 'that was dreadful, more than dreadful. It was devilish. Really evil. I left him with his beads. May they be his cross—his albatross.'

'Never mind, John. I know,' and we went off together for one of our long walks. During it he talked unexpectedly and at length, and discoursed on duty and the sergeant having no choice. He also said that the sergeant was uncertain and uneasy now in the presence of Irishmen, and was to be pitied.

'All the same,' I said, 'I feel like murder.'

'And I feel like a drink,' said Big Jim.

We had one, my thoughts hovering about Dublin.

And now I was saying good-bye to Jim and my other sergeant friends. They massed drinks before me. I heel-tapped. They advised and joked at me alternatively. A grave old colour-sergeant from Limerick reminded me of my own traditions as an Irishman. I was to keep them among the strangers. 'Be yourself, and be no one else,' he growled. He was a good type, and had once discomfited a crowd of Orange chums of his who offered him an Orange lily on the 12th of July by taking it, and then handing it back again with the words:

> *O let the Orange lily be*
> *Your badge, my patriot brother.*
> *The everlasting green for me,*
> *And we for one another.*

I escaped from the mess with Jim, and we stood outside in the darkness. He came near to me and demonstrated his affection for the only time by pressing my upper arm with a hand that half-paralysed it. I said: 'Oh, we'll meet again, Jim,' and releasing me he said: 'No, Johnnie, because from now on we move in different circles. Good luck.'

He stood away rigidly, cutting the line between officers and other ranks, and then saluted me, and said: 'Good luck, sir.' I laughed nervously, shyly acknowledged his salute, and said: 'Many thanks, old thing. Good luck, Jim,' and I walked off to the officers' quarters.

Before mounting the steps on the opposite side of the wide barrack-square I looked back, and Jim was still standing there, motionless against the lighted windows—the personification of comradeship between men, and a symbol of all his kind for me— the case-hardened war-time members of the sergeants' mess, the senior non-coms. who were the backbone of the army, who soldiered well automatically, and fought and led in war without supervision when their officers were killed.

I was proud now to be an officer, but prouder far to have been a Regular sergeant with those chaps.

EPILOGUE

Immediately on receiving my commission I was told
to be ready to go back to France within a month. I
spent a comfortable four weeks at the depot, carrying out ordinary routine duties, and the casual polite-
ness and easy manners of my new comrades made
life very pleasant. Many of these officers were war
veterans recovering from wounds, and a large number of them were well known to me. Others had never
been to the front, and among them were certain
Reserve officers who had fought against the 'rebels'
at Dublin in 1916. One of these latter was very
gloomy because his orders for the front had come at
last, and he complained that he, at any rate, had no
hope of returning alive from France, because he felt
that, if the Germans did not get him, some southern
Irishman might shoot him down surreptitiously in
battle for the part he had played at Dublin. By some
curious trick of fate he was killed in his first action.
He left the British front trenches to attack with his
men, but did not arrive at the German front line,

and his body was not recovered. Already the Sinn Feiners were earning a name for never forgetting.

I confess I was rather indifferent to this officer's fate, because he was an Irishman and should have not fought against his own people. His end impressed me because I went over the top on the left of his company at the same time, and afterwards other officers confirmed that he had confessed to his old fear before advancing.

My own mind was in a questing state preparatory to committing myself to war again. I wondered how I would acquit myself as an officer. In the depot mess we computed that the average life of a front line second-lieutenant was only three weeks. One thing I did decide, and that was to go all out in any attack. That was not difficult for a professional, but it was not enough.

An old captain of ours was chatting with me on behaviour under fire, one night after dinner, and I could not help saying to him: 'You always appear to be calm and collected, whether at peace or war.' He looked at me in genuine surprise, and said: 'My God, no. I'm generally wind-up in battle.' Then I remembered the last time I saw him under fire, and related the incident. The C.O., he, and I were sitting in a brick outhouse which served as battalion headquarters. This building was the only one untouched thereabouts, and was only two hundred yards behind the front line—an inviting cockshy for the German gunners. I hated it, and used to wonder why it had not been flattened out. The C.O. and he were arguing about the necessity of reporting a relieved battalion careless in handing over trench stores, and I was writing painfully with a copying pencil on a field-message pad, writing out a situation report, when a very low and sudden raking swish followed immediately by a bang made us all three duck our heads. The Germans had put over a whizz-bang which skimmed our roof. It was too close to ignore. 'That sounded unhealthy, where was it?' asked the captain. 'Just over, sir,' I answered, and waited for them to shift out of the house and into the trench in rear. They did not stir, and their resumed discussion was cut short by a louder bang, this time in front of our house.

'Hell!' said the captain. We all three now knew that we were closely bracketed by enemy gun-fire, and that the third shell would probably blow the house to pieces. They continued to sit and talk. I swore to myself at their pride and folly, and quaked. I could not show cowardice, but I slipped to the edge of my stool ready to dive to the floor, though I felt sure I could not beat the shell. In an exasperatingly ordinary voice the captain took up his plaint: 'Not good enough, really, sir. Too much stuff missing. Six coils of barbed-wire, several crowbars, pick-axes and shovels, and the Lord knows how many sandbags missing. We must report to brigade, sir. I'll do another check if you like.' 'Yes,' from the C.O. 'Another check would be advisable. We don't want to be unfriendly, and——'

Epilogue

'Suffering God,' I thought to myself, 'am I to be blown up listening to a conversazione? Blast that battalion and their barbed-wire!'

I wasn't having any. I rose quickly, interrupting them with 'Situation report due, sir,' and I dived out of it into the signallers' dug-out, a few feet from the door, without waiting for any officer's signature on my report. A gust of laughter welcomed me into the dug-out. A Corporal claimed a bet from the operator on duty. 'Hand over the cash.' And then to me: 'I knew you'd hook it first, Sarge. Are the others still in there?'

'None of your blasted insubordination, Corporal!' I said. 'And that's no way to speak of officers.' Internally I was swearing. Outside there was a pattering. We peeped out carefully, and saw the C.O. moving at a fair turn of speed down the trench towards his own dug-out. After him the captain strode imperturbably along the duck-boards. The third shell shrieked to explosion behind his back. Its smoke eclipsed him. He never even turned his head, but continued to march away steadily.

The shell had missed the house completely.

'Now,' I asked the captain, as he peacefully quaffed a whisky and soda in the mess at home, 'what about that?'

'Good Lord,' he replied, smacking his knee, 'we were waiting for you to get up and out of it first, and we both had the breeze up properly.' I was really surprised, and stuttered: 'But you walked away as if you were strolling down Regent Street.'

'I don't know about that. Thanks if that is the impression you got of me,' said he, laughing and coughing, 'but actually, in that very position I was so nervy that I couldn't function properly for about four days.'

'Well,' I said, 'I blasted you. I was in a frightful dither.'

'Were you indeed?' he asked pleasantly, 'I thought you were much too cool a hand, and I was fed up with you for keeping us waiting there. But as you were a sergeant, we had to kind of hold ourselves in.' This interested me, and also bucked me up, and we had another drink on our mutual confession of 'wind-up'.

In July 1917 my orders for the front came through. I was ordered out with a draft due to leave at the end of the month for my old battalion, which was once more fighting in the salient. I received the news with mixed feelings. A sense of nervous horror seized me at the idea of moving up the dreadful Menin Road again to take part in the hopeless fighting on Passchendaele Ridge—the most dismal of the battlefields.

That sombre fighting ground was my doleful Ninth Chasm, and the opening words of Dante's twenty-eighth canto of the *Inferno* is fit introduction to that place of misery: 'Who, even with words set free, could ever fully tell, by oft relating, the blood and the wounds that I now saw? Every tongue assuredly would fail because of our speech and our memory that have small capacity to comprehend so much.'

I took a few days' leave home, and bade my people good-bye. 'This is farcical,' I said, pretending to be cheerful. 'I am always saying "Good-bye", and I always keep on coming back. I'm fairly sure to come back again.'Inwardly I knew that thousands of others, now dead, had said the same.

My brain, made ready, now clicked down on the warmth of home, and in the first sacrifice of my second departure for war ruled out rigidly all temptations to live in comfort. I ruled a line through every appeal to the senses, the furniture and carpets, the soft eyes and faint scents of women, the deep encouraging voices and proud looks of the elder men, and occupied mind and time with my preparations. I took delight in my officer's kit and equipment, and in the second-hand revolver that now replaced my rifle and bayonet. It had belonged to an officer killed on patrol.

A few days later I was standing in the mud outside a camouflaged tent near Vlamertinghe with two other subalterns.

When darkness fell we walked up to Ypres, and the guide, a muddy rifleman, recognizing me, came out from shell cover: 'Hello, sir. I'm glad to see you again.' 'Hello, Hayes. Still alive.' 'Ah yes, sir. You can't kill a bad thing.'

I ordered the others to follow at the required interval, and led on up the Menin Road, talking to the guide. Before we covered the first mile to Hell-fire

Epilogue

Corner I had all the information I wanted. A mile and a half ahead the battle line flamed and thundered, and dancing Véry lights and flickering shell-bursts made a steady band of light above a seven-mile crescent from Saint-Eloi in our right rear to Pilchem on the left.

From my knowledge of the place I knew the line was practically in the same position as it was over two and a half years ago.

According to the guide the battalion was having a hard time. The shelling was awful. One company was caught out before it got into position. The medical officer had also been killed on the road up. Battalion headquarters was isolated during daylight. No one could get near it on account of 'five-nines' falling about it. It was packed stiff with wounded waiting for darkness to be evacuated. A lot of gas too. The battalion was in support close up to the front, and the men said an attack was coming off soon, because the conserving reserve of officers, including the C.O., and a number of N.C.O.s as well, had been left behind in bivouac.

We went on steadily, and as we penetrated the battle area shells of all calibres swished, roared, whined and exploded on and about the road. From time to time I shouted back to the nearest officer, and he in turn called to the other behind him, and reported all well.

On either side of this doleful road forward batteries of field-guns were lined in close array. An amazingly satisfactory sight to me, who had hitherto seen only a few widely dispersed guns thereabouts. The British were coming on. Gun-fire flashes showed the weapons to be so numerous that they appeared to stand wheel to wheel. An encouraging sight. Groups of silent men and rumbling carts hurried along past us in either direction, the fear of the road on them.

Near Hooge we took to the mud of the open country on the left of the road and followed a duckboard path. Fresh white wood-splinters showed dimly where shells had burst within the last few minutes. This was the bogged area where men wandering from the double duckboards became submerged and engulfed in the mud. Above us the night sky screamed with the passing of shells, the trails of many shown by thin streaking lines of light like falling stars. The salient was stoking up for something big.

Eventually we arrived, pretty well tired out, at a semi-collapsed German pill-box—battalion headquarters.

A small section of wrecked trench, cluttered with half-opened boxes of grenades and ammunition, surrounded it.

Inside it was dimly lit with candles, the air thick with tobacco and charcoal fumes, and I had to step carefully over wounded men packed side by side like sardines on the damp concrete floor to get to the adjutant, who was sitting, pale and tired-looking, with dishevelled hair and pouched eyes, writing at a table. The C.O. was out looking at the company positions. The two new officers were sent off at once to their companies with guides. My guide was late and I had to wait. I moved back to an unoccupied ammunition box near the pill-box door. On my way several standing men plucked my sleeve or grasped my hand—old friends, the regimental sergeant-major, a battalion runner, a clerk. I waited a long time sitting on my box—the assistant adjutant leaning over to me from a top bunk, speaking in a suppressed monotone, so that the men might not hear.

The battalion was deployed in support on Ballewarde Ridge, less than half a mile from the front line —the ridge a morass of waterlogged shell holes, under heavy fire. The clayey ground impossible to dig. Any digging merely collected surrounding water. This surely was the nastiest position in the salient, and the third battle of Passchendaele was in full blast.

The moans of the wounded worried me, and I looked down at the nearest face lying near my boots. The eyes opened on that reversed face, and in the dim light I saw with pain that it was Spud, the 1914 signaller. Recognition was mutual. He could not see my badges of rank, and called me as he knew me last: 'Sergeant Lucy.' There was a fluttering at his right side, but his welcoming hand collapsed weakly halfway out from the covering greatcoat. I reached over and pressed his hand. It was cold. Spud was dying. I looked back at the assistant adjutant, who nodded slowly three times. Murphy closed his eyes again.

A rattle of accoutrements at the door and a voice:

Epilogue

'Guide for Mr. Lucy!' 'Right. Coming,' and to the adjutant: 'I'm off, sir. Cheerio.' 'Cheerio, Lucy.'

Another half-mile of mud brought me to a small trench in which two officers were seated—the O.C. 'B' Company, Captain Collins, and a Lieutenant Malone, both Wexford men. Collins was very cheerful. He warned me not to knock over the little wall of mud along the parados which was keeping out the surface water.

'Come in,' he then said, 'and have something to eat.' An orderly appeared with cold bully beef stew, potatoes, a bottle of sauce and some earthy bread, and promised a cup of tea to follow. I had to fish for saliva before I ate. Rain began to fall steadily.

All next day, 9th August, the Germans hammered our shallow support trenches and shell holes on the ridge with an incessant bombardment, and kept us immobile. There was no communication between companies or with battalion headquarters. Telephone wires were broken, and no runner could come through the storm of steel that broke all day to a depth of almost a mile backwards from the front line. Machine-guns sprayed our ridge and the ground behind.

The Germans knew we were going to attack them. Night came and with it definite orders for the advance in the morning, and I moved out to a near-by trench to find my platoon and make myself known to them. I collected the sergeant and the section commanders and explained the plan of attack, which was very simple.

The battalion would go forward in an hour or so and take over a section of trenches from the English holding the front line. At the first streak of dawn the British creeping barrage would come down on our front, and we would go forward at once, following the barrage, and occupy the German first line. Then there would be a short pause, and we would follow the barrage to the German second line, which we would hold and consolidate. I reckoned the German second line was about three hundred yards from our front line, and the map showed that directly in front of my platoon was the village of Westhoek, which we would take in our stride.

Extra shovels were issued and strapped to the backs of selected men. Empty sandbags were dished out, extra grenades and bandoliers of ammunition, and water-bottles were filled from petrol-tins. Greatcoats were rolled and dumped at company headquarters trench.

We arrived thirty strong in the front line, and the English went out, back to support. Rations, tobacco, and rum came up and were distributed, and a double tot of rum was saved up to be taken by each man just before zero hour.

I was glad to see my sergeant cheerful and carrying himself well. One of the corporals also attracted me. He made a bet that he would reach the second German line before me. I took him on, though later in the night I asked him to be careful about himself in the morning, as I found him going along the trench extracting promises of their rum ration from the tee-totallers in the platoon. Some of the men were rather quiet, and I went along talking to them, and telling them I had done this kind of thing before, and that all would be well. The main thing was to get out of the trench quickly and keep up with the covering barrage.

I told every one except sentries to get down and to rest as much as they could. I noticed with satisfaction that the Germans had outranged our trench in previous bombardments, and was glad to be off the ridge behind, where the English battalion was getting it hot.

Hardly any one slept that night. There was too much coming and going. Runners, stretcher-bearers, gunner officers, signallers, stoke-mortar teams, and others made perpetual traffic during the darkness. I sat up and wrote a last letter home by shaded torch-light. A dismal epistle, in the form of a last will and testament. Then and there I could do nothing better. Even the ridge we had left looked impossible to get back over, and I was about to go the other way, forward into the more concentrated blast of an attack in a few hours.

The sergeant roused every one an hour before zero, and repeated orders to sections. Rum was issued. I went along to inspect the men. Bayonets were fixed, cartridge clips and grenade pins loosened. Some men had collected boxes, others had dug holes in the trench side, or placed small ladders to help them to clamber out. They stood facing the parapet, jaw muscles rigid, bayonet-points under cover—waiting.

At two minutes to zero I took a good swig of neat whisky, saw the nearest men all tensed ready to climb out, and put my whistle to my lips. My heart thumped heavily.

Exactly to the second pandemonium broke loose. I blew my whistle and was up and over looking back to see my trench rapidly emptying. Only two men were still struggling to get out—slipped off boxes or something. Good enough for me. I broke forward into a trot, gripped my whistle between my teeth, pulled a bomb from my haversack, and threw away the pin. With my ready bomb in my right hand and my revolver in my left I speeded up. Concussions jostled me in my stride. The German counter-barrage was down. A shell blew a black fountain a few yards to my left front and knocked me down. I rose and went on. Another heavy concussion threw me off my feet. I fell sideways, all my bones singing, and lay breathless. I said to myself looking at my right hand: 'What a fool I was to throw away the safety pin of my grenade!' I hung on to the dangerous bomb, rose and went on again. I intended that bomb to explode in the German trench before I got into it, with revolver changed to my right hand. My boots struck hard on road metal —part of Westhoek, and I did not know it. There was

not a brick left upon a brick. Now I became exhilarated. My men appeared to be going well. On my
right they were in advance of me, and some of them
had entered our own creeping barrage. Overhead
the skies were ripped by tearing shells going both ways.
terrific sounds lost individuality in the high roar of
modern battle. Our massed machine-guns contri-
buted their screaming undertone, falling and rising
as they weaved their interlacing sprays of bullets just
over our heads. Before us a heavy pall of smoke hid
the German position. Dim figures with hands up tot-
tered towards us out of the clouds. We waved them
on to the British line. Then the British barrage checked
according to plan. The sudden withdrawal of that
tumultuous noise gave me a physical shock, and gave
me the sensation of being deaf. I found myself with
about twelve men standing where a German trench
had been. Battle gear and odd rags of uniform lay
scattered about the torn earth. Parts of bodies stuck
into the air above a zigzag grave—the trench. Only
a few small groups of enemy, most of them bareheaded
came to us with hands upstretched. We waved them
away back to our lines. They thanked us in gestures
with their descending arms.

The barrage crashed again and on we went, and
again it stopped, and again we found a trench line
flattened out. My men poked round, heads down,
looking for cover and firing positions. On my left my
Lewis-gun section clambered on to the roof of a German pill-box, and one of our own shells came and

blew the whole team off it. Most of them rose and appeared to be unhurt. The pill-box was occupied by Germans, who began to stream out, hands in air. A young subaltern suddenly appeared from the left, attracted by the procession, and went to meet the Germans, poking his gun at them. A tall German officer suddenly stepped forward from behind his men, fired his parabellum at our officer, and missed him. The subaltern fired back, but his hammer clicked on an empty case. He coldly broke his gun, loaded up, and killed the enemy officer. The German men scattered like hens in fear. The young officer collected and counted them, and gave a signed note to one of them showing he had captured them.

I turned away in loathing, went farther forward, and getting into a shell hole examined the ground in front through my field-glasses. I had thrown away my unwanted grenade.

The country in front was remarkably quiet. One silly British gun kept placing a shell on the ground behind our backs. The co-operation aeroplane suddenly appeared from the rear, flying very low, and I lit three flares. It wheeled away right.

I brought my Lewis-gun over to my right, and was surprised to find its crew reduced to one man, a redheaded country boy named Kelly. We made a small emplacement for the gun, and were working away when he gave a shout and pointed to a low slope some distance from the left corner of a high wood to our right front. There in a small gap I saw a stream

374

of German infantry in clean uniforms leisurely march-
to the end of a trench, crowding there, and dropping
in one by one under cover. Reserves coming up.

I judged them to be six hundred yards away, and
said to Kelly: 'Come on. On to 'em.' He aimed and
fired and only a single shot came from the automatic.
He tried again with the same result. I snatched the
gun, twisted the magazine, pulled the cocking handle,
and fired—again one shot. I dropped the gun and
ran shouting to the riflemen, who got into action.
Using my field-glasses I counted aloud as the Germans fell over. We got fifteen of them. Had our Lewis-
gun been in working order we might have wiped out
a company, because, though the Germans appeared
to be men freshly brought on to the battlefield, they
seemed tired and listless, and at no time hurried to
get into the trench.

After this incident Collins, wounded through the
arm, came up and said: 'Hallo, Luce. How goes it?'
I told him. Then he asked quizzingly: 'Have you any
idea where you are?' I said: 'Not the faintest.' 'Well,'
he said, 'all the other platoons are behind you, and
you had better get back into line, you have gone too
far forward.'

This surprised me, and at the time I could only
feel foolish at being carried away by the excitement
of the attack.

About now the Germans realized that they had
lost their trenches, and they opened with their guns
on the captured ground. I moved back with six men,

and told the sergeant to cover me from any ground attack, and to follow with the rest. We lost four or five men in that simple operation, and it was only when I got back in line with the other platoons that I saw I had but eight men left out of thirty. The ground about showed the reason. It was covered with a close network of concrete pill-boxes, whose garrisons must have raked us with machine-gun fire as we passed through. We took station in a small trench on the British side of one of the captured pill-boxes. Exhaustion and reaction came now. We dug a little to improve the post. Stretcher-bearers appeared from the rear, and moved openly across country collecting the wounded. My little command slumped down and most of them fell asleep. One man had to be dragged into the trench from the open, where he lay spread-eagled on his back, snoring loudly under a fresh enemy bombardment which increased in intensity every moment.

We were relieved that night and marched back from Ypres to rest and reorganize in billets—a small unit of seven officers and one hundred and forty men. Three or four officers and a hundred men joined us there in the following three weeks. No more were forthcoming from Ireland. The rebellion had checked recruiting. Collins was taken to hospital.

Towards the end of October I got the pleasant news that I would be granted leave home for a week, and also that I would probably remain in reserve during the next battle, though no one knew when this would take place.

Before going home I rode into Béthune one evening to dine, accompanied by one of our captains—a temporary officer called Jackson. He was a doughty fellow, still in his early twenties, and he wore three decorations for bravery. I could never quite understand him. He hated the Germans and he was a killer. In action he was ferocious, and was always ahead of his men pistolling and bombing the enemy. The entire garrison of one German trench surrendered to him in one attack before his own men arrived at the trench. The troops adored him. He was very good company when he was not berserk. At dinner I noticed that his hands were very shaky, and I hinted that perhaps he wanted a rest. He had been over two years in France. Then he broke down embarrassingly and became incoherent. 'I miss Collins,' he said. 'And now I have to lead every blasted night patrol in my company. All my officers are young. Will you come to me. I will give you a good time.' Here was one of the bravest officers I knew turned into a sad nerve case. I soothed him, told him how Ryan's death had bowled me over, and advised him strongly to go sick and have a rest. He was very indignant at the suggestion, and asked me if I was wind-up too. I said I would take what was coming, but did not look for trouble, and that perhaps I was less keen than three years ago. I admitted patrolling put the wind up me. That was a job I would prefer to do alone, or with one clever N.C.O. or man, and not with five or six awkwardly moving troops clanking their equipment in my vicinity, and frightening me far more than any enemy. Although junior in rank, I pointed out that I was second-in-command of my company, and had many privileges—very useful in war. I was not therefore the type who would transfer to him merely in the dangerous capacity of patrol officer. He was too fond of patrolling anyway, and thought his company had to keep up a name for being outstandingly aggressive. I knew that constant or capricious patrolling might easily have the opposite effect to that desired, and ended coldly by confessing I could not possibly fit in with his scheme. We dropped the subject, and then he drank too much and became affectionate. He was killed four months later in hand-to-hand fighting, surrounded in his turn by an enemy party who outnumbered him and excitedly gave no quarter.

The night before I left for home I joined the medical officer's roulette party, and lost every franc I possessed. I had no money left for my leave at the end of the evening and had to borrow from the M.O.

At home I had a good time on what was to be my last leave from France. Every one I knew made much of me. I had all kinds of commissions to perform for my fellows in France, one special request being to bring out a supply of Irish flags with harps only inscribed on them. I bought them in an umbrella shop in Cork. Our battalion was due to be transferred to the Ulster Division, which was considered to be poisonously loyal by many of our southern officers, hence the flags.

In London, on my way back to France, I was met by some school-day friends, and one, a girl, took me off for a meal at her house. She gave me a silver medal of the Madonna, which I wore inside my jacket from then on, and she rather surprised me by weeping uncontrolledly when I got aboard the train for Folkestone. Feeling very awkward I got out of the train and kissed her, and she gave me a great hug in return.

The battalion was in bivouac east of Arras, in reserve for the battle of Cambrai when I got back, and it had already been transferred to the Ulster division. We gave a great dinner the night before the battle, and invited a good many officers of the Ulster division to join us. They came, and affected no surprise at our very Irish table, decorated with green flags and other national emblems, and we had a very merry evening.

Outside our temporary mess heavy tanks, still a novelty, were lurching up the country roads under cover of night to their places of assembly for the first famous tank attack in France.

Two mornings later their engines woke us before dawn, and we could distinguish some of them leaving cover and lumbering forward to their zero-hour starting-points. My platoon, detached from the battalion, had the job of filling in friendly and enemy trenches in the wake of the tanks, so as to allow our front field-guns free passage forward. A gunner officer was with us to show us where to bridge the trenches. There was no preliminary bombardment to warn the Germans of their danger. In the first light of morning rows of tanks crept forward, crossing no-man's-land, and guns opened simultaneously. The names of the villages we could see beyond and along the German front were made historical in the next ten minutes—Mœuvres, Graincourt, Havrincourt.

Above them the long stretch of Bourlon Wood blazed and smoked under the hurricane of our shells. In a few moments the tanks had driven over and flattened out wide lanes through the intricate barbed-wire of the German line, and most of them had gone on and were through the vaunted Hindenburg trenches behind.

Two tanks perambulated along the nearest German trenches, rolling the whole wire system flat. A few got bogged. One crashed through a bridge while crossing the Canal du Nord. Most of them lumbered straight ahead, engines roaring, and we witnessed the astounding sight of whole sections, and even platoons, of our infantry strolling up the opposite enemy slopes behind them.

A few German batteries opened spasmodic fire. The enemy infantry panicked and fled from the massive war machines, or streamed down the slopes towards the British lines to surrender. We watched the scene fascinated.

Epilogue

'Come on,' said the gunner officer, 'our time now.' I fell in my platoon, lifted tools, and off we set up a narrow sunken road, followed by the second platoon.

German infantrymen streamed past us, lifting their hands as they did so. We hardly looked at them, and, quickly going on, filled bridges in the British trenches, and then strode over no-man's-land to make similar passages through the enemy front line, now abandoned. Odd shells were falling, and one tank came back downhill persistently pursued by the missiles of one German field-gun. As we finished each trench we passed along the little road to the next place for filling, already marked with little flags by our energetic gunner officer working ahead of us to indicate the passage for his guns. German dead and wounded lay about.

We marvelled at the success of the attack. The forward British troops had advanced over three miles from their own trenches on this part of the battlefield. It was rumoured that our cavalry had got through, and were playing merry hell miles behind the German front. I looked round and saw some of my fellows wandering and standing about chatting and smoking in what was the centre of a formidable enemy defence system that morning. I collected the silly fellows and marched back gaily to bivouac. When we got back we heard that the battalion was in reserve near Mœuvres, west of the Canal du Nord. It attacked that village three days later without tanks, and captured most of it, but some enemy strong points held out, and our chaps were ordered back to the southern outskirts, where they dug in. The battalion suffered one hundred casualties.

The battalion came out of action the next day, and we marched away back to the other side of Arras, in bitter wintry weather with snow and sleet falling, but we were happy enough, feeling that we had played some part in what was already acclaimed to be a very important victory.

Then to cheer us further there was a rumour that we were bound for Amiens for a long rest. Fate ruled otherwise. The great German counter-attack at Cambrai took place as we were moving away, and we were ordered back into a battle we thought was ended.

We hastened back to Cambrai by train and route march, and we were put into the line in the southern sector before the village of Marcoing, which the Germans had recaptured. Farther south they had made much more headway, and had broken right back through the British lines. On the northern sector where we had fought the British repulsed the counter-attack and held on to the ground won by them. We were disappointed and annoyed at having to remedy the defeat of other units. The immediate order was to hold the shattered front at all cost. A brigade of our division took over and we relieved one of its battalions and the remnants of an overseas regiment on the night of the 3rd of December. The main

front trench was a colossal anti-tank trench with deep
firesteps on either side. We struggled into it in the
small hours of the following morning. Companies
going out passed us by in the great trench and I
asked: 'Hallo, are you the Skins?' A young officer
promptly answered: 'No. The Royal Inniskilling
Fusiliers to you, if you don't mind.' I did mind, and
growled: 'Well, you needn't be so haughty about it.
You'd be surprised to know who we are.' He grunted,
and clattered on with his men. Farther along our
Colonial guide passed left into a branching trench.
'Is this a communication trench?' I asked. 'No,' he
answered, 'front line.' Even in darkness I could see
it was a rotten, hastily dug trench with a poor parapet and no fire-bays. I took over from a sergeant, who
gave me very little information beyond the general
direction of the enemy. He was undisguisedly wind-
up, and his men were shaken. He complained: 'They
attack us every night, and come in, and take prisoners. We have not enough men to man the whole
trench.'

I did not want my men to hear him. 'Out of the
way,' I said, 'and let my platoon in.' He hurried off,
his men crowding after him.

I posted two platoons along the bad trench, warned
the men about enemy patrols, found touch with the
company on the left, and went back to the enormous
trench seeking my company commander to report
the relief completed. Some men in the large trench
said it was part of the Hindenburg Line, others said

the Siegfried Line. I turned left to explore farther,
and a sentry stopped me at a block. 'You can't go
any farther, sir. There are Germans on the other
side.' I turned back, found company headquarters
quite near, and went down a deep dug-out to the
company commander, who was sitting half asleep by
a lighted candle. I told him our position appeared
to be very queer, and that as far as I could make out
the front line was a right angle, and that at the apex
we shared the main trench with the enemy. I told
him the nearest Germans must be only about twenty
yards from where he was sitting, as his dug-out was
close to the apex. I pencilled a rough sketch. He was
not greatly concerned, and he said: 'Ah, leave it
alone. Keep the sentries lively, and we will have a
good look at it in the morning.' At the dawn 'Stand-
to' I prowled round near the block. On our side of it
the big trench was a shambles. Freshly killed, muti-
lated bodies of Irish of another regiment were laid
along the fire-step, and a hand of one protruding into
the trench had all the fingers neatly sheared off as if
by a razor blade. Beyond our block the Germans had
built their own block, and from behind it they began
to fire pineapples at us. Then British shrapnel burst
over us, and we found ourselves getting a dose of
morning hate from our own guns. 'Good heavens,' I
said weakly, and I sat down.

I had the most depressing feeling of coming calamity, and was not at all surprised to hear later that
our third officer in the company had been wounded

and taken away. He had been hit outside the company commander's dug-out by a splinter of pineapple. I had a fall and stabbed my knee on wire.

An hour after dusk I was on duty looking out over the top near a sentry. The moon climbed slowly directly to our front, and rising clear of the horizon exposed six or eight Germans in line coming towards us—one of them was silhouetted directly against the full moon. I sent the men on either side of me to pass the whisper: 'Stand to! No one to fire until they hear my revolver.'

I went round a bend to see the Lewis-gun mounted, and passed word for the gun of the right platoon to get ready. The German patrol came on slowly and steadily, and when I judged them to be less than fifty yards away I fired my revolver at them, as a signal. A burst of Lewis-gun and rifle-fire floored the Germans, and their cries of 'Kamerad' came to us. We ceased fire and watched. No movement could be seen, and I told the men to keep to their trenches. I sent a runner to company headquarters to report the repulse of the patrol, and presently he returned saying that the commanding officer phoned up that I was to come and see him.

I limped back painfully about three hundred yards to battalion headquarters, where I was given a drink, and ordered to fetch in any dead Germans. I objected, and there was a shocked silence among the headquarters staff. My reason please? I said—the very reason that gave me the opportunity to shoot the

2B   385

Germans—a bright full moon! I also reminded the
C.O. that the Germans had the nasty habit of covering their recent dead with machine-guns to prevent
identification. Then the C.O. said he would sooner
lose six men than the chance to identify. I compro-
mised by saying I would take advantage of any
clouds, and go out on the first opportunity that offered.
It was two hours before we got a chance. I lagged behind the patrol as I could only make poor headway
crawling on my bandaged knee. This was coupled
with an entire lack of enthusiasm. My spirit had gone
somehow. The sergeant coasted well ahead with one
of his points, and nothing could be found. The Germans had made a quick clearance of their casualties.
I sent in a report to that effect. The enemy dared not
raid us after that.

The following day was fairly quiet, except for
bombing in the main trench. The British guns lifted
their fire, urged by the execrations of the C.O., and
some good improvement work was made on the
trenches.

On the fourth morning I became queerly fascinated
by the trench block, and attracted by the situation
there. The Germans could be heard talking, and they
began to worry our men seriously by altering the
range of their pineapples. These bombs were heavy
high-explosive missiles which burst on impact, and
were of the shape and size of pineapples. Any hit in
amongst the men would create havoc. I knew that
the enemy often took the hint at threatened reprisals,

so I got showers of hand- and rifle-grenades going at and over their block. My scheme did not work. The enemy stubbornly increased to rapid fire, and a bomb fight followed.

All the German bombs went over our block party and no one was hurt. We then had to conserve our ammunition, and resorted to replying with a rifle-grenade to every pineapple. So the affair simmered down. This was really a problem for a trench mortar. I remembered I had not inspected rifles, and ordered the block party to show theirs one by one. A rifle inspection at such a time appears silly, but actually such inspections retain a desirable normal atmosphere, and have a steadying effect.

I foolishly stood away from the block as each man came with his rifle. One man who was not a rifle-grenadier had a dirty barrel. He stood facing me, his back to the block. The sergeant, slightly forward on my left side, looked on, and we formed a little group of three. I had begun to tick off the soldier for neglecting his rifle, and at that moment I was knocked over on to my back.

I saw my two feet above my head for a moment. I heard no explosion, but to myself I said: 'This must be it.' It was. I was benumbed, and I did not feel the slightest pain. Actually there were sixteen holes in me. The man I had been scolding was dead, and the sergeant was lying still near my left shoulder. I came slowly to my feet, and was relieved to find I could stand. My face was covered in blood, and blood dripped from the fingers of both hands. I felt my head all over quickly, and then each limb. Nothing felt broken or swung loose. That was good. Then my left leg began to quiver and weaken. Men had rushed to hold me up. I looked down at the two still lying. The men said that the man was dead. The big bomb had burst behind him, and most of the pieces that hit me had passed first through his body. The blood on my face was his.

I asked about the sergeant, and he, hearing me, looked up and smiled. A corporal made a sign, and two men half-lifted, half-carried me into the entry to the company dug-out a few paces away. They wiped away the blood from my face and hands, and opened up my clothes to staunch my wounds with field-dressings. Part of my left buttock was blown away. A large lump of metal had passed through one thigh and bruised the other. Another piece was sticking in the bone of the side of my left knee. There were two wounds in my left arm, a small hole in my stomach, and my back was bleeding in a couple of places. I had various minor cuts and bruises else-where, and my face and left hand were peppered with fine metal dust.

My left leg and thigh stiffened rather rapidly as I was being taken down to the battalion aid post lean-ing on the shoulders of two men. There the medical officer tidied my dressings and said: 'Well, that's not too bad. I'll get a stretcher to take you out.'

I said: 'Please wait a moment. I want to ask you

a serious question. I wish to know if my stomach wound is serious. I'm not worrying about the others. They feel as if they would heal.'

He hesitated. I urged him: 'Oh, come on. I'm an old hand, and it is purely a matter of convenience. I like to know, and I can bear it if I am going to pass out.'

He was fellow officer as well as doctor, and though he looked very grave he was kind enough to say: 'I don't know if that wound is bad. It may not be. I dare not probe a tummy wound up here, but I'll tell you this—you will be in danger if you sick up. That would mean penetration.'

I was then loaded on to a light motor ambulance and taken out at a casualty clearing station, where I passed into the hands of a very cheerful American doctor. He was super-efficient. Two knife slashes through my laces, and my muddy boots dropped off. All my wounds were examined, cleaned and bound up anew. The American chatted casually all the time. 'Nasty business up there now, I believe,' he said, 'but you wait. Our boys are coming.' When he had finished he asked me if I wanted anything special. Yes. That tummy wound. I'm afraid I had something to eat. What about it?

He roared with laughter. 'Oh, that's nothing. Outer skin only. You'll do.'

Then he said: 'Anything else?' 'Yes, my revolver. I want that.' He stuck it under my pillow. He held up my trench coat, which was slashed to ribbons on the front and on the left side from the waist down. 'You may like this—to look at later—as a souvenir.' He packed it in my haversack.

He put a cigarette in my mouth and lighted it. Then he patted me on my unwounded shoulder and said: 'You're a good kid.'

I thanked him very much and I was put into a larger motor ambulance with three other lying cases, and one more officer who sat on a flap-down seat near my head. A heavy shell bumped the road a good way off as we started. The sitting case emitted a low whine and pleaded: 'No. No.' I put my hand out on to his knee, and he turned his face towards me in a series of small jerks. It was fallen in and blank with terror, and both lips were jerking—a bad case of shell-shock. I said: 'Never mind that. It was miles away. Cheer up, old thing. You're for home.' His mouth opened, but he was incapable of speech.

I do not know what happened next. The American must have drugged me. I do remember lying on a stretcher clad in pyjamas outside an operating theatre, and I remember being stripped and having my whole body X-rayed. Two men in white turned me round and round, tracing the metal bits inside me. From time to time they put heads together to look collectively at some discovery, and one of them said: 'Mark,' and I was pencilled. It was 'Mark', 'Mark' until I said in a silly way: 'Mark cock,' and they both laughed.

Epilogue

Another train ride, and a bed with white sheets in a quiet ward of No. 8 General Hospital, Rouen, where I first landed in France. A friar came rather shyly and asked to hear my confession. I had enjoyed a general absolution before going into action, which bound me to confess at the first opportunity, but I felt somehow that I wished to avoid the atmosphere of a confession in bed. Too suggestive of last moments, and I would not concede anything to death. I therefore bilked and said: 'No thanks.'

I lay stretched helplessly with my legs under a cradle. I did not want to move. There was a gentle buzzing in my ears—pleasant. An orderly came and gave me a bed bath with warm water. My attendance at this performance seemed unreal, and 'Very nice', I thought impersonally. I was semi-conscious, and did not know that I was sinking and on the seriously ill list. The matron had written home about me, always a danger sign. But somewhere inside me, in the core of my being, there was a hot spot. That only was me. I receded deliberately into it. Refuge there, and a great determination to expand and live again some time later when I felt less weak. Thus I planned as consciousness rose and sank in slow waves.

One day an urgent call from my neighbour pulled me completely back. 'Do me a turn, like a good chap. I feel pretty bad. I have a back wound and want to know about it. They turn me on my right side. Do have a look when they come round.' The next time the doctor and assistant sisters came dressing wounds

Epilogue

I had a look. I saw a hole where the left kidney should have been, the edges blue and greeny-yellow —gangrene. They went. 'Well,' he asked, 'how does it look?' 'There's a hole,' I said. 'It doesn't look too bad.' 'It feels dreadful—dreadful.'

They took him out at night so that the other patients would not notice. He had died quietly. Alone.

The last dead man I saw in France.

At the end of December I was transferred to England in a hospital ship, my accompanying case sheet marked: 'Shell wounds; very severe—knee, buttock, thigh, abdomen, back, and forearm.' At Southampton some one came to my stretcher and asked me if I wanted to go to London (the Mecca of all wounded officers, where rich private houses were opened as hospitals and convalescent homes), and I said: 'No. Please send me to Ireland.' They said: 'We can't do that right away, but we will send you part of the way.'

A smooth-running hospital train brought me to Exeter, where some St. John's men put me into a small ambulance van, alone, and shut the door. The car started with a jerk, and my body slid through the bandages on my main wounds. I started to bleed afresh. The blood was showing on some bandages when I was put to bed, and the V.A.D. on duty said she dared not dress me. She sent for another V.A.D., who was also afraid to tackle the job. I asked for the doctor, and they said he would not appear until morning. I then asked them at least to bind fresh bandages tightly over the old ones, and this they did very nervously.

Then they left me, and I cursed and cursed, intensely and audibly. A tired, protesting voice from some wounded officer said: 'Oh, for goodness' sake, please shut that row.'

In the morning the matron came and inquired for the angry Irishman. The war was over before they cured me.

I had seen the travail which God had given the sons of men to be exercised therewith, and at the beginning of life it was proved to me that great calamity is man's true touchstone.

THE END